PRAISE FOR *FUTURE TENSE*

'Tony Leon is not only an experienced politician but also a talented writer, and this book is the highly readable result of that combination. His analysis of the last two decades in South Africa is honest and penetrating and his views on the handling of the Covid pandemic are persuasive. He demonstrates very clearly that change will be needed for widespread prosperity, freedom from corruption and reliably good governing to be achieved. This will be an important book for South Africans who want to ensure their country succeeds in the 2020s, and for so many in the rest of the world who are urging them on to reach their true potential.'
– *Lord William Hague, former British Foreign Secretary and Conservative Party leader*

'From the vantage point of years in active politics, Tony Leon provides a lucid analytical balance sheet of SA Ltd 2021. Eschewing political correctness Leon tells it as he sees it. The consequence is a book that will promote much needed rational debate about the direction that the country needs to take.'
– *Judge Dennis Davis*

'*Future Tense* unflinchingly anatomises what has gone wrong in South Africa since the heady days when Tony Leon entered politics. As the former leader of the country's main opposition party, he was never going to pull his punches when describing the dismal decline of the African National Congress. But he is just as critical of his own party's failure to translate popular dissatisfaction into votes and political change. Anyone who wants to understand South Africa today – a country so beautiful, yet so broken – simply has to read this book.'
– *Niall Ferguson, Milbank Family Senior Fellow, the Hoover Institution, Stanford, and author of* Civilization: The West and the Rest

'Tony Leon's passionate and informed account of South Africa's decline from the world's new democratic hope two decades back to its capture by corrupt big men who rode roughshod over its constitutional promises is essential reading. Not just for South Africans, but for people everywhere who need to heed the warning on what happens when the ruling party trumps the state and when populism fuels economic decline. In the midst of many current crises, Leon also points the way for a more hopeful future for a country which needs to succeed to prove that democracy and the rule of law can still flourish in a multi-ethnic, historically conflicted and potentially rich nation.'
– *Bill Browder, author of* Red Notice

'Even his political opponents must confront Tony Leon's jarring questions about whether South Africa can be rescued from corruption, cronyism and continued economic decline.'
– *Peter Hain, former anti-apartheid activist and senior Labour Party cabinet minister*

PREVIOUS BOOKS BY TONY LEON

Hope and Fear: Reflections of a Democrat (1998)
On the Contrary: Leading the Opposition in a Democratic South Africa (2008)
The Accidental Ambassador: From Parliament to Patagonia (2013)
Opposite Mandela: Encounters with South Africa's Icon (2014)

FUTURE TENSE

Reflections on my Troubled Land
South Africa

TONY LEON

Jonathan Ball Publishers
Johannesburg · Cape Town · London

Originally published in South Africa in 2021 by
JONATHAN BALL PUBLISHERS
PO Box 33977, Jeppestown, 2043

This edition published in 2021 by Jonathan Ball Publishers
An imprint of Icon Books Ltd,
Omnibus Business Centre, 39-41 North Road, London N7 9DP
Email: info@iconbooks.com
For details of all international distributors, visit iconbooks.com/trade

ISBN 978-1-77619-142-0
ebook 978-1-77619-075-1

Quotes, including from speeches, that aren't directly sourced or
referenced, refer to personal communication with the writer, ad-
libbing in speeches at which the writer was present and taking notes,
and/or communications during Q&A sessions following official
speeches.

Cover photographs: Reuters/Gallo Images (top),
Gallo/Getty Images (bottom)

Printed and bound in Great Britain
by Clays Ltd, Elcograf S.p.A.

To Michal

'Most of us have only one story to tell. I don't mean that only one thing happens to us in our lives: there are countless events, which we turn into countless stories. But there's only one that matters, only one finally worth telling.'

JULIAN BARNES, *The Only Story*, 2018.

Contents

Preface

'I know how dangerous it is to make personal experience your main basis for authority.'[1] So says Yuval Noah Harari, author of bestselling blockbusters *Sapiens* and *Homo Deus*.

Danger acknowledged, the book in your hands, *Future Tense: Reflections on my Troubled Land*, is very much my own singular take on select themes and events, and some of the personalities – some outsize, some obscure – who shaped the core happenings that led South Africa to the place it finds itself in in 2021, and how these may impact our future.

It has been my great good fortune to have been present at key moments when the door to the future swung on the hinges of history, and I encountered some of the more remarkable characters in our national story, and some of the players in the wider world, who shaped us and who offer useful pointers for the future.

I had the privilege of serving the longest period to date as leader of the official opposition in democratic South Africa, from 1999 to 2007. And after leaving Parliament in 2009 I was engaged in international diplomacy as South Africa's ambassador in South America, to Argentina, Uruguay and Paraguay, and more recently as chairman of a local communications company and advisor to overseas consultancies. These postings provided distance from and lent perspective to the rough and tumble of public life in which I'd been engaged for over twenty-five years.

Dozens of books have appeared on local shelves chronicling what went right in the brave and inspiring new dawn of democracy in South Africa in 1994. Even more volumes have been published on what's gone wrong since – the vertiginous slide from Nelson Mandela and Desmond Tutu's Rainbow Nation to the Republic of Resentment and Decline. This book is, I hope, different and also more refreshing than depressing.

Neither of these destinations, utopia or dystopia, was inevitable or even, before their occurrence, likely. Both of them, and the stumbles between the two roads open to South Africa twenty-five years ago, were navigated by men and women of zeal. Some were zealous in a good sense – selfless, committed and singular in purpose – while others were greedy, corrupt and entirely selfish. Among those who ploughed our national path in more recent times were some committed to decent ends – albeit occasionally pursuing irrational and self-defeating means to achieve them – a few who were prisoners of dogma, and yet others who proclaimed high principle and collective purpose to conceal their own predations. Another category muddled along in the middle, hoping for the best without preparing for the worst outcomes.

In the tussle in history there are two threads that determine outcomes, according to *Beyond Great Forces: How Individuals Still Shape History* by Daniel Byman and Kenneth M Pollack. On the one hand there are the great men and women, 'individual leaders, both famous and infamous', who drive events; on the other there's the 'structuralist zeitgeist' where huge sweeping forces trump the power of personality.

Both matter. But consider the United States and the world today had Hillary Clinton prevailed over Donald Trump, as she nearly did in 2016. Or if David Cameron had not chosen to call a referendum on Brexit earlier in the same year …

Here at home, you can play the 'what if?' game by asking the likely outcome had nature not intervened in 1989 and felled reluctant reformer and hard-line securocrat President PW Botha, via a ruptured blood vessel in his brain, paving the way for FW de Klerk; and you can take this further by wondering the outcome – given, as Byman and Pollack put it, 'the ruthless domestic politics in a country roiled by civil war and a regime's inherent desire to survive' at the time – had De Klerk not stepped down.

And, more recently, what about if Nkosazana Dlamini-Zuma had prevailed at Nasrec in Johannesburg in December 2017 and become President of South Africa?

This book, informed by my own experiences with the challenges of leading a political party in South Africa for thirteen years, is a reminder of the power, and the flaws, of human agency in determining the fate of nations and the political tribes who live in them.

In Britain when David Cameron's precipitate decision on Brexit looked certain to lead to his resignation, journalist Janan Ganesh presciently observed that leadership in politics is 'not quite the only thing that matters but almost. A party with a good front man or woman can afford to get everything else wrong and probably will not. Most other variables – policy, strategy, organisation – flow from the leader.'[2]

I was to discover the potency of that prophecy in local terms when the unhappy circumstances in which the Democratic Alliance (DA) found itself in 2019 led to my being called in to interrogate its leadership. This book also deals with that story.

There are as many variants of political correctness as there are categories of victims, and South Africa is a world leader in both.

Plenty has been written about the wide variety of groups and the historical events that swept away the *ancien regime* of apartheid, but little is addressed to the concerns of the middle-class tax-paying backbone of the nation. I'm not politically correct and have no claim to victimhood but I recognise the real hurt felt by those who endure the lash and legacy of discrimination, of whatever sort.

I'm categorically middle class by income and liberally minded by inclination. I'm also – and I'm reminded daily of the fact in the cacophony of the local noise that often passes for commentary – white. From this – my – demographic much is demanded and, for some of us, the future is cloudy. Regarded by our political overlords with suspicion, advised daily to 'check our privilege', our pockets are pillaged by the fiscus, and we're often pilloried as unpatriotic or worse. We have, simultaneously, the best and the worst of the new South Africa; some of us have thrown in the towel and departed. This angst gets an airing here since I am of this tribe, even though I've always regarded nationality, language and culture as far more essential to my identity than my race.

Perhaps the greatest threat to the future of freedom in this country, and in far more enduring democracies beyond its shores, is the grim realisation of British philosopher Bertrand Russell in 1928, that we have two kinds of morality, side by side: one that we preach but do not practise, and another that we practise but seldom preach. In a country and world being tested by the plague of the coronavirus and its aftermath, tempted by the quick political cures of populism and magic money trees, and slideaways from constitutionalism and sound money principles, these words, written nearly a century ago, now have an urgent relevance.

Writing this book during the covid-19 pandemic was a profound experience. Beyond the intimations of mortality the virus induced in us all, it did at least allow a concentrated focus on the vital issues that have left South Africa so battered by the effects of the lockdown. The flip side was the dilemma of writing about contemporary topics amid such a huge upheaval – but, as this account suggests, the personalities, policies and politics of South Africa predated, sometimes by some decades, the imposition of the national lockdown in March 2020.

I'm deeply grateful to Jonathan Ball and Jeremy Boraine of Jonathan Ball Publishers for suggesting this book and guiding it to completion, our third such happy collaboration; to Tracey Hawthorne, for the very helpful editing and shaping of this book; to Geordin Hill-Lewis, who provided valuable advice on interpreting the data of the National Treasury; to Dr Anthea Jeffery, who offered useful guidance on expropriation without compensation; and to Paul Wise, for proofreading and additional fact-checking.

Much appreciation, too, to the Thursday Zoom Durban cocktail sessions with Steve and Kirsten du Toit and Mike and Phillida Ellis, who sustained my writing effort with encouragement and humour. And, as always, my wife Michal filled the indispensable roles of constant muse, chief critic and best partner in the world. This book is dedicated to her.

Any mistakes in these pages are, irritatingly, mine.

Tony Leon
Cape Town
January 2021

PART I

PRESENT TENSE

CHAPTER 1

—

Long fuses, damp squibs:
The false new dawn

A travel tip I heard too late was to never go to New York City during the United Nations General Assembly week in late September. It's a misery of barricaded streets, impassable roads and overcrowded subways because every world leader, from the good and the great to the despotically awful, descends on the Big Apple. If Madame Kleptomaniac, First Lady of the Republic of Thievery, wishes to go shopping, the city police obligingly close off a main road, with attendant traffic chaos.

However, a US firm for whom I was an advisor correctly viewed the week as an opportunity for endless meetings with the corporate and political types flooding the city. So in September 2018 I was assigned to address them on matters South African, or how the country was faring with Cyril Ramaphosa at the helm in his first year as president.

His nail-biting, against-the-odds victory in the election for the presidency of the African National Congress (ANC) in December 2017 had allowed him to shove the vanquished Jacob Zuma from the state presidency some six months before, and expectations of deliverance from the dread Zuma years were sky high. But

Ramaphosa's defeat of the charismatically challenged Nkosazana Dlamini-Zuma, favourite of her ex-husband and the radical brigade, had been extremely narrow, and purchased at great cost.

His razor-thin winning margin of just 179 votes (out of 4 776 voting delegates) at the ANC Conference meant he was, in the words of one party veteran, 'in control of just 51% of the entity'. And this was mirrored in the delegates' choice of the other 'top six' positions: alongside Ramaphosa in the high echelon were some very dubious, indeed arguably criminal, characters: new secretary-general Ace Magashule, the Guptas' Free State enabler, was generally believed to be deeply corrupt; the shadowy deputy president DD Mabuza had been the subject of a detailed *New York Times* hatchet job which covered allegations ranging from warlord activities in his province of Mpumalanga to embedded graft and larceny;[3] and the deputy secretary-general was Zuma holdover and staunch defender Jessie Duarte.

It was Mabuza who'd broken with the so-called 'Premier League' of provincial barons aligned with the Zumas to give Ramaphosa his narrow win. And it was reckoned that between the two candidates – Ramaphosa and Dlamini-Zuma – around R1 billion had been spent to win allegiances, suggesting that the ANC conference 'wasn't an election but an auction'.[4] Ramaphosa had taken money from some of the most compromised and corrupted companies in the land, notably a tender-milking entity, Bosasa.[5]

HALF A WIN

Midweek, and mid-afternoon, I zigzagged around various obstacles to arrive at the InterContinental Hotel, where Cyril Ramaphosa was the guest speaker at a business conference hosted by the South African Embassy.

The venue, on the mezzanine level, and the event itself, gave an indication of where the country and its new president stood in the world. Bearing in mind that Yankee Stadium was at its 60 000-person capacity in 1990 to welcome Nelson Mandela after his release from prison, and that Mandela's successor, Thabo Mbeki, would have attracted a belt of heavy-hitting corporate CEOs and chairmen from the major companies, this medium-sized ballroom with its many empty seats told its own story.

The warm-up act was compèred by trade and industry minister Rob Davies, whose fashion choice of a maroon shirt and green tie somewhat deflected attention from his remarks. He had on stage representatives from two big companies, consumer-goods corp-oration Procter & Gamble and tech company IBM, whose task was to parade South Africa's business attractiveness. But instead of top-level CEO endorsers, the two speakers were senior-management types.

Still, as we waited for Cyril Ramaphosa to commence speaking that afternoon in New York, a grizzled American lobbyist on Africa sitting near me said, 'It doesn't really matter what he says. The whole point of this afternoon is that he is speaking and not Zuma.'

'Not Zuma' was indeed Ramaphosa's only international calling card at the time, as his partial victory had meant he was saddled with policy pledges to implement land expropriation without compensation (EWC) and nationalise the Reserve Bank, among other delights plucked from the 1960s socialist playbook.

But what, in fact, were Ramaphosa's own views and values on the most important and pressing reforms needed to right-size South Africa and unite it after a decade of division and misrule? Did he have a vision of what the country needed and what to do to achieve it?

THE CHAMELEON

Here the view was deeply occluded. Ramaphosa had both a chameleonic resumé and a paradoxical outlook: 'a representative of both sets of black South Africans who [had] done well since 1994'[6] – the trade unionists and the black economic empowerment (BEE) millionaires – he came from both groups and was hardly likely to upset either. Trade unionist, one-time communist, business billionaire, he had variable and excessively vague views on the most urgent issues. His own alleged pro-business standpoints were often more the imaginings of his millionaire backers than the result of any entrepreneurial flair or grit on his part. His vast pile of cash was the result of BEE receipts and major board appointments and share options: he held great wealth rather than having created any.

Ramaphosa's most noteworthy accomplishment before national politics was his stewardship of the National Union of Mineworkers (NUM) from 1982 to 1991. In his time there, the industry employed 500 000 people and its gold mines were producing 504 tonnes of the metal from sixty-five mines. By 2017, I was advised by one audience member embedded in the industry, we were down to 110 tonnes from just nine mines, a drop of more than eighty percent in two decades, with plummeting job losses. Eskom power cuts and tariff hikes (a surge in pricing of 500 percent in a decade), populist unions and the cost of very-deep-level mining had extracted a fearsome price.

Around the same time as Ramaphosa's New York foray, mining veteran Jim Rutherford, a one-time director of mighty Anglo American, spoke for many when he told a local mining conference in Johannesburg, 'South Africa does not feature on the international investor radar.' International mining equity investors had 'largely given up' on South Africa, and saw better opportunities elsewhere, he said.[7] (In early 2020, after a hundred years as the icon of mining in the country, AngloGold Ashanti, the latter-day incarnation of Anglo American's gold mining, exited the country completely.)

Although immediately following Ramaphosa's election there'd been a surge of economic optimism, dubbed 'Ramaphoria', among suburban matrons and in the 'chattering classes' – intellectuals or artists who tend to express liberal opinions – who normally were staunch in opposition to his party, was he really a non-racialist in the mould of Mandela? After all, he'd warned voters in rural Limpopo in 2013 that not voting for the ANC meant 'the boers will come back to control us'. (He later 'clarified' this attack as directed at 'the apartheid regime' and said that it was 'unfortunate' that his statement had caused offence.)[8] And this is by no means an isolated instance of Ramaphosa's 'doublethink', where the speaker simultaneously espouses two contradictory views, à la George Orwell's *Nineteen Eighty-Four*.

An old political acquaintance, Dr Mario Oriani-Ambrosini (who died very prematurely in 2014), related in his memoir that during the constitutional negotiations in 1994, Ramaphosa had told him the ANC had a '25-year strategy to deal with whites'. 'It would be like boiling a frog alive, which is done by raising the temperature very slowly. Being cold-blooded, the frog does not notice the slow temperature increase.' Ambrosini took this to mean that 'the black majority would pass laws transferring wealth, land, and economic power from white to black slowly and incrementally, until the whites lost all they had gained in South Africa, but without taking too much from them at any given time to cause them to rebel or fight.'[9]

The facts, from a raft of legislation to proposed constitutional amendments, lent credence to this account. And in late 2018, with the '25-year strategy' nearing its end, Ramaphosa lashed out at what he termed 'lackadaisical' whites for their attitude towards transformation, and warned in a radio interview that 'we need to use a multiplicity of pressure points'.[10]

LOUSY DIAGNOSIS, GOOD DOCTOR

That September afternoon in New York, Cyril Ramaphosa eventually took the stage but his speech was more word salad than menu of thoughtful ideas and bold actions. Having the day before advised *The Wall Street Journal* that 'we were too slow with some reforms [but] now the reforms are coming fast and furious,'[11] he certainly didn't announce any in his speech that day (and, indeed, we still await a sign of them two years later). Instead, in a curious note to strike to wary potential American investors, he invited those present to join South Africa on its 'journey of transformation'.[12]

Some in the audience had already been on this particular ride: policy uncertainty, stringent BEE codes, rigid labour laws, and soon a highly intrusive and interventionist competition policy aimed at foreign investors. Many had dismounted and disinvested. But Ramaphosa that day did what he did best: he offered emollient reassurance in dulcet tones of trust and confidence, and he doled out the charm.

I'd formed the view, watching him over the years and based on occasional interactions, that he was like an old-style doctor – the diagnosis might be lousy but you trusted the GP.

But what was far less persuasive was another note: he sidestepped any responsibility for the failures of policy and execution of what was by that point two and a half decades of ANC governance. For example, while he correctly acknowledged 'a lamentable crisis in education and the country's skills deficit', instead of manning up to his party's 24-year failure on this front, he blamed the whole mess on apartheid. Ramaphosa, while far more articulate than Zuma (who famously couldn't properly read out a set of figures in public), was essentially cut from the same blame-game/avoid-accountability mould.

I left the hotel in New York reminding myself this was the first time I'd seen Ramaphosa in action as president, and thinking that, like most of the addresses I'd heard him make in Parliament years before, it had been fluently delivered but content light.

PROMISES MADE …

The early days of Cyril Ramaphosa's presidency suggested pre-varication and fudging on the critical issues and a retreat into the safe harbour of the past; rhetorical thrusts were never matched by decisive action. And those early-warning signs would, over the next two years, harden into a deadly inertia, with the president's response to the cascading economic crises confronting the country being not to confront the roadblocks to a reform agenda in his own ranks, from the unionists to the communists, but to call conferences and summits. Balancing factions might have been useful for party-unity purposes, but was fatal when it came to moving forward the country and its economy.

In his 2019 State of the Nation speech in Parliament, the normal high, breathless expectations of dramatic changes were antici-pated by media blowhards. Ramaphosa announced none. Rather, he referenced no fewer than nine commissions or committees or summits or panels to deal with the challenges and crises facing the country.

I had, the week before, been in England and tramped around the bucolic estate of Winston Churchill's Chartwell home in Kent, where his famous 'Action This Day' philosophy was everywhere in sight in the ghosts of the rooms where he'd plotted the fight against Hitler's Germany, and before that his willingness to stand alone against the forces of appeasement in his own party. Ramaphosa was fond of quoting Churchill but he never followed the British leader's bold examples of moving assertively to restore both confidence and growth, and ignoring, or even sidelining, internal party rivals.

Ramaphosa also invoked the spirit of Nelson Mandela to justify his compromises and consensus-seeking ways. He told Parliament, and his growing band of detractors, 'Achieving consensus and building social compacts is not a demonstration of weakness. It is the essence of who we are.'[13] Left unmentioned in all this was that at more important moments in recent history, from starting secret negotiations with the apartheid government to undertaking a U-turn on economic policy, and even retaining the Springbok rugby symbol, Mandela had led first and achieved consensus later.

Ramaphosa's early-2019 promises of moving South Africa twenty places up the World Bank's 'ease of doing business' index, on which it was then a lowly 82nd, instead saw it slide down to 84th place the following year. His promise of 'lower debt trajectory' was observed only in its breach: the country's debt-to-GDP ratio was forecast to shoot up to 85.6 percent by 2021, rising to 95.3% by 2025 – its highest level ever.[14] And the 'million paid internships' in three years he promised in the touted Youth Employment Service had by 2019 reached just 32 248, leading opposition member of Parliament (MP) Geordin Hill-Lewis to tell Parliament that at that rate it would take eighty-eight years to reach its target.[15]

Whatever Ramaphosa's limits, for his ravaged party he was its 'get out of jail' card in the 2019 general election. He managed to present himself, notwithstanding sitting atop an atrophying and hugely corrupt machine, as the face and force of welcome change.

When the votes were counted in the May poll, South Africa's sixth democratic election, the ANC had triumphed by less than before (57 percent of the total) but had held onto its eight (of nine) provincial redoubts, if only by a fingernail in the heavily contested Gauteng province. But the unambiguous below-the-surface numbers were hardly reassuring: more than nine million eligible voters hadn't bothered to register for the poll, and of those who did, over a third (34 percent) simply stayed away from voting.

For all the ANC's vaunted self-belief of being a vanguard 'people's movement', it had won the election with the lowest voter haul on the lowest percentage poll against the highest non-registration of eligible voters in twenty-five years. This meant its outsize parliamentary majority (234 of a total 400 seats) masked the fact that in reality only 26.5 percent of all voting-age South Africans had turned out for the governing party.

And even Ramaphosa's clear ability to deliver electoral salvation for his party remained contested within it: ANC election head Fikile Mbalula said that without Ramaphosa at the helm, the party would have lost badly, polling in the region of only 40 percent, by his estimation; yet his and Ramaphosa's *bête noire*, party supremo Ace Magashule, denied this, claiming the party win was due to 'the collective'.

In the months following the election there was little if any sign that Ramaphosa would 'do a De Klerk', shorthand for how, in the last white election of 1989 (which elected me to Parliament), after the mighty National Party (NP) led by FW de Klerk was humbled by its lowest voting percentage in thirty years, De Klerk declared that the general election had placed the country 'irrevocably on the road of drastic change'.[16] He then greenlighted the most monumental changes ever witnessed by the white Parliament in one speech on 2 February 1990, including the unbanning of the ANC, the release of political prisoners and the end of the state of emergency.

After the May 2019 election, finance minister Tito Mboweni published a series of suggested – incremental and modest – reforms: independent energy alternatives, local control of ports and harbours, some minor privatisations, and telecommunications liberalisation. He also warned on the need for debt reduction through culling the public-sector wage bill. Ramaphosa appeared to back him but shied away from implementing any of the items. Mboweni became so frustrated about his agenda not being realised that he took to late-night Twitter sessions to complain about the paralysis at the heart of government.

When it came to Ramaphosa's own suggested minor reforms, from energy independence and breaking up Eskom, to more rational visa regulations, either they were never implemented or they were done in half-baked fashion. Instead, he contented himself with conjuring, to an ever more incredulous nation, fantasies such as 'smart cities' (in spite of the fact that most municipalities were bankrupt), bullet trains (the passenger rail service had effectively by then collapsed in Cape Town) and sovereign wealth funds (at the time the country was borrowing R2 billion every trading day, according to former finance minister Trevor Manuel, just to service its soaring debt load). It was almost as if he believed that mere assertion would deliver results.

ONE-WAYS AND U-TURNS

Little wonder, then, that when credit-rating agency Moody's Investor Services cut the country's final rating into junk territory (or below investment grade) in late March 2020, it cited missed opportunities for its long-awaited decision: 'Unreliable electricity supply, persistent weak business confidence and investment as well as long-standing labour market rigidities continue to constrain South Africa's economic growth,' the agency noted.[17] In the wake of this, and an expected sell-off of local bonds, the currency crashed at one stage to R18 to the US dollar, an extraordinary tumble: when I'd returned from Argentina in late 2012 it was at R8.

Still there was no discernible shift on the real reform front by the president, who maintained his silence at these seismic eruptions on the economic landscape. On the losses to the fiscus, with a hole in revenue collection north of R350 billion, Mboweni noted, '[Following majority decisions] sometimes feels like swallowing a rock.'[18]

Ramaphosa made no attempt to defend his minister, who by then was being referred by the party for disciplinary measures for going against its decisions.

Tito Mboweni was one cabinet member I remembered fondly

from the early days of the democratic Parliament. He was then labour minister and I his shadow on the opposition benches. Unlike most of his political brethren, he had enormous doses of self-confidence: sometimes wrong, never in doubt. But he was one of the few ANC ministers who never resorted to racial name calling, and even after a fiery debate (and we had many) would invite me out after the session for dinner or a drink.

But as finance minister in 2020 he stood isolated. All economic measures were, increasingly erratically, being enacted on the hoof by trade and industry minister Ebrahim Patel, a staunch communist and micro-manager of note. He felt empowered enough to dismiss bleak economic forecasts offered by Mboweni's ministry of the post-covid landscape as 'a thumb suck'.[19]

During the government-imposed national coronavirus lock-down, Mboweni lost every round to the faction that Ramaphosa was trying to appease, notably that of Nkosazana Dlamini-Zuma, on whose arrogant command the entire disaster management of government rested. She saw the lockdown as an opportunity to change the economy completely, and even spoke in revolutionary terms of 'class suicide' to achieve this.[20]

The lost revenues from her ban on the sale of cigarettes and alcohol exceeded the R70-billion loan the government was forced to obtain from the International Monetary Fund (IMF) in July 2020. (The IMF promotes international financial stability and monetary cooperation, facilitates international trade and sus-tainable economic growth, and helps to reduce global poverty, among other things.) Perhaps the lowest moment of Ramaphosa's entire presidency was when Dlamini-Zuma simply countermanded his announcement that cigarette sales would be allowed in the next (stage four) level of lockdown. He meekly defended her U-turn of his decision, invoking the myth of 'the collective'.

There was something frankly pusillanimous about Ramaphosa.

While he abided over the conversion of millions of law-abiding cigarette smokers and drinkers into overnight criminals (since most sourced their smokes and booze via the flourishing black market), and while an estimated R13 billion in cancelled projects by brewing companies and glass manufacturers rendered laughable his vow to attract new investment, he blinked when challenged by a far more powerful and often violent lobby – the taxi owners.

Covid-19 regulations insisted that the thousands of taxis that clog our roads had to limit the number of commuters per vehicle to interdict the spread of the disease, and prohibited them from crossing provincial boundaries. In exchange, the taxi industry was offered R1.3 billion for lost revenues. In defiance, and as a demand for more cash to be stumped up by an essentially insolvent government, the SA National Taxi Council (Santaco) simply flouted the regulations. No crackdown followed, since the taxi owners were too powerful and the government too weak to respond effectively.

This led commentator William Saunderson-Meyer to observe:

> It's difficult to think of any other country where a mafia will inform the nation on Sunday that it intends on Monday to cause the eventual premature death of hundreds, possibly thousands, of citizens unless it is paid a massive ransom. Where else, except South Africa, would the response to such criminal, homicidal blackmail not be the declaration of martial law, mass police deployment and pre-emptive arrests of the ring leaders?[21]

Where else indeed?

LIGHTING THE LONG FUSE

Many, including himself, said Ramaphosa was playing 'the long game'. In one interview, Ramaphosa compared himself to the heroes in the 1978 British-American war movie *Force 10 from Navarone.* He told *The Economist:*

> British commandos try to blow up a dam so that the water will sweep away a bridge that the Nazis want to use. When the explosives go off, nothing happens. The commandos are furious. 'It didn't work!' they say. But the explosives expert tells them to wait. The dam is structurally damaged and will soon collapse, he says. Once the fuse has been lit, there is no going back.[22]

The exception, troublingly for those who thought his leadership would point the country in an economically sound direction, became manifest during the coronavirus crisis. He advised a Mayday gathering in Stanger on the north coast of KwaZulu-Natal that 'the gloves are off' in terms of constructing a 'new economy' and said it 'is time to stop playing around the edges' and that 'radical economic transformation' (a phrase plucked directly from the Zuma lexicon) was the best route forward.[23]

This gave encouragement to the economic Talibans in his party. They were determined to use the excuse of a health emergency to perfect their schemes for economic utopia. For example, ANC 'manager for research, strategy and policy analysis' Dr Mukovhe Morris Masutha – a Zuma acolyte – argued that the coronavirus crisis had delivered 'an unprecedented opportunity' to defeat the 'tyranny of "investors" and "lenders"'. He warned that a careful study was needed of 'the past 26 years of democracy', which he described as 'our nation's failed neoliberal experiment'. He urged his party to 'guard against the tyranny of the markets, defend democratically elected leadership and put the wellbeing of the nation first, even if it means risking everything.'[24]

You don't need to be a Nostradamus to suggest that 'risking

everything' could indicate what was in store for the country post-covid-19.

Incidentally, Masutha, a colourful character who had dated a daughter of Jacob and Nkosazana Dlamini-Zuma, had, variously, led the #FeesMustFall campaign (a protest movement that began in 2015 to stop increases in student fees and increase government funding of universities) at my alma mater, the University of the Witwatersrand (Wits), and, according to a media report, been a spy for the State Security Agency, the government's intelligence arm, at the time – allegations to which he did not respond.[25]

Higher up the party food chain, cabinet minister and South African Communist Party (SACP) boss Blade Nzimande (who'd been instrumental in the rise of Zuma but had clung tenaciously to office under his successor) lambasted the Mbeki-led 'Growth, Employment and Redistribution', or Gear, economic policies as having 'left the economy increasingly dependent on volatile and speculative investment', neatly eliding the fact that the policies had produced the highest growth and job levels in a generation. He also warned that in the aftermath of the pandemic (whenever that might be) 'we can't go back to the crisis before the crisis'.[26]

Licking his ideological lips, too, was Nzimande's colleague, SACP deputy secretary-general Solly Mapaila, who was even more explicit about who was in the party's sights post-pandemic: 'The covid-19 crisis provides an opportunity for the state to be empowered to discipline capital and the private sector,' he harrumphed, noting that the private sector, an engine of growth and opportunity, was now 'at its weakest'.[27]

Ramaphosa himself entered the lists on this debate, telling a very rare press conference on 31 May 2020 that the current economic set up was 'colonial and racist'.[28] This was the system that had enabled him to become a billionaire – clearly a case of 'do as I say, not as I did'.

These were clear signals that fundamental anti-investor, business-hostile, growth-negative economics was in the offing. Mainstream economists by this stage feared that financing this new economic revolution, at a time when the state had raked up huge deficits, would likely only happen by raiding pension funds, imposing swingeing 'wealth taxes' and/or reimposing capital controls. The last option – printing money – was, happily, unlikely, given the tenacious independence of the Reserve Bank.

The prospect of the country going to the IMF for a loan was another possibility, but the leftists in control of economic thinking in government loudly foreclosed this option, fearing a 'threat to national sovereignty', as the international lender would likely impose 'structural reforms' on the country.[29] The grant of a low-cost loan by the IMF in July 2020, by way of a rapid financing instrument (RFI), was certainly less onerous and conditional than the straitjacket of structural adjustment but could be a harbinger for the future.

(An IMF RFI provides rapid financial assistance for countries with urgent balance-of-payment needs caused by, among other things, natural disasters, and requires repayment at low interest rates within three to five years. By contrast, an IMF stand-by arrangement (SBA) is much more expansive, and may require critical reforms of policy to restore macroeconomic stability and growth.)

An ANC policy document on post-covid economic recon-struction, published in May 2020, codified thinking in the starkest terms: 'the developmental state and its hegemony' were front and centre of it all, once again and notwithstanding the appalling track record of the preceding twenty-six years.[30] This led *The Economist* to note, 'There is seemingly no problem for which the ANC does not see the state as the solution.'[31]

This was yet another paper, one of an endless stream, which, whatever its merits or likely demerits, arrived on a landscape already littered with them. Veritably, the country was, in the words of the Brenthurst Foundation, 'policy rich but implementation poor'.[32]

WEAK OPPOSITION

Finally, it remained, certainly for outside observers, a puzzle, given the multiplicity of failures or missteps by government and the wasteland of the Zuma years, why the opposition parties couldn't better capitalise on the situation to their own advantage.

Award-winning columnist of *The Times* of London, Jenni Russell, hitherto a hopeful pundit on the country's prospects, in January 2020 made the funereal observation that 'lights are being switched off in South Africa'. Her gloomy conclusion was referenced to, in part, the poor performance of the opposition at the polls, which removed from Ramaphosa a potential trump card:

> The opposition parties are so weak that the ANC is still guaranteed its majorities. Ramaphosa cannot use that as a lever or a threat. If he cannot persuade, threaten or cajole his party into thinking beyond their own greed and wealth, the future of the country will be bleak.[33]

CHAPTER 2

Opposition blues:
What happened in the DA

The ANC's holy grail, the 1955 Freedom Charter – drafted largely by white communists – commenced with the clarion call that 'South Africa belongs to all who live in it – black and white'.

This was matched and internationalised a few years later by the declaration of civil-rights warrior Martin Luther King Jr who, with deep eloquence, stated that the US would bend the long arc of its discriminatory history toward justice when people would be judged not by the colour of their skin 'but by the content of their character'.

A GOOD QUESTION

'So how can a white man lead a political party in a country that's eighty percent black?'

This was the question that Tim Sebastian, the rightly feared inquisitor of the BBC World TV news programme *HARD Talk*, asked me again and again during our half-hour interview recorded in May 2004 and broadcast later across the world. And he was hardly alone in wondering about this.

My BBC interview happened just weeks after the 2004 South African elections, when the DA consolidated itself, for the second time since the 1994 first democratic elections, as the official opposition party – but way behind the ANC of Thabo Mbeki. Once again, the terms of electoral trade had been race determined: the black majority held to the ANC, while the minorities mostly united behind the party I led, the DA.

I'd pondered a lot on the *HARDTalk* question long before it was posed, and increasingly afterwards as I had to deal with a great din of background noise within the party and the crude barbs of the ANC outside it. This meant that, notwithstanding constitutional niceties about equal citizenship, political reality dictated that to succeed in South Africa the opposition needed to be led and perhaps largely populated by representatives of the majority group.

One contrary view from outside the narrow and ever more stifling debate on race in South Africa came in the form of the Brazilian ambassador to South Africa, a man of easy charm and cynical disposition. He arrived by appointment one day in the early 2000s in my parliamentary office and cheerily advised me, 'If you were a political leader in Brazil, you'd probably be president.' He went on to inform me that despite nearly half of Brazil's huge 211-million population being black, 'we only have white presidents'.

In 2008 Barack Obama famously, and against the weight of his country's conflicted history, became the first black president of the United States. But in both that contest and his 2012 re-election, Obama got a huge turnout among the minority cohorts of the electorate – blacks, Latinos, university graduates, etc – but lost the white vote by more than twenty percent to his unsuccessful and white Republican opponents.[34]

CHANGE AT THE TOP

When I stood down after thirteen years as leader of the DA in May 2007, the party was still grappling with mixed results on how to square the circle, if indeed it was capable of resolution: how to maintain its majority support among minorities, and increase its meagre voter share among the black majority.

My successor as party leader, Helen Zille, commenced with many advantages I'd lacked. She inherited a relatively large and well-functioning party, and her resumé of activism and journalism during the apartheid era suggested that she could reach parts of the electorate beyond my grasp. And, although she'd been alongside me in the party since 1999, and was in fact seven years older than me, she did objectively signal leadership rejuvenation.

But she too grappled with our one essential sameness – the country's primary opposition party, never mind its diverse membership and caucus composition, was still white led.

She addressed this dilemma in two ways, with decidedly uneven results.

First, in the run-up to the 2014 general election, she spearheaded a 'Know Your DA' campaign video and pamphlet. It drew commendably on Helen Suzman's legacy but omitted entirely my own role as the only other living party leader, and obliterated the leadership of other founding spirits such as Colin Eglin and Zach de Beer. I was irritated by the omission but offered, to those who asked me about it, only the comment, 'If you get into a contest about the past, the ANC will beat you every time.'

My former chief of staff Gareth van Onselen was less constrained. Drawing attention not only to who'd been omitted from the campaign materials, but also who'd been highlighted in them – a pantheon of ANC heavyweights, from Mandela to Albert Luthuli – he noted:

> The video attempted to position the DA's legitimacy entirely on the ANC's terms, drawing wholly on ANC endorsements [of Helen Suzman, for example] and recognition, as evidence of the party's moral worth.[35]

It was easy to poke holes in the attempt by the DA, awkwardly and selectively, to position itself on the 'right side' of history but the electoral results in terms of attracting new black votes were very modest: the party did advance overall in the election, to a total vote of 22.23 percent (compared with 16.6 percent in 2009). However, subsequent research indicated that it received an improved but still disappointing 3.2 percent support from the black electorate.[36]

SHORT-CIRCUITING HISTORY

The second attempt by Zille to colour the party leadership was on display just before and immediately after the 2014 election, and indicated just how hazardous an attempt to short-circuit the fuses of history can be.

It was a function at the stately Mount Nelson Hotel in February 2014, some three months before polling day, that the grandees of opposition politics gathered for the launch of Robin Renwick's book on the life of Helen Suzman. The event drew Mangosuthu Buthelezi, FW de Klerk, myself, the mayor of Cape Town Patricia de Lille, and the newish and young leader of the parliamentary opposition Lindiwe Mazibuko. But all eyes that night were on two of the speakers at the launch, Zille and former principal of the University of Cape Town (UCT), Mamphela Ramphele.

The day before the book launch, Zille and Ramphele had announced that Ramphele would be the party's 'presidential candidate' in the election. Although no such post actually existed, it was Zille's attempt to ensure the campaign was spearheaded by a well-known black female. But within five days of the announcement, Ramphele had reneged on the position by refusing to sign a party membership card.

I found the whole exercise ludicrous. On the one hand, Zille had often and with feeling described to me just how difficult it was to work under Ramphele, as she'd done when employed at UCT. But beyond Ramphele's lack of empathy, there was the question of achievement: she'd held high but brief office at the World Bank and started various business ventures that had emphasised her connection to the late Steve Biko more than her economic acumen. I once described her as 'the Zsa Zsa Gabor of politics' – famous for being famous rather than for noted achievements beyond her medical background.

Indeed, she proved built not to last. And after her split with the DA, she went on to lead her Agang party to a huge defeat in the polls (achieving just 0.28 percent of the vote), then refused to take up one of its two seats in Parliament, leaving her party both in the lurch and saddled with great debt.

On the other hand, I understood Zille's problem: how do you dramatically indicate to wary voters that the party has really changed its leadership profile and isn't simply the movement the ANC suggests it is – a home for recalcitrant, even racist, reactionaries?

THE HORNS OF THE DILEMMA

I had experienced Zille's dilemma: as leader it's necessary to marry principle, of which you're chief standard bearer, with a ruthless pragmatism to advance the party – not an easy mix. Indeed, at that Mount Nelson book launch I'd mentioned to Suzman's daughter, my friend Francie Jowell, that her mother had never sought the party leadership and was an example par excellence of a doughty, conviction-led politician. Her work and legacy were thus relatively uncontaminated by the messy compromises of party management and the need to expand the base of her movement (which for thirteen years held just one seat of 166 in Parliament).

My great colleague of yore, who died very suddenly in 2016, Dene Smuts, suggested the way to expand leadership was 'to grow your own timber'. But cultivating such trees or saplings inside the party forest proved to be difficult or too long term for a party in a hurry to change the race dynamic.

If Mamphela Ramphele was a brief and misplaced dalliance that did little damage, two other guests at the Mount Nelson Hotel, both promoted by Zille with the same motive, incurred great cost to the party, and to her, when they departed amid much acrimony later. The weapons for advancing the party proved to be boomerangs in the cases of Mazibuko and De Lille.

In 2011 there was a mid-term caucus election to reaffirm the party's parliamentary leader, Athol Trollip. Zille couldn't fill the post, as she'd elected to be provincial premier, so Trollip had been chosen in 2009 to replace my close friend Sandra Botha in the role. That first bruising contest pitted two other friends of mine against each other – Trollip and Ryan Coetzee, both with very different skills sets. In the event, Trollip won and Coetzee went on to be Zille's key advisor in her role as premier of the Western Cape.

But when Trollip faced his reselection process in 2011, Coetzee and a group of young turks in the party, David Maynier, Gareth Morgan and Tim Harris, decided to run Lindiwe Mazibuko, with just two years' experience in politics and Parliament, against him.

Trollip, a party veteran for whom I had both regard and affection, but whose parliamentary leadership was apparently intellectually average – although excellent on the emotional-intelligence front – would very probably have retained his post but for one hugely significant intervention which tipped the scales against him. Zille decided that the optics of a young black woman being bested by a middle-aged white man would be disastrous.

As one undecided MP described it to me by email, 'One by one we were rounded up and asked to visit the Premier and Leader [Zille] at Leeuwenhof [her official residence in Cape Town]. And there we were intellectually waterboarded by her to support Mazibuko.'

Trollip lost the contest – notionally to Mazibuko but in reality to Zille. It was the second such defeat at her hands, as she'd beaten him for the party leadership when I'd stood down in 2007. This second defeat would have huge consequences, as the party unravelled after the 2019 election. But in the short term Mazibuko became the youngest leader of the official opposition and the first black person to hold that post.

However, beyond these metrics, trouble loomed. First, Mazibuko's caucus management was, to be polite, suboptimal. She led the party to support the Employment Equity Amendment Bill of 2013, which stringently tightened and increased the criminal sanctions of the 1998 version that the party and I had so strenuously opposed. I was amazed at this U-turn and well remembered how staunch Helen Suzman had been in supporting my opposition to this 'pernicious piece of racial and social engineering', as I put it at the time.[37]

My former researcher, now editor of PoliticsWeb, James Myburgh, led the charge against this spectacular desertion by a party of liberal principle by asking, 'Has the DA just put a bullet through its brain?'[38] And when I called Mazibuko to protest this, it seemed to me that she hadn't read the legislation properly and wasn't bothered by the clear slide away from party principle that festooned the new bill.

All this proved too much for Zille, who forcefully intervened and insisted the party reverse course on what she called 'a plane crash that should have been avoided'.[39]

By then the strain between the two leaders was telling, and suggestions started circulating that Mazibuko had designs on Zille's post, something hypersensitive Helen wouldn't have countenanced.

Shortly after Zille led the party to a successful outcome in the 2014 elections, Mazibuko stunned the DA by announcing her departure from both Parliament and the country, to study abroad.

ADDITION BECOMES DIVISION

The De Lille saga also originated with Zille's desire to import influential outsiders to augment the party's leadership, but the strategic rationale for rewarding Patricia de Lille with the plum post of Cape Town mayor in 2011 was never clear.

When De Lille and Zille, previously sworn political enemies in the City of Cape Town, where De Lille aligned her small Independent Democrats with the ANC against Zille, announced a tie-up, I wrote to Zille from Argentina. I suggested the marriage would hit the buffers soon enough due to De Lille's super-sized ego and her antipathy to liberal ideology – she'd been a leading member of the Pan Africanist Congress (PAC) and had trafficked in significant anti-white rhetoric.

Zille wrote back assuring me that she could control the situation, and reminded me of my phrase that 'we should be a party of addition not division'.

De Lille led the party to success in two municipal elections. But during her second term after 2016, she began to foment discord in her caucus and ride roughshod over councillors, and was fingered by the party in a range of misgovernance and suspect processes. The allegations against her included irregular tender procedures for buses with a Chinese company, that she'd influenced the appointment of the city manager and that she'd halted the heritage protection of the Bokaap – all based on two reports by the law firm Bowmans.[40] The party managed to botch all attempts to remove her from her post.

During the great Cape water crisis of 2018 there was growing alarm in the party leadership that De Lille was not satisfactorily handling the situation, and DA leader Mmusi Maimane was inserted into the campaign, partly to restore his profile and relevance. But Maimane's publicly taking control, as party leader and not a city councillor, eroded the barrier he had himself accused the ANC of lowering between party and state. He also effectively signalled a usurpation of the role of Mayor De Lille in the process.

I had some empathy with the DA, having back in 2001 forced the resignation of a previous Cape Town mayor, Peter Marais, for destroying the internal unity of his caucus and for being involved in a vote-rigging scandal relating to his desire to rename Adderley and Wale streets, among other matters.[41] While the ousting of Marais did damage to the DA at the time, and saw us on the receiving end of a court judgment, from its commencement to his resignation the process lasted all of six weeks.

De Lille, by contrast, dug in for eighteen months and finally only quit in October 2018, launching GOOD, her third party in ten years. It obtained a paltry 0.4 percent of the vote in 2019 (but she was rewarded with a seat in Ramaphosa's cabinet).

Before she left the mayoralty, De Lille humiliated the party in a series of adverse court rulings against the DA, failed motions of no confidence against her (with a few DA councillors either supporting her in the council votes, or abstaining), and hugely damaging publicity, which punctured the myth that the DA was a party of clinical efficiency and effective government. This would reflect in the results of the 2019 election.

RISING WITHOUT TRACE

At first sight there was much to admire in Mmusi Maimane. He was young (in 2015 he was only 35), tall, handsome, highly articulate and extremely personable. He would also prove to be, aided by his background as a television performer and church preacher, highly telegenic. He radiated and personified non-racialism, augmented by his attractive white wife Natalie.

His admirers hyped him as 'the Obama of Soweto' and his back-ground story – a son of Dobsonville, child of working-class parents, university graduate – could have been written in Hollywood. His life story brimmed with the promise of a more hopeful future unburdened by the struggles of the past.

His dizzying ascent up the ranks of the party meant that he never really got a footing in any of the many posts he held between his recruitment in 2010 and his election as national leader in 2015. He hopscotched from the Johannesburg City Council in 2010 to provincial-premier candidate in 2014, and in the same year entered Parliament for the first time and was promptly installed as parliamentary leader, without a day's experience in the legislature.

In 2015 Helen Zille was wavering as to whether to continue as national leader, and wasn't reassured when her key lieutenants equivocated on supporting her re-election. So at the party congress in Port Elizabeth she stood down from its leadership. The congress, with strong support from Zille's entire inner circle, elected Maimane as its new leader with nearly 90 percent of the votes.

Despite some sharp disagreements between us, I felt Zille's leadership had indeed been crowned by significant achievement. I was surprised to read in her subsequent autobiography that she and other members of her circle thought I had been 'captured' by the New National Party (NNP) faction of the party in the mid-2000s, and that I'd spearheaded the campaign against her election as leader.[42]

Neither of Zille's claims was correct; I joked to a colleague that sections of her book should be classified under the category 'science fiction', not 'non-fiction'.

A FALSE DAWN

In the run-up to the local elections in 2016, I had two telling encounters that pointed to a sharp change in the electoral weather. First, I addressed an eve-of-election rally for DA Johannesburg mayoral candidate Herman Mashaba, at his request. Houghton Primary School, my old polling station when area MP, was packed with many old-timers from my campaigns and a sea of new faces.

Mashaba spoke at inordinate length in a flat monotone about himself, rather than the party and its election platform, perhaps because few expected him shortly to be elected mayor of the city: my efforts on his behalf would, in time, confirm the aphorism 'no good deed goes unpunished'.

The second encounter, shortly before polling day, was when I met, on an unrelated matter, with veteran ANC cabinet minister Jeff Radebe at the Union Buildings. He advised me that the prospects for his party were very uncertain, with a divided leadership in Pretoria and a horrific record of governance in Port Elizabeth. 'But,' he said, 'Johannesburg is in the bag for us – we won't lose there.'

In the event, all three cities fell from the grasp of the ANC. But the huge success achieved under Maimane's baton in the elections, which saw Port Elizabeth (Nelson Mandela Bay), Pretoria (Tshwane) and Johannesburg instal DA mayors, disguised other factors. And while to the leader go the laurels of victory, Maimane had little to do with assembling the impressive DA electoral 'blue machine' and its mighty funding base, both of which predated his leadership.

There was, moreover, inside the DA a fundamental misreading of the auguries from the electorate.

First off, far more than an enthusiastic embrace of the DA with its first black leader at the helm, the voters who'd turned out in that poll were registering their disgust with the presidency of Jacob Zuma, then in the nadir of his rule. Maimane, to be fair, had led the public charge against Zuma, memorably (courtesy of a magnificent parliamentary speech authored by my later business partner, MP Gavin Davis) calling Zuma a broken man leading a broken country.[43]

Moreover, the dramatic results of that election flattered to deceive: on the surface the ANC total vote had fallen to an all-time low of 53.6 percent, and the DA had risen to a new high of 26.9 percent – its best result to date. This was achieved, though, on a relatively low turnout (58 percent), and the fall-off in ANC support was attributable largely to an intense poll in opposition-supporting suburbs and a stayaway in ANC township strongholds.

And, second, most of the switch in support from the ANC to the opposition went to the EFF rather than the DA, although the latter did grow its black support to a 'high' of 5.9 percent. It was sobering, after all this effort and leadership turnover, to recall that when I first led the newly formed DA in local elections in 2000, we achieved 4.9 percent from the same demographic, suggesting just how long the climb and how far from the summit the party remained sixteen years on.[44]

The party was, however, pumped up by its local and unexpected successes, leading it to the false conclusion that it could, with more effort and less principle, reach national power in 2019 as the head of a coalition government. It misread the electoral map and never factored, among a range of other elements, what a huge difference would occur when the despised Zuma was ousted and it would be Cyril Ramaphosa, not the 'corrupt thief' from Nkandla,[45] against whom the party would face off next time round.

THE HOLLOW MAN

While Maimane spent the next two years tirelessly traversing the country, he essentially outsourced strategic and policy decisions to paid advisors and a group of core MPs. When called on to make a tough decision, he generally equivocated or rushed to a quick judgement which soon enough was reversed.

In consequence, when Helen Zille, still the premier of the Western Cape, issued an ill-judged tweet on the consequences of colonialism in March 2017, Maimane condemned her before speaking to her. And when the party determined that the premier should be sanctioned, he announced a series of half-measures that left her in place and attempted to minimise her influence in the party and with the public. This landed up offending her considerable body of supporters both in the party and outside, and did nothing to mollify the faux-outraged woke brigade who'd demanded her head.

On the policy front, Maimane was even more equivocal. He tinkered with core principles, such as the supremacy of the Constitution and gay rights and, on the hoof, made extreme commitments, such as doubling the funds for child-support grants.[46] David Maynier, who was the DA's finance spokesman at the time, told me that he'd never been consulted on this social-grants announcement, and that should the DA achieve power, the costs of that commitment 'would bust the Treasury and we would have to go cap in hand to the IMF for a loan'.

Mindful of growing disquiet about his temporising and the party's half-baked policy proposals, towards the end of 2017 Maimane asked me to chair a two-day workshop to determine opposition economic policy. During the workshop we heard a series of highly sensible proposals (and others less so) from some top-notch experts. Maimane was inspired by the proceedings and promised to arrange, early in the new year, for the key thoughts to be translated into concrete policy proposals. I never heard another word about them and nor did the party.

The only direct result of our gathering was his decision to appoint one of the participants, the impeccably liberal and whip-smart Gwen Ngwenya, as the new director of policy. This commitment was followed through, but after arriving in office, Ngwenya was starved of resources. And when she did offer a necessary corrective to the party's flirtation with BEE and employment equity, suggesting these had no place in the DA, she was shut down; a few months later she resigned. (She returned to this post in 2020, after Maimane resigned.)

The leadership vacuum at the top quickly percolated its way down through the provincial and municipal ranks of the party, which became contested ground between the liberal element and the more recent arrivals who believed the only way to win new support was to make the DA more aligned with ANC ideology.

In Johannesburg the DA mayor, new recruit Herman Mashaba, made common cause with the EFF to stay in power. When questioned by his caucus members about a range of dodgy tender processes, or by the party about his request for the DA to instal the EFF in power in another 'hung' municipality, he bristled with indignation and labelled his critics racist. He used the same smear when his caucus colleagues requested services for the suburbs that had voted for his party.

Not only had ANC rhetoric become the mode of defence for underperforming DA leaders, but the entire party, in its lurches and equivocations, began to be labelled, not inaccurately, 'ANC-lite'.[47]

Maimane explicitly endorsed this shift with a series of interventions denouncing 'white privilege',[48] backing the assault on Afrikaans-medium schools and universities,[49] and suggesting that when an underprepared rugby host stormed off a television set, he was a victim of racism (a thorough investigation of the conduct of Ashwin Willemse led by a black advocate found no substantiation for this claim).[50]

The most devastating public judgement, which resonated with a growing circle of critics inside and outside the party, was the label Gareth van Onselen stuck on Maimane: 'the hollow man'. While Gareth backed up the charge with facts and statements, the most incontestable was this: until Maimane joined the party for the first time in 2010, he'd never once voted for it in any preceding election.[51]

Little wonder that Maimane embraced Thabo Mbeki in acts of public fealty and ignored the devastating aspects of his presidency – he had voted for the ANC, not the DA, back in 2004.

It's a good and necessary thing for a political movement to attract new recruits, unless it wishes to remain a small cult of true believers. But to hand over the top post of the principal opposition party in the country to someone who has no background in, nor long-time sympathy with, its core convictions is reckless.

FAMILY MATTERS

Increasingly, Maimane's indecisiveness alienated major figures in the parliamentary party. This meant the paid personnel (rather than his political colleagues), in the form of party CEO Paul Boughey and strategist Jonathan Moakes, became the key deciders.

I had two direct intimations before the 2019 election of how badly matters had gone awry.

Political leaders are well served by having a 'kitchen cabinet' of trustworthy and smart advisors. Given the intensity of the environment, its members are like close family – you argue furiously but always have each other's backs. My core inner team were indispensable – Douglas Gibson, Joe Seremane, Ryan Coetzee, Mike Ellis, Greg Krumbock, Russel Crystal and James Selfe (long-serving party federal executive chair, equivalent to secretary-general).

I'd known Selfe since arriving in Parliament in 1989, and he had an intense work ethic and a deep attachment to the cause. Twenty years in the same post was, however, in my view, time enough, and Maimane thought the same. However, Maimane recoiled from speaking to Selfe directly about standing down at the forthcoming congress. I found this inability to hold difficult conversations a negation of leadership, and was surprised when Maimane asked me to approach Selfe on his behalf and suggest he retire.

Selfe declined my advice and told me he would stand again and win, but added the killer comment, 'Why doesn't Mmusi have the guts to speak to me directly?'

Selfe was duly re-elected alongside Maimane, and now the two top posts in the party were filled by people who held each other in mutual suspicion and disdain. By then, all the key players who'd enthusiastically backed Maimane two years before were in varying stages of disassociation from him, and he appeared more isolated than ever from leading influencers inside his own caucus.

A week after the Congress I was in London when I heard that my dear father, Ray, had passed away peacefully in Durban at the grand age of 93. His long and good life had been studded with achievements and emblazoned by firm attachment to liberal principle, as both a Supreme Court judge and as chancellor of the University of Natal (today the University of KZN). But it hadn't been without controversy, especially regarding his sentencing of ANC guerrilla Andrew Zondo to death in 1986. (I dealt with this saga at length in my book *Opposite Mandela*, published in 2014.)

One of the first messages of condolence I received from home was a warm text of support from Maimane, and he later sent flowers.

The news of my father's passing quickly made news in South Africa. While obituaries from the fulsome to the inaccurate appeared in the papers, there was no public word at all from the DA or its leader. I was advised by a participant in the daily telephonic management meeting of the party leadership that when my dad's death was flagged as an issue meriting party comment, an appropriately deathly silence followed and no statement was issued.

Ironically, given their different places on the moral and political spectrums, Dad died within days of Winnie Madikizela-Mandela, both a hero of the Struggle and a convicted criminal for kidnapping and a range of other crimes catalogued by the Truth and Reconciliation Commission. In my 2008 autobiography, *On the Contrary: Leading the opposition in a democratic South Africa*, I wrote at length about her complex role in the country, describing her as both 'a profile in courage' at best and, at her worst, 'a Madame Defarge on steroids'.

Unlike my father, a lifetime supporter and funder of the DA and its predecessors, Madikizela-Mandela had held the party in high disdain. On her death, though, the DA and Maimane issued a statement of condolence which, as one commentator noted, was 'without a single reservation, criticism or moral qualm'. She was simply, according to the DA leader, 'a great South African ... who stands as a bright light'.[52]

Pandering to the racial populists to whom this DA statement was presumably directed – and not offending this group – was the unarticulated reason for the silence on my Dad.

This was too much for Zille, who sent me a note while I was attending the funeral in Durban. In part it read:

> At caucus this morning, I lambasted the DA for its failure to speak up formally about the issue [of your father's death and related matters], but that is ... what the party has become. It took me a while to work it out. We used to stand by the principle, and deal with the consequences. Now we predict the consequences (amongst people who would never vote for us anyway), and then ditch the principle. It is really infuriating, and it must have compounded your grief manyfold.

REVERSAL OF FORTUNE

Going into the 2019 election, in addition to all these false steps and inner tensions, the DA performance in local governance gave the lie to its claims for sound administration.

In Port Elizabeth, Athol Trollip's mayoralty had collapsed. The party's indifferent record in Tshwane was underlined by the decision of its mayor, Solly Msimanga, to abandon ship there and seek to become premier of Gauteng. The Cape storms over the departed De Lille were fresh in memory.

In Johannesburg, any visit to its CBD and suburbs suggested the city was, literally, a mess, aggravated by massive billing errors that infuriated its ratepayers, the DA core voters. Spotting the difference between the ANC and DA was often difficult at local street level.

Facing a resurgent ANC under the new leadership of Cyril Ramaphosa, the DA decided to double down on both the abandonment of principle and the extravagant claims of its electoral aims, presuming, perhaps, that the former would help the achievement of the latter. It broadcast its intention to win 30 percent of the national vote, oust the ANC from power in Gauteng and the Northern Cape provinces, and retain the Western Cape.

The self-delusion that gripped the party high command was apparent when I was invited to lunch a few weeks before polling day by Paul Boughey and Jonathan Moakes.

Party CEO Boughey had worked in my office years before, in the 2000s, as my chief of staff, a role he'd performed very competently and without controversy. But my set-up had consisted of just six or so people, including the tea lady. By contrast, the DA in 2019 was a complex and comparatively sprawling operation, with hundreds of staffers and clashing egos and simmering ambitions. Boughey was the lightning rod for much tension, and apparently generated a great deal of it himself.

When we sat down to lunch under the oaks of a Constantia wine estate, the two repeated the claims made on the party's behalf. When I pressed them about the electoral damage flowing from the De Lille saga and other missteps, I was assured that their polling indicated that they'd put the difficulties of the last year behind them.

However, as the real purpose of the lunch became clear, it was evident that the party's head honchos were more worried about the situation than their outer confidence suggested. 'Our core voters do need some reassurance and reinforcement,' Boughey told me, 'and Mmusi and I would appreciate it if you would go out and publicly campaign for us. Your presence will reassure our traditional supporters.'

When the duo advised me that their nemesis, Helen Zille (Boughey had been at the forefront of moves to terminate her membership of the party), had been roped in as well, I realised that there must be some real panic in the leadership about the impending outcome, despite the surface confidence evinced by them that afternoon.

I felt slightly conflicted about their request: it would hardly be helpful to my work commitments as chair of a communications company and independent newspaper columnist; and anyway I had doubts as to whether anyone's last-minute intervention could tilt the result, as most voters' allegiances are formed long before voting day. But this was my party, and I had devoted most of my life to its success, so I set my qualms aside and agreed to a pared-down programme of public events on its behalf.

The night before the polls opened on 8 May I called James Selfe to find out the final party forecast. He assured me the DA would obtain 'as a minimum' 25 percent of the national vote, less than its rosy early prediction but still ambitious, given the circumstances, compared to the 2014 total of 22 percent.

In the event the party achieved just 20.77 percent, its first vote-shedding since 1994. It lost support everywhere and in all communities.

The DA had failed to achieve three of its four self-proclaimed targets, and even its retention of the Cape was achieved on a reduced vote in comparison with 2014.

CHAPTER 3

The DA pile-up … and the panelbeating

The small conservative rural town of Schweizer-Reneke in the North West province has a population of less than 50 000, including white Afrikaners. When the votes there were counted after the May 2019 poll, the DA had lost every polling station there, after twenty years of strong support.

What's more, the loss of some 450 000 votes across the country could be attributed, in some measure, to the windstorm created from an initial squall there in January, when a photograph appeared on social media showing small children in a pre-primary class at Laerskool Schweizer-Reneke, a multiracial Afrikaans-medium school.[53] The facts that later emerged were that four Tswana-speaking 5-year-olds were placed at their own table, separate from the rest of the class, to enable the Tswana-speaking teaching assistant to translate the introduction of the teacher, young Elana Barkhuizen. The picture was taken by another teacher to send off to parents to show them that the children were settling in happily.[54]

When, without any supporting facts, the photograph appeared on Twitter as an example of egregious discrimination, the DA republished it with condemnatory statements and factual errors. The DA's youth leader, Luyola Mphiti, announced that he would visit the school where Ms Barkhuizen, to DA applause, had been suspended as a teacher.

She was later exonerated and reinstated, indeed praised for her caring approach.

COUNTING THE COST

The affair cost DA around five seats in Parliament. Anchen Dreyer, a staunch liberal and outgoing party vice chair, noted:

> The Schweizer-Reneke incident was a travesty of justice. The dishonesty of the DA attack on an innocent teacher and school was the final nail in the coffin for the DA among many Afrikaans voters; it has direct influence on the dramatic loss of hundreds of thousands of DA votes in the 2019 general election.[55]

Dreyer later presented a report on the party slideaway, which contained no fewer than thirteen other events and incidents where the DA had abandoned the legitimate interests of its Afrikaans supporters or even insulted them. This suggested that Schweizer-Reneke was – in her words – the 'straw which finally broke the camel's back'.[56]

Initially, the party appeared indifferent or unconcerned.

I was alarmed when I saw how the right-wing Freedom Front Plus was making electoral hay out of the DA's miscue, when it launched an aggressive social-media campaign around it, and I phoned party chairman Athol Trollip to express my disquiet. He was by then deep in the bunker and drinking of the party Kool-Aid, and he expressed confidence that the issue was a storm in a teacup and that he'd never 'seen such enthusiasm and party activity on the ground'.

This 'on the ground enthusiasm' had proved elusive when I'd hit the trail on the party's behalf. I'd addressed a string of meetings in

Gauteng and Cape Town. At one of them, in Centurion near Pretoria, just two weeks before election day, I'd been joined by my old political comrade Douglas Gibson, like me a veteran of many past campaigns and with heightened political antennae. During the Q&A following our speeches, audience members had peppered us with queries and doubts about the party, its standpoints and even what its offer to the electorate consisted of.

I turned to Gibson afterwards and said, 'You know that these are not the sort of questions voters should be asking just before election day. It seems that many of our people are very doubtful about the party.'

He didn't disagree.

In the aftermath of the 2019 electoral results, in which the DA suffered its first reversal since 1994, the party, led by Athol Trollip, attempted to shield Mmusi Maimane from responsibility. Curiously for a movement that championed individual rights and accountability, Trollip announced – grim faced after a federal executive meeting – that the party took 'collective responsibility' for its defeat. Other statements emanating from key operatives spoke of 'a winning loss', in one instance, and suggested, in another, 'good riddance' to its deserting voters.

I felt the party needed to take itself by the scruff of the neck and stop avoiding the hard questions, so a few days after the results I phoned Maimane. I'd pondered at length the predicament of the party, especially as media calls proliferated seeking my views on its performance and about Maimane's position. He sounded disconsolate and said he felt 'terrible' about the loss of support and the calls for his head.

I tried to buck him up by reminding him what Boris Becker had said after losing his crown at Wimbledon in 1987: 'Nobody died. I just lost a tennis match.'

He gave a nervous laugh in response.

THE PANELBEATING

I suggested to Maimane that the party needed a deep dive into what had gone wrong and how to fix things. I also advised that this couldn't be done by 'the usual suspects' in the DA's top echelon, whose misreading of the electoral tides had beached it. Outside experts with a broad loyalty to the party and its causes were needed to do a no-holds-barred investigation.

He seemed gripped with this idea, and a few days later he asked me if I would serve on a proposed review panel.

I noted that the review panel would need robust and clear terms of reference and 'nothing should be off the table' – diplomatese for ensuring that the issue of leadership would be interrogated.

Given what eventuated, perhaps I should have heeded the advice of then CEO of Resolve Communications, Nick Clelland, not to serve on the panel. I was chairman of Resolve and wasn't seeking new headlines or controversies, both of which followed after I decided to ignore Clelland's view. However, I felt so deeply invested in the DA project, and so certain that it needed right-sizing, that simply standing aside at its moment of deep peril wasn't an option.

I expressed my view in *Business Day.*

'How do you go bankrupt?' asks a character in the Ernest Hemingway novel, *The Sun Also Rises.* 'Gradually and then suddenly.'

This is a handy warning for the Democratic Alliance. The DA needs to boldly interrogate its results. It did not clearly capitalise on the past nine years of abject state failure and it could not counter the Ramaphosa effect. Of deep concern is that in the election it shed nearly 500 000 votes.[57]

I then warned, noting the siren calls inside the party for it to ignore its loss among bedrock white supporters:

> If the DA gets caught in the vortex of racially preferencing its supporters on a simplistic and electorally disastrous decision of going for 'either/or' rather than 'both/and', a temporary setback will become over time an electoral rout.

Mindful that I could soon serve on the panel reviewing its future, I offered:

> Alone in the ring, the DA is a multiracial party. There are few examples in our racially polarised country of institutions which have managed to provide a home for all without being rent asunder by race holding. But a strong value system and its refurbishment is a clear essential on the path to DA renewal.

Extraordinarily, given that the political ceiling had fallen on his head, Maimane dithered around in finalising our brief and finding panellists. One name after another had apparently declined to serve, and I had yet to receive instructions. When I finally obtained the reference points, I discovered that the proposed 'broad-based review' would be done by just three of us: banker and party donor Michiel le Roux, Ryan Coetzee and me.

Coetzee has several intellectual gifts, prime of which are his clarity of thought and concision of expression. These were reflected in our terms of reference, which he drafted and on which Maimane signed off. The terms were unanimously agreed by the party's federal council, and read in part:

> The review will investigate the underlying drivers of the party's performance in the 2019 election and will encompass

the capacity of the party's leadership ... its political identity, policy platform, strategy, structure, processes and operations, as well as any other considerations relevant to achieving the party's objectives.[58]

Michiel le Roux is one of the tiny handful of dollar billionaires in South Africa, a status he reached entirely on his intellect and business smarts. He certainly was, in appearance and manner, the most modest and soft-spoken member of this elite group I'd ever encountered. His razor-sharp mind, steely resolve and unflinching integrity would serve us well.

The three of us agreed that the party was navigating dire straits, and couldn't afford to proceed on its previous path of half-measures and evasions of hard choices. But before we reached any final judgement we would receive the evidence – and weigh it objectively.

THE UNBURDENING

A centre of excellence in Mmusi Maimane's office, the cheerful and uber-bright Sandy van Hoogstraten, was deputed to assist us, and we set about our task, which by the end of the process absorbed over 300 hours of my time, *pro bono publico*, as the saying goes.

Over 200 written submissions poured in, and we sat for days in Johannesburg and Cape Town hearing the views of more than forty national and regional party leaders, and from a sample of the DA's donors and some leading members of civil society. For many it proved cathartic, and one leading party light told our panel that his interview was akin to 'marriage counselling', as he could unburden himself of his deep concerns on his relationship with an organisation 'I love but which is in deep trouble'.

On the contested issue of the party leadership, it was clear from all quarters, even those most sympathetic to him, that Maimane's irresolution and essential passivity on crunch issues and personnel matters was the cause of many of the party's travails. A typical comment from one submission reflected a widely held view:

> There is a lack of decisive and proper leadership at the centre; Mmusi is not coherent on what he wants … he is dithering, indecisive, lacks self-confidence and is conflict averse.

Even a staunch supporter of his advised our panel, with some sorrow, 'Problems will not be easy to fix with Mmusi at the helm, but there is no one waiting in the wings to take his place.'

On the even more vexed issue of policy confusion and values and party ideology, one of the key outsiders we interviewed – a black intellectual – summed it up: 'The DA has been captivated by the racial and nationalist narrative of the ANC.'

While we found a lot of tension on racial matters and their projection inside the party, we didn't think them insurmountable. But this came with a fat proviso: unless the party developed a 'coherent and principle-based approach to race that allows it to make clear, consistent and communicable decisions, especially when hard choices are required',[59] it would fail on all fronts, with both its members and voters. Such an approach – and we offered the detailed outline of one – would have to replace the current offer of 'slogans and generalities'.

Our final report didn't duck its central purpose. I drafted the conclusion, in which I noted:

> It is our view that, in the absence of a step-change along the lines of [the panel's] recommendations … the Democratic Alliance's current travails will intensify and metastasise to the huge disadvantage of the democratic project in the country and could over time lead to the destruction of the DA as a political force for good in SA.[60]

The most controversial of our recommendations was:

> The overwhelming view of those who made submissions ...
> is that the party leader, while immensely talented,
> committed to the cause, hardworking and widely liked, can
> be inconsistent, indecisive and conflict averse, and that this
> has led to a lack of clarity in the party's vision and direction,
> confusion about the party's position on key issues [and] the
> erosion of the party's unity of purpose.[61]

Flowing from this essential and wide-reaching finding, we recommended

> that those ultimately responsible for the leadership and
> management of the party – the leader, chairperson of the
> federal council and chief executive – step down and make
> way for new leadership.[62]

Since the chair, James Selfe, had by then been moved into a lesser
position, taking a role as head of the party's governance unit for
local authorities, this left CEO Boughey and leader Maimane in the
frame. (Boughey would resign before the conclusion of the process.)

THE LEAKING SHIP

Right through the process, we, the panel troika, kept a tight lid on
our hearings and conclusions. However, as we were finalising the
report in late September, Coetzee kept receiving anxious messages
from Maimane and his lieutenants. Maimane then requested the
panel meet with him in his office on 30 September 2019.

I was very doubtful about the wisdom of such a meeting: if we
shared with him our central finding, that he quit his post, weeks
before the presentation of our report to the federal council on

19 October, endless mischief and distortions could leak out, to the detriment of our process and of the party.

Le Roux, on the other hand, from a position of good faith and not damage control, was of the strong view that as a matter of honour it behoved us to advise Maimane that we would be recommending his exit, to give him time and space to consider his position and perhaps seek another high position in the party, such as the provincial cabinet, where his talents could be deployed.

Coetzee hoped that Maimane would see the hopelessness of his situation but as a good soldier to the cause would seek to manage matters in the best interests of the party, and his own.

So I found myself in a familiar place, outside the large office of the leader of the opposition on the second floor of Parliament's Marks Building, on a crisp Monday morning, alongside Ryan Coetzee and Michiel le Roux.

A secretary advised us, 'The leader will see you now.' Such grandiosity indicated that status and title weighed heavily on my embattled successor. The perks of his office had also been the subject of recent press reports, which detailed how Maimane occupied a house purchased in murky circumstances on his behalf by party donors,[63] and his use of a fancy vehicle lent to him by disgraced Steinhoff boss Markus Jooste.[64] The leaks of these lurid details, clearly by his internal enemies, were disgraceful but did underline questions about Maimane's judgement and probity.

On entering the familiar wood-panelled lair of the leader, I was surprised by two enormous paintings, identical in composition, one of Maimane and the other of Mandela, seeming to suggest that Maimane was cut from the Madiba cloth of leadership which was, to put matters at their kindest, a stretch.

Maimane listened as we outlined our central findings, and he kept notes on an iPad, but offered little or no comment. He was most exercised that we refused to allow the party executive to 'workshop' our recommendations or leave behind a copy of them. On the issue of his leadership he declined any commitment, as indeed was his right.

The meeting became even more surreal when he insisted we be joined by the deputy chairman of the executive, Thomas Walters, a person given to obtuse and lengthy soliloquies, who also urged that we share our thinking with the federal executive a week before the final meeting of the larger federal council. I wasn't at all convinced this would achieve anything beyond endless manoeuvring and further leaks but we agreed to this process in order to not be seen to have some or other hidden agenda.

Within hours of departing Maimane's office, I received a disturbing phone call from John Steenhuisen, the chief whip. I hadn't shared any of the findings of our panel with him – but someone else had, and in a destructively divisive fashion.

'Tony,' a rattled Steenhuisen said, 'Mmusi just called me and told me that your panel is to recommend that he, I and all the DA metro mayors [those of Johannesburg, Pretoria and Cape Town] should get the chop.'

I was flabbergasted. Here was the leader, whom we'd just visited in good faith and at his urging, deliberately distorting our conversation: his fightback was to join up an imaginary cast of fellow-victims to destroy any chance of our report being accepted.

I told Steenhuisen that there was no such contemplation in our report and declined any further insight of its contents; and I took exactly the same line when the media, subject to the same distorted background briefing as Steenhuisen's, began to call seeking comment.

It had been well over a decade since I'd last appeared on the front page of the *Sunday Times* but the edition of 6 October 2019 compensated for my long absence with the screaming headline 'Leon's secret Mmusi mission'. The article below it repeated the canard that we were seeking the removal of DA mayors. In addition, the piece suggested that the call for Maimane to quit was not only in our report but that our visit to his office had been at the initiative of influential outsiders, not a consequence of Maimane's invitation.[65]

THE MAYORAL ACCIDENT

The day before we were to engage with the federal executive ahead of the meeting of the full federal council, on 10 October, an email arrived from Maimane that suggested that cooked-up conspiracy theories had become standard fare in the DA kitchen. This one, though, made the 'Illuminati controls the world' shtick seem unimaginative.

Maimane's email requested my comment on a letter he'd received from Johannesburg mayor Herman Mashaba, a missive riddled with errors and reeking of self-justificatory bile. Mashaba claimed that I'd sought to solicit, on behalf of a client of Resolve Communications, services with the City of Johannesburg 'at an annual cost of R300m'; that I'd done so at a meeting with him at his home on 5 April 2019; and that his failure to act on this 'solicitation' had caused the review to recommend 'the collapse of our coalition governments'.

Other than the date and place of my meeting with Mashaba – I had enjoyed, at his invitation, a very pleasant dinner at his home on the night in question while on the campaign trail for his party – this fantastic confection bore no resemblance to the facts. But the letter had been written to be leaked, as it duly was, in the Sunday edition of *City Press*, two days after I first saw it, earning me another front page in another Sunday paper.[66]

As I indicated to Maimane and Mashaba in my response, nothing improper or untoward had been discussed during that evening, and I noted:

I hardly need to point out that who the City of Johannesburg decides to contract with is entirely the business of the City following all lawful processes. It is not the business of the company I chair … we manage relationships in an entirely open and transparent fashion.

But it was our findings on the EFF, on which matter Mashaba was relying on an inaccurate and distorted leak of our verbal presentation to Maimane of our key findings, that had clearly got the mayor's goat. He stated that the review proposed to end the relationship, which indeed was doing enormous harm to the DA brand.

I pointed out in my letter of response the true position of the review panel, which proposed to conduct a poll among DA voters to assess their appetite for the continuance of this extraordinary relationship with the DA's ideological enemy. I wrote:

It is entirely untrue that the review panel proposes the collapse of any governments. If Mr Mashaba is confident in voter sentiment regarding his coalition, then he will have nothing to fear from the proposal to undertake an opinion survey of the voters in Johannesburg.

I also observed that Mashaba was curiously oblique in his mode of operation: he'd never approached me to express any concerns on any aspect. He also didn't show up the following weekend when, as a member of the federal council, he could have, had he so chosen, advanced his own case on his coalition arrangements. Clearly, his bold volubility on Twitter and in the press wasn't matched by a willingness to directly confront his adversaries, real or imagined.

(Following his exit from both the mayoralty and the party, a hagiography by Michael Beaumont on Mashaba was published in June 2020, entitled *The Accidental Mayor*. In my view, and given my experiences, *The Mayoral Accident* would have been more accurate.)

THINGS FALL APART

The meeting of the federal executive took place on 11 October 2019 in Cape Town. All the members of the federal executive attended, including the federal leadership, all nine provincial leaders and various other office bearers. Each member of the executive was handed a copy of the panel report, which they had in front of them for the duration of the meeting, and then had to hand back at its ending.

The meeting itself was worthy of a scene in the political theatre of the absurd. Maimane led off with a speech of incoherence that did not deal with any of the essentials in our report.

Then the provincial and other party leaders spoke, in turn, and most of them in largely self-referring, myopic terms. The candour our review panel had seen when we'd obtained their evidence was mostly missing from their inputs at the executive meeting. Their courage to face reality was clearly confined only to forums where their party colleagues were absent.

In addition, initially, both Trollip and Maimane were enthusiastically in support of both the review process and our modus operandi, including our investigation into the capacity of the party's leadership, yet when the findings were emerging, Trollip suggested that our determination on the leadership 'was an overreach', while Maimane, who'd put his signature on these very instructions, claimed, 'It must be made clear the review panel is not a referendum on the leadership of the party.'[67]

When we left the meeting, Coetzee, Le Roux and I were severely depressed at the lack of statesmanship evident in the room, and the descent into mediocrity that several of the party leaders evidenced.

The final act of this melodrama played out the following

weekend at the party's vast and expensive new headquarters in Bruma in eastern Johannesburg, where the full federal council gathered to deal with our report and elect a new federal executive chair. Up for the post were Athol Trollip, former deputy chief whip Mike Waters and current deputy federal chair Thomas Walters – and, in a surprise announcement just before the deadline for nominations was reached, Helen Zille.

I realised that her election would, in large measure, together with the review report, determine the party's course. The very forces who opposed her were the most negative about implementing the root-and-branch changes our panel had identified as essential to right-sizing the organisation.

Into this toxic mix arrived, yet again, Herman Mashaba. He let it be known that a 'right wing' element, housed in the Institute of Race Relations (IRR) and headed by Zille, was determined to seize control of the party, and that he would have no part of it. On the eve of the gathering, on Friday 18 October, a headline in *The Sowetan* proclaimed 'Black DA pushes back against Zille'.

This threat, of his impending departure in the event of her election, indicated that a blackmail of sorts was underway. I was now convinced that only Zille's election would see our report being operationalised rather than filed in a back drawer at the party office.

But first our panel would air our proposals, and I was keen to see the reaction of the 150+ party delegates. Maimane and Selfe both seemed determined to constrict our report's ventilation, however, and Coetzee pushed back hard against a madcap proposal from the duo that no copies of the report should be handed to delegates, but that it should be viewed by the delegates on slides, to prevent the full contents being leaked.

In the event, our report was surprisingly well received. When Ryan Coetzee outlined its essence with his customary skill, especially that the party target its redress policies 'at people who currently suffer disadvantage as a consequence of past discrimination and does not use race as a proxy for disadvantage',[68] it bridged a lot of divides.

It fell to Michiel le Roux to deliver, in low-key cadence, the most deadly line of the day: 'Mmusi is a nice guy, but he's not a good leader.'

For my part, I advised the gathering, 'This report might seem to be like chemotherapy in some of its conclusions, but believe us, it's necessary to ensure the survival of this party.' Less dramatically, but anticipating that the party leadership might pick and choose the more digestible bits and disregard the rest, I warned that the full report needed to be implemented. 'It's not a smorgasbord,' I said.

After answering a few questions, we left the venue and the party to its fate. The meeting apparently argued deep into the afternoon, but to my surprise we were later advised that the full report had been adopted, followed the next day by Zille's election. She defeated Trollip by a significant margin.

(Zille had pledged that she would stay in her lane and not interfere with the remit of the leader, whoever that might be, and would busy herself with backroom administration. Subsequent events proved this to be a vain promise. In June 2020 she dragged the party, consequence of yet another controversial tweet, into a truly extraordinary fight and race-baiting war over her quite wrong assertion that there were more racial laws after apartheid ended than before. Another distracting and divisive blow-up now dragged the party from the front foot of its energetic pushback against government overreach during the height of the coronavirus pandemic to a defensive crouch on its commitment to non-racialism.)

In choosing Zille over Trollip, the party had put Maimane in an even more precarious position, as he knew that she would implement all the panel recommendations with vigour.

The day after Helen Zille's election, Herman Mashaba

announced that he was quitting the mayoralty, and denounced the party and Zille. Open-mouthed, I watched Mmusi Maimane, the leader of the DA, lifting Mashaba's arm after this announcement, like a prize fighter, declaring him a 'hero'.

This couldn't go on, and indeed it didn't. Two days later, in an even more surreal event, Maimane announced he was standing down as federal leader. Despite bemoaning the organisation he'd led for five years, he said he intended to stay on as its parliamentary leader.

His caucus, quite correctly, rebelled, and he quit all his posts the next day.

Stranger still was the decision of Athol Trollip who as party chair (not to be confused with the chairmanship of the federal executive and council) was the most senior elected official after the leader, and would likely have been elected interim leader of the party after Maimane's exit. Instead, he quit. I never heard from Trollip afterwards, so have no insight into his decision; antipathy for Zille, against whom he'd lost three rounds over twelve years, was likely high on his list.

The man who inherited Trollip's role, John Steenhuisen, said to me later, 'Athol held a royal flush, and I had a pair of twos. But he threw in his hand.'

In November 2020, in a coronavirus-induced virtual congress, the DA confirmed its leadership, with Steenhuisen elected by the entire party with a hefty 80 percent mandate (young black provincial legislator Mbali Ntuli went up against him; her lively campaign excited media interest but garnered relatively few votes), and Zille confirmed as the federal council chairperson.

A SIGNPOST, NOT A WEATHER VANE

No democracy worth its name can endure without an effective and independent opposition, and South Africa's precarious democratic project certainly needs the best one on offer to succeed, even if its prospects of achieving state power are remote.

A former leader of the parliamentary opposition, Frederik van Zyl Slabbert, once said that for this job you need 'iron in the soul'. The new leader of the official opposition – the eighth since democracy dawned in 1994 – John Steenhuisen, needs that quality.

Often mocked by his opponents for having no university degree (he dubs himself 'the most famous matriculant in South Africa'), he is a keen autodidact and intellectually curious. He's come up through the party ranks and done the hard yards in three different legislatures. He does, as I jokingly remind him, 'suffer a birth defect' – he's a white male in a country where demography is seen as a determinant of destiny, personal and political.

Politicians can usually fit into two categories: weather vanes, which switch and turn with every popular or populist gust; and signposts, which don't bend and buckle at important moments. The opposition cause is, in my view, always better served and led by the latter, and Steenhuisen certainly anchors his politics in the founding principles of the movement.

CHAPTER 4

——

The Constitution of Big Men: Joining the dots

I was gripped, and furiously made a series of notes, when in 2016 I read *Red Notice: How I Became Putin's No 1 Enemy* by Bill Browder. It was an extraordinary story that on the face of it had nothing to do with South Africa. But it was a vividly recounted cautionary tale of what happens when the rule of law is replaced by the rule of men.

In 2006, when Vladimir Putin, in the first of now endless terms as president of Russia, arrived in our Parliament, I was part of a delegation of office bearers invited to take tea with the 'great man'. My ANC colleagues regaled the Russian head of state with effusive, obsequious outpourings of appreciation for the role played by the Soviet Union in the liberation struggle. This was hardly grounds on which I could compete, so, when invited to offer some words, I piped up, 'I'm the only South African here who can boast a Russian grandmother.'

At this Putin seemed genuinely intrigued. He asked from where in Russia my granny, Tamara Drusinsky, hailed. My answer, that she was born in Sebastopol, Crimea, revealed a shaky knowledge of geopolitics: 'Sadly, Crimea is no longer part of Mother Russia,' Putin told me.

Eight years later he invaded the region and illegally annexed it to his motherland.

A TALE OF TWO MURDERS

Bill Browder didn't have tea parties with Putin. Instead, he and his investment-company team in Hermitage Capital Management were victims of the dark and lethal arts of Putin, a former KGB officer, and his apparatchiks.

Browder had all the attributes for success in the freewheeling casino capitalism of Moscow in 1990, shortly after the fall of communism. His grandfather had been leader of the US Communist Party in the 1930s, but Browder's rebellious nature meant that instead of following his parents into socialism and academia, he decided to become an arch-capitalist. Armed with an MBA degree and high intelligence, and a background in banking, he was one of the very first people to understand that assets in Russian companies were undervalued, and were being sold for a song. So he went to live in Moscow, where he put his intuition into practice and hit paydirt. His firm became the largest foreign investor in Russia and he personally pocketed north of R6 billion in the process.[69]

But in 2007, after butting heads with Putin's cronies in the companies in which he was heavily invested, it all went wrong. Because Putin and his circle effectively controlled the police, the judiciary and the tax authorities, it was easy for the state apparatus to hit Browder hard. He and his company were accused of acting for foreign agencies, being spies, and committing 'crimes against the state'.

Browder and Hermitage became victims of what he termed 'state corporate raiding' during which some R3.8 billion paid by his companies in taxes were, effectively, stolen by the government. Browder was arrested at the airport and banned from Russia. When he tried to enforce his rights, the real trouble began.

His tax lawyer, Sergei Magnitsky, whom Browder described as

the 'bravest man I've ever known', refused to leave Russia with the rest of the team and stayed to enforce the company's rights. He declared his faith in the legal system. For his belief he was arrested on trumped-up charges, detained in horrific conditions and, on 16 November 2009, beaten to death in his cell by eight guards in riot gear while he was handcuffed to a bedrail. The state then concocted a fantastical cover-up story.[70]

As I read this gripping and harrowing tale, events in South Africa were taking a sinister turn. A report had appeared in the *Sunday Times* concerning public protector Thuli Madonsela, who'd officially reported the unlawful spending on Zuma's private Nkandla estate, and who'd triumphantly weeks before had the report endorsed by the Constitutional Court, which in March 2016 held that the president – 'the personification of this nation's constitutional project' – had 'failed to uphold, defend and respect the Constitution'. Zuma had thumbed his nose at the imposition by the public protector of an order to repay a portion of the money for the cost of the upgrades, which included 'a cattle kraal, a swimming pool, a chicken run, a visitors' centre and an amphitheatre'.[71]

The Sunday newspaper indicated dark forces at work against Madonsela: she was 'living in fear for her life' since she'd received credible information that a 'revenge hit' on her had been arranged in exchange for R740 000 to the killers, who would do her in by way of a car 'accident'.[72]

The plot went no further but a barrage of media assaults was launched to discredit Madonsela. On the same day as the hit-job report appeared, social development minister Bathabile Dlamini – herself a convicted criminal[73] – harshly criticised Madonsela for 'politicising her office'. Since a core element of Madonsela's brief had been to investigate abuse of office by politicians, this was an absurd claim. But it was part of a sinister narrative from the ANC high command.

The State Security Agency at the time was investigating the public protector on allegations of 'spying', and the egregious one-armed deputy minister of defence, who'd deserted an ANC camp while employed there as a cook, Kebby Maphatsoe, had declared Madonsela to be 'in the pay of the CIA'.[74]

After reading Browder's book, I wrote a column weaving together the two narratives. On the one hand, South Africa's rule of law was battered but less degraded than in Russia. On the other, in both cases it was a fragile instrument capable of capture by wayward politicians – such as Putin and Zuma – who used the state and its resources as sites of personal plunder, not as instruments for social progress.[75]

The publication of my column led to a public rebuke by the Russian Embassy, which was predictable enough. What I hadn't anticipated was direct communication from Bill Browder himself. And so we developed a relationship, and on my next visit to London I spent some time with him at his offices in Soho.

Browder was disarmingly direct and friendly, and fantastically well informed. The horrifying murder of Magnitsky had converted him into a human-rights crusader and he'd become, in the intervening years, the most potent external opponent of Putin. I told him that reading his account of the killing of his tax lawyer and the cover-up that followed reminded me of the murder in detention in Port Elizabeth in 1977 of Steve Biko, the black consciousness leader. He advised that this parallel was exact, and revelatory.

He told me that at the height of his crisis with Putin and after Magnitsky's murder, he and his wife were in desperate need of a holiday, and they decided to visit Cape Town for the first time. On the plane over and to familiarise himself with the country, Browder read Donald Woods's account of Biko and his life and death, *Cry Freedom*. He was struck then by the eerie parallel between the two murders and was very keen to obtain more first-hand information.

On discovering that Donald Woods had died some years before, he reached out to the newspaper reporter who'd uncovered the circumstances of the Biko death, Helen Zille, by then premier of the Western Cape. 'I was absolutely amazed,' Browder told me, 'that this busy, high-profile woman readily spent a morning with me going through all the essential details.' It was entirely typical of Helen, in fact.

Browder was so taken with Cape Town that he decided, on the spur of the moment, to buy a home in Camps Bay. I asked him when he'd last visited Cape Town. 'I won't set foot in South Africa while Zuma remains in power,' he said. 'He'd ship me off to the Russians in an instant.' Indeed, Russia had issued a 'red notice' for Bill's arrest anywhere in the world. The close association between Zuma and Putin connected, apparently, to a proposed nuclear deal was well known; Bill's caution was perhaps advisable.

Realising that the murder of Biko in custody had been the catalyst of the international campaign of sanctions against the government of South Africa, Browder set about using the anti-apartheid template as a model for his own campaign against the assassins of Magnitsky, promoting the passage of the so-called Magnitsky Acts, targeting the assets and movements of the Russian principals involved in the crime.

Since 2016 the US version of the Magnitsky Bill has been widened beyond targeting the killers: it now authorises the US government to sanction those deemed human-rights offenders, freeze their assets and ban them from entering the US. In a delicious twist, in 2019, the US used this legislation to impose wide-ranging sanctions on the three Gupta brothers, and their business associate, Salim Essa, aptly described as 'the spider at the centre of the state-capture web'.[76]

THE GOOD CZAR

My fascination with Russia was due not just to my Russian grandmother, nor to my encounters with Bill Browder, nor to the uncomfortable parallels between the local state-capture project and Putin's empire and network based on cronyism and the use of democratic instruments for authoritarian and corrupt ends.

The oft-held view in that vast land that its government consists of 'a good czar and bad boyars'[77] (senior officials) had a local echo. The idea that some great leader could guide a country to better outcomes, and was stymied in so doing only by poor ministers and bureaucrats, would be a widely shared view on the presidency of Cyril Ramaphosa.

Before Ramaphosa took the helm, the excitement that greeted his election was all of a piece with a far earlier South African trend: the belief that redemption would arrive with the right leader at the top. Concern for the institutional health of the apparatus of government always excited less attention and interest.

This also allowed an army of disillusioned ANC supporters and media camp followers to deprecate the extremities of Jacob Zuma's misrule as an unfortunate aberration rather than the predictable outcome of prioritising party above state, and investing the head of state with extraordinary power should he choose to use and abuse it. It also allowed faith to be kept with the ANC in the belief that salvation would be at hand after Zuma's departure.

There was always a nostalgic lament for the golden age of Mandela. He'd used his vast authority lightly, famously spurning pleas to serve a second presidential term.

A truer reflection arrived with Mbeki, who realised that the locus of power rested in the party, and not in Parliament, or even in the executive arm of state. He thought his expiring second term as country president could be alchemised into continuing his hold on power by getting re-elected as party president in 2007. His bid was defeated, ushering Jacob Zuma in to the presidency of the party, and soon enough, the state.

Under Zuma's sprawling kleptocracy, not only were the state and its institutions captured for ideological reasons; as one of his predecessors, FW de Klerk, wryly noted, 'While the SACP and Cosatu were trying to capture the state for the National Democratic Revolution [NDR] and for socialism, he succeeded in capturing it for himself.'[78] And, of course, for his family and friends.

Zuma's predations in office were mightily assisted by the ANC resolution in 2007 to disband the hugely successful corruption-busting law-enforcement agency, the Directorate of Special Operations, or the Scorpions – precisely because of, not despite, its 93.1 percent conviction rate in cases it prosecuted.[79]

At the same time, nearly a third of the new national executive committee (NEC) elected to supervise the party and, effectively, govern the country were either convicted criminals, or were under investigation by the criminal-justice authorities, or had resigned from public office owing to ethical lapses.[80]

The following year, Parliament had rubber-stamped the death sentence on the one truly successful corruption buster in the country. In so doing, the ANC ignored a petition of 98 000 signatures and 7 978 written submissions calling for the retention of the Scorpions.

The replacement agency, the Hawks, was far more pliable to corrupt governing-party interests than its predecessor, and far less minded to investigate or prosecute real crimes and high misde-meanours, from the Guptas to the bevy of cabinet and party enablers who facilitated the capture of the state.

PARTY ABOVE ALL ELSE

During the terrible covid-19 winter of 2020, public rage against ANC officials pilfering procurement contracts and the skewing of health-equipment tenders to close family members erupted. And, lo, even the same ANC NEC that had so eagerly defanged the Scorpions now suggested their resurrection.

In his typical conflict-avoidance style, Cyril Ramaphosa decided to appoint a committee to investigate.

But the real face of the Hawks was revealed not by its inaction and incompetence on the crime and corruption fronts, but in something even worse: the top law-enforcement agency had become, in the furious phrase of a leading journal, 'a rabble who believe their main job is to act as private security for cretinous politicians'.[81] This was a reference to how the Hawks had swooped to arrest the errant wife of the egregious and disgraced former cabinet minister Malusi Gigaba, for scratching a luxury car of his friend, and the jailing of a spurned lover of a serving deputy minister, David Masondo. As the *Financial Mail* correctly observed, 'It's a terrible message: you can pillage the fiscus and kill without consequence. But cross our politicians and the dogs of war will be let loose.'[82]

It was easy enough to parody Zuma as heading an 'ineptocracy' (a system of government where the least capable to lead are elected by the least capable of producing), but Zuma's view gained wide traction in his organisation, which regarded itself as the fount of genuine authority as exemplars of the 'people's will'. As he said at a gathering in KwaZulu-Natal in late 2015, 'I argued one time with someone who said the country comes first, and I said as much as I understand that, I think my organisation, the ANC, comes first.'[83]

And Zuma had long held the view that the party should trump not only the country but the Constitution as well. In 2016 I shared a platform in Cape Town with an old acquaintance, Mosiuoa 'Terror' Lekota, by then the leader of the Congress of the People (COPE), and he recounted an incident from the mid-1990s, when Zuma was chairman of the ANC, and he'd fired Lekota as premier of the Free

State. Lekota's offence? Dismissing a member of the cabinet who'd stolen public funds.

When Lekota advised the ANC high command that he'd acted well within his constitutional rights to dismiss such an errant member, Zuma told him that the ANC was more important than the Constitution; the Constitution was only there to 'regulate matters', he'd said.[84]

ANC consistency on the topic didn't end with Zuma's demise. Today, a search of the Twitter profile of every cabinet minister, including Ramaphosa, yields an interesting continuum: each preferences their ANC office ahead of their constitutional title. And this isn't merely symbolic – the diktats of the party are the supreme authority. Parliament and the other checks and balances, bar perhaps the courts, prove to be expensive but largely toothless adornments.

When, in the early stages of the covid-19 pandemic crisis, health minister Zweli Mkhize (Twitter profile: 'Former ANC Treasurer General Current Minister of Health') publicly upbraided the gormless executive member for health in the Eastern Cape for failing to fill the crucial post of director of public health in the Nelson Mandela municipality, she responded that she was 'waiting for ANC secretary-general Ace Magashule to approve a name'.[85]

MOSENEKE WARNS

The year 2016 marked twenty years of the enactment of the South African Constitution. Our future may have looked increasingly imperilled, but retreading, often mythologising, the past was always a crowd pleaser.

At a 'People's Consultative Assembly' I attended, implacable ANC veteran and former constitutional court justice Zac Yacoob denounced Jacob Zuma, then entering his final years in office, and warned that the country should never again elect a president who would 'steal so much and lie so much'.[86]

While such a stark character assassination was fully justified by the known facts, a more searching critique was offered by Yacoob's former judicial colleague, retired deputy chief justice Dikgang Moseneke. It was significant that the impeccably well qualified and legally admired Moseneke had been overlooked by Zuma for the top judicial office in favour of Mogoeng Mogoeng as Chief Justice. The latter lacked Moseneke's judicial seniority and certainly his struggle credentials (Moseneke had been imprisoned on Robben Island while Mogoeng had served as a prosecutor in the bantustan of Bophuthatswana), and he couldn't match his legal accomplishments, but Zuma no doubt thought – erroneously, as it turned out – that his appointee would prove tractable.

Freed from the constraints of judicial office, at the People's Assembly Moseneke (whom I'd first met in Geneva in 1991 at a World Council of Churches seminar on South Africa) made the most telling point of the day. He précised his remarks from a speech first delivered at a university symposium some years before, which went to the heart of the issue: the huge powers the Constitution invests in the person and office of the president. 'The anecdotal account is that at the time of the formulation of the final Constitution, whenever there was a dispute about who should appoint a public functionary, the negotiating parties were happy to leave the power in the incumbent, President Nelson Mandela. He, after all, would do the right thing.'[87]

During those epic constitutional negotiations in which I was so immersed between 1991 and 1996, our influence was marginal – Cyril Ramaphosa infamously described the 'sufficient consensus' criterion for the Kempton Park negotiations brutally: once the ANC and the NP had agreed, everyone else could 'get stuffed'.[88] But a warning voice kept echoing in my head, and it was amplified by my Democratic Party colleagues. It was the voice of my constitutional law professor at Wits, Johan van der Vyver, who told our class way back in 1980, 'If you ever get to write a constitution, make sure that you have in mind what will happen if your worst enemy, not your best friend, gets into power.'

Some thirty-five years later Moseneke stated it was time to revisit the 'dispersal of public power' and in whom and how it was allocated. He noted the 'vast powers of appointment' allocated to the president, and to the national executive, which the president appoints and dismisses, were both problematic and dangerous.[89]

It was a Constitution fashioned around Mandela, driven into a ditch by Zuma.

CHAPTER 5

___

Unpopular populists:
A red warning

French statesman Charles de Gaulle drew a sharp distinction between patriotism and nationalism, even if in modern times they seemed one and the same: 'Patriotism is when love of your country comes first; nationalism is when hate for people other than your own comes first.'

Demagogues need a rallying point to provide a ready enemy, or handy alibi, to explain the pain and misery and mistrust felt by many voters. In India, for Hindu nationalist entrepreneur prime minister Narendra Modi, the target was the Muslim minority. For another incipient authoritarian, Hungary's Viktor Orbán, international Jewish financier George Soros was the bogeyman. And for Donald Trump in the USA it was Mexican immigrants.

Protectionism, or autarky, was their promised economic cure-all.

A BUNDLE OF FREEDOMS

The smug assumptions embedded in long-established, largely western, democracies were poleaxed by a series of electoral shocks in the 2010s which had political consequences of both economic and cultural origin.

In June 2016 a referendum was held in the UK asking voters whether the country should leave or remain in the European Union. Unexpectedly, the 'leave' side won by nearly 52 percent to 48 percent. 'Brexit' – 'British exit' – rent asunder nearly fifty years of ever closer union between Britain and Europe. That outcome had been the life's work of one man, the pub-friendly populist Nigel Farage. When Prime Minister David Cameron, who'd campaigned hard against leaving, fell on his sword, he might have rued his early dismissal of Farage and his party as 'a bunch of … fruitcakes and loonies and closet racists'.[90]

A strikingly similar note was struck by Donald Trump's opponent and the odds-on favourite to beat him in the November 2016 American election, Hillary Clinton, who derided many of his supporters as 'a basket of deplorables'.[91] Many Americans and the world were shocked when Trump was elected president of the USA.

And the results of the Brazilian presidential election two years later, in November 2018, seemed confirmatory of the perils of conventional wisdom – although in that election both the polls and the pundits had agreed that the winner would be obscure far-right populist congressman Jair Bolsonaro, the self-proclaimed 'Trump of the Tropics'.[92]

This had much to do with Bolsonaro's predecessor but one, Luiz Inácio Lula da Silva, universally known as 'Lula'. In November 2012, shortly after my return to South Africa from South America, I noted on Lula's visit here at the invitation of the Congress of South African Trade Unions (Cosatu) that he'd achieved a rare trifecta in the world: his two-term presidency was credited with high growth, expansive political freedoms and falling inequality – the exact ingredients largely missing in South Africa. But I'd missed the acute observation of Lula's predecessor, Fernando Cardoso, that 'Lula-nomics' consisted of 'government by cash dispenser'.[93]

Lula sat out the 2018 Brazilian election in a prison cell, convicted in the greatest corruption scandal in the world at the time, 'Operation Car Wash', which dwarfed the local version of state capture by multitudes of billions. His once-admired state proved to be bloated and thieving, fiscally ruinous and utterly enfeebled at law enforcement.

Little wonder, then, that Bolsonaro triumphed: he offered a heady mix of dubious nostalgia (admiration for the achievements of the military dictatorship of three decades back) and extreme measures against crime, and he disparaged gays, blacks and women.

The core for any demagogue, such as Trump, is a base of true believers. As US philosopher Eric Hoffer wrote in 1951, 'All active mass movements strive ... to interpose a fact-proof screen between the faithful and the realities of the world.'[94] Belligerent nationalists, right and left, use popular grievances, traffic in falsehoods and exploit a pervasive sense of disempowerment to unite supporters and identify villains and scapegoats.

This issue was identified by Helen Zille in 2015 in a presentation to Liberal International,[95] a world federation of liberal political parties. Her talk was noteworthy for the fact that she's the daughter of refugees from Nazi Germany, which had been the ruinous apogee of this sort of destructive politics. The assassins of democracy often operate from within the citadels, and use the system to trample over its foundations.

SONS OF THE SOIL

The Economic Freedom Fighters (EFF) was founded in 2013 by ex ANC Youth League leader Julius 'Juju' Malema, a year after he was expelled from the ANC when a disciplinary committee found him guilty of fomenting divisions and bringing the party into disrepute.

The dire metrics in South Africa – huge unemployment, vast inequalities and a history of dispossession – suggested fertile political ground for the EFF to till. Yet its radical economic and racial prescriptions were strikingly unsuccessful with the voters. In the 2019 general election, held after nine years of Zuma's misrule, against which the EFF had been the most vocal opponent, it netted only 10.79 percent of the national vote. In local elections three years before, in which voters directly elected members of municipal councils, it failed to amass enough votes in any single ward, beyond Rustenburg in the country's platinum belt, to elect a councillor directly.

While it would be easy to dismiss Malema and his red-overalled members and supporters as 'unpopular populists', in 2020, with the local economy crashing to depths unseen since the Great Depression, there was some echo of the dynamics of Weimar Germany of that time. In that country in 1928, under relatively secure conditions, most Germans viewed the Nazi Party as the lunatic fringe and awarded it with a paltry 3 percent of the vote in national elections. But in 1933, shortly after the Great Depression struck, the party won 44 percent of the vote and became the largest faction in the Reichstag, and soon thereafter took over the government.

Back in 2014, when the EFF first brought its street tactics of mayhem and chaos into the hallowed halls of the National Assembly in Parliament – a trick it would wearingly repeat for the next six years – ANC secretary-general Gwede Mantashe used the Nazi analogy on the EFF. While the mishmash of EFF policies, drawn from the ruins of Hugo Chávez's Venezuela and Robert Mugabe's Zimbabwe, hardly added up to anything beyond a gaseous concoction of economic populism, they completely lacked the unique evil of the Nazi Reich. But there was something in the analogy in the EFF's tactics of thuggery – disrupting Parliament, labelling a journalist a 'bloody agent'[96] and calling Ramaphosa a 'bastard'[97], trashing retail outlets, brandishing firearms in public, and invading private and public land across the country.

In his *Concise History of Nazi Germany* Dr Joseph Bendersky points out in immaculate detail how the Nazi Party conducted itself in the Reichstag between 1928 and 1932 when, like the EFF in South Africa, it had little political support but enjoyed outsize attention, not least through its outlandish tactics. The party disrupted and paralysed the political system and electoral processes to win control of the very system they were so energetically undermining. 'They intimidated their opponents, they created disorder in the streets ... and they kept themselves in the public eye,' Bendersky notes.[98] Malema was certainly doing, with modern African characteristics, a good job copying this strategy.

The EFF was blatant in its attempt to vandalise Parliament and upend its dignity through the tactics of shock-and-awe disorderliness – spurious points of order, singing and shouting, intimidation and disruptions. On one occasion, in July 2019, EFF MPs physically rose and surrounded a minister, their *bête noire* Pravin Gordhan. One analyst described this 'threatening violence in Parliament' as 'a new low'.[99] But the ANC in South Africa was made of sterner stuff than the weak governing parties of Weimar Germany: in the latter days of Zuma it regularly used white-shirted security bullyboys to expel riotous EFF members from Parliament.

This attitude of contempt had not always been the case. Nelson Mandela had, for example, made himself accountable to Parliament and showed the appropriate deference. Frene Ginwala, speaker of Parliament during his presidency, remarked that in place of his normal batik-style shirts, Mandela 'always wore a suit to Parliament as a sign of his respect for the institution.'[100] And it was not just his sartorial choices that mattered, both in the House and in the courts of law. He pitched up, did his duty, answered questions, and even took the occasional judicial and political bullet against him.

The years since Mandela had, however, witnessed a vertiginous decline in the accountability and decorum of the executive; the loutish behaviour of the EFF inside and outside the chambers of

Parliament simply underlined the Potemkin village, with an outer façade hiding an inner emptiness, that Mandela's successors had built.

And the ANC was no slouch in undermining Parliament itself. For example, in 2014 – and this trend was to continue – only 17 percent of oral questions to ministers were actually answered, and 53 bills were steamrollered through Parliament 'of which only 20 were properly debated in just 28 hours'.[101] In any event, all decisions of consequence were debated outside Parliament, in the inner sanctum of ANC national executive and subcommittees.

By the time of the coronavirus in 2020, all decision-making in the country was concentrated in the hidden bowels of the National Coronavirus Command Council. Rule by decree, strikingly like PW Botha's State Security Council during the 1980s state of emergency, had become the new, undemocratic, normal. And this left even less oxygen for the shock-and-awe spoiler tactics of Malema.

The second caution in drawing too much solace from the EFF's underperformance at the polls (where on its best day it managed only half the support of the moderate, centrist DA, for example) lay with the ANC. Since the EFF was, in effect, a tributary of the ruling party, another way of reading the same election results was simply to combine the ANC and EFF totals, which measured almost exactly the vote for the ANC in 2004, or 67 percent of national support.

TICKLING POLITICAL EROGENOUS ZONES

While the EFF was unburdened by any of the compromises of governance, its extremist populism reflected, and often spurred, an attitude that pervaded the inner councils of the ANC as well. That is the best explanation for why a slew of EFF positions – such as EWC, ratcheting up the pressure on employment equity, a refusal to countenance privatisation of state assets, and importing the rhetoric on 'radical economic transformation' (RET, defined by one critic as 'a severe dilution of property rights, massive intervention by a corrupt and incompetent government, and a concerted assault on the legitimate rights of millions of South Africans solely on the basis of their race')[102] into the government policy mainstream – had all been adopted by the ANC in 2020.

The threat from the EFF at the polls might have been slight – although the shattered post-covid economic landscape suggested all future bets were off – but the EFF tickled the erogenous zones of the body politic in many other ways.

While many prognosticators imagined an electoral future when, after thirty years of misgovernance, the ANC would finally be pushed below the fifty-percent support line in 2024, it didn't require feats of imagination to contemplate that the most likely combination for a coalition in that event would be the rejoining of the EFF wayward child back into the mother party. The real point of speculation is what would be the price tag, on both sides, for readmission.

There was little, as well, to choose from between the parties on the corruption front. The media made much of the conspicuous consumption of the EFF – Malema proudly sported a Breitling watch and lived high on the hog in a Sandton home where his lifestyle was allegedly funded by an illicit-tobacco baron. Credible, meticulously detailed reports of the proceeds of the looted assets of the VBS Mutual Bank — which collapsed into insolvency — appeared in the bankrolls of Malema and his deputy, Floyd Shivambu, enabling the latter to have purchased Gucci loafers, a Range Rover and a holiday in Zambia. While, by October 2020, seven people had been arrested in connection with the looting of the bank – and the case had been postponed to January 2021 to allow 'police to make additional arrests' – no action had been taken against Malema or Shivambu by law-enforcement authorities.[103]

On the issue of race, Malema beat this drum with relentless fury, and with much crudity and offence. He fused Indians into his diatribes against minorities, on one occasion accusing Indians of seeing blacks as 'subhuman' (as evidenced by the low rate of interracial marriages.)[104] Sometimes, in his attempt to discredit minister Pravin Gordhan and the revenue authorities who were delving into Malema's unpaid taxes, he took aim at 'a small clique of Indians who are in bed with a group of Afrikaners in SARS', in this way merging two hate groups for the price of one slice of rhetoric.[105]

But it was whites who served as an all-purpose punching bag and handy alibi for his explanation for black failure and dispossession. In her 2015 presentation to Liberal International, Helen Zille noted, 'It is easy ... to mobilise a populist agenda on the basis of race in South Africa,' and suggested that whites 'fulfil all the criteria for becoming a scapegoat for contemporary South Africa's problems and policy failures'.[106]

At the EFF's seventh-anniversary celebrations in July 2020, after greeting his 'fearless ground forces of the revolution', Malema – the 'commander in chief', as he styles himself – offered up his usual fare of fear and loathing, of which the following extract was sample gruel: 'We must break the hypnotising of 1994, that has made us accept a fake unity in this country while our economy remains in the hands of our oppressors.' Telling his listeners that an 'arrogant race of people arrived in South Africa and assumed themselves as superior', he reminded them that 'for as long as the land remains in the hands of the white minorities, we will never rest. We want the land to be returned in the hands of the rightful owners.'[107]

THE DRINK OF LOSERS

While Julius Malema rallied his 'fighters' to wage an 'aggressive war against capital and corruption',[108] it was an article written in

October 1937, five years into Hitler's rule in Germany, and in a vastly different South Africa of seventy years ago, by Dr HF Verwoerd, then the editor of *Die Transvaler*, that provided a significant clue on the limits of Malema's appeal, despite his incendiary rhetoric.

At the root of the argument between Afrikaners and Jews, maintained Verwoerd, was material interests. 'The Nationalist does not hate the Jew,' he wrote, but added that the Afrikaner had found that commercial and industrial undertakings were mostly in 'foreign' hands, 'latterly mostly Jews'. Verwoerd accused Jewish businesses of employing only fellow Jews, thereby hindering opportunities for Afrikaners.[109] In similar vein, areas of conflict between the two groups had been exacerbated by, he said, Jews moving into the professions, thus blocking Afrikaner advancement.[110]

As a solution, Verwoerd advocated 'to remove the source of the friction' – in this case, the disproportionate domination of the economy by the Jews – by ensuring that Afrikaners received a share of commerce and industry 'according to its proportion of the white population'.[111]

In democratic, ANC-dominated South Africa, some seven decades afterwards, just such a proposal was embedded in a slew of enacted laws, from employment-equity legislation to prescripts for public-sector appointments and promotions. In 2020 the government signalled its intention to accelerate and intensify these. Verwoerd's original idea of fixed racial percentages was now dressed up as 'representivity', with different targets – the old lived on in the new South Africa.

Here, then, was one reason why, shorn of its radical language and wilder ideas, some of the core ideas on the topic offered by Malema were already settled policy by the government he disparaged.

In his 2019 biography of American diplomat Richard Holbrooke, author George Packer warned of the perils of nationalism, whether African or Afrikaans – or, in this case, Serbian. 'It had the irresistible taste of bitterness flavoured with the sediment of ancient grievances distilled to a dangerous potency that induced hallucinations of purification and revenge,' he wrote.

Packer also universalised the concept and limits of such nationalisms, whether in South Africa or Serbia: 'It was the drink of political losers. Maybe that is true of nationalisms everywhere.'[112]

CHAPTER 6

———

Myths and legends:
The price of free speech

The pink colonnaded grandeur of the Mount Nelson Hotel at the foot of Cape Town's Table Mountain provided the setting for my encounter with a famous political figure. Frederik Willem de Klerk had shaped many of the country's recent political contours yet, like the proverbial prophet, by November 2019, on the afternoon of our get-together, he enjoyed little honour in his own land.

While De Klerk was indisputably one of the key founders of the liberal democratic constitution that was inked in 1996, he was by inclination and acknowledgement a conservative nationalist. I first met him in Parliament thirty years ago, when he was president and I a junior backbencher. He was always courteous, indeed warm, yet there was sometimes a slight edge in our encounters. Perhaps this was because the NP, the party of which he was a famous scion (son of a leading apartheid cabinet minister, Jan de Klerk, and nephew of hard-line apartheid prime minister JG Strijdom) and later leader, had been forced to disappear into the folds of the Democratic Alliance (DA).

In July 2000 I had led the Democratic Party into this merger with the NNP, then helmed by De Klerk's chosen successor as leader, Marthinus van Schalkwyk. I became the first leader of the new DA, and for Van Schalkwyk's short stay with the party, he was my deputy. It was a very unhappy union, and in November 2001 Van Schalkwyk and his top lieutenants withdrew from the new party and relaunched the NNP as a separate entity. It did disastrously at the polls, although Van Schalkwyk parlayed his own role rather well, becoming premier of the Western Cape and then an ANC cabinet minister.

De Klerk played an ambivalent role throughout: at first he was supportive of the DA, but when Van Schalkwyk withdrew, he (De Klerk) accused the DA of embarking on 'the course of traditional, competitive opposition politics' and expressed 'sympathy' for the NNP decision for closer cooperation with the ANC.[113] He embraced a cooperation agreement between the ANC and the NNP in 2004, but when Van Schalkwyk formally merged the NNP with the ANC later that year he resigned from the party.

ANATOMY OF AN APOLOGY

On that benign early-summer afternoon at the Mount Nelson Hotel, De Klerk and I were on stage before a well-heeled audience. This had become his new métier: a comfort zone in which, in exchange for a handsome honorarium, he could tell a truly re-markable story of a political apostasy that had, arguably, as much as the inspirational and visionary leadership of Nelson Mandela, pulled the country back from the brink of a racial civil war and worse.

The Owners Forum is an international club of ultra-wealthy privately owned family companies, which includes among its members the Oppenheimers, the Ackermans and the Motsepes of South Africa. On that day, though, most of the audience was from overseas. For them, De Klerk symbolised someone who'd relin-quished power and presided over the against-the-odds transition that had catapulted South Africa from polecat of the world into an admired member of the comity of nations.

On 2 February 1990 – my first-ever day in Parliament – De Klerk had metaphorically detonated a political explosion of such thermonuclear intensity that its aftereffects are still being felt today, thirty years later. That morning, in undramatic tones, he upended over 350 years of political history, announcing the unbanning of the ANC, the SACP, the Pan Africanist Congress (PAC) and related organisations; the imminent release of Nelson Mandela; and the commencement of full-scale constitutional negotiations.

As a consequence, he was, on the one hand, reviled by the governing party for being the 'last apartheid president'; he was also, to them, an inconvenient reminder that, far from its mythologised armed struggle having ended apartheid, the demise of the system in some considerable measure was attributable to this unlikely reformer.

On the other hand, to many of his own former supporters – the white voters who'd lifted him to the presidency in 1989 – De Klerk was a sell-out who'd offered his supporters a false prospectus. The Constitution that he'd promised would prevent untrammelled majoritarianism from extinguishing core rights, such as the preservation of Afrikaans schools and property rights, was under siege.

My role that November day was to pose questions to De Klerk to elicit some of the flavour and colour of the momentous times in which he led South Africa from 1989 to 1994. I commenced my rather gentle interrogation of the then 82-year-old but still spry and engaged De Klerk with an underarm delivery, asking him to comment on a recent encomium on his achievements by US academics Daniel Byman and Kenneth M Pollack. They wrote:

> If De Klerk had remained committed to apartheid, the most likely outcome would have been South Africa's descent into

even greater racial violence or quite possibly an all-out civil war not much different from what is happening in Syria and Venezuela today.[114]

De Klerk was rather modest in accepting this consolation from two foreign historians. But he was more forthright when I upped the tempo slightly, suggesting that he suffered from the Mikhail Gorbachev paradox. Like the last Soviet leader, I offered, he'd dismantled the system of privilege he'd been entrusted to safeguard, earning both the scorn of those who benefited from the change and the enmity of those who lost out in the process.

De Klerk rebuffed the suggestion, advising the audience, 'The difference between Gorbachev and me is that I apologised for apartheid, and in respect of communism he did not.'

The nature and quality of that apology was to be interrogated just three months later – by a far less hospitable and appreciative audience than the wealthy worthies gathered that day at the Mount Nelson Hotel.

CRIMES AGAINST HUMANITY?

The problem for the ANC, ever attuned to its place and those of its paladins in the vanguard of history, was that to commemorate the 30th anniversary of the release of Nelson Mandela from 27 years' incarceration in February 2020, it had to acknowledge the fact that he didn't march out of Victor Verster prison because he chose to do so on 11 February 1990. It was on the order of President De Klerk.

President Ramaphosa decided to split the difference by using the anniversary occasion to remind South Africa that it had been the forces arrayed against De Klerk that had compelled his decision and, on his version, that it owed nothing at all to 'the kindness of [De Klerk's] heart'.[115]

It was quite striking how the reformist De Klerk inspired such contempt in the ANC, even though on any version of history he had helped bend the country towards the arc of change and reconciliation. Yet his predecessor, the hard-line PW Botha, had been almost mythologised as one of the good and the great by some of the same forces of liberation. For example, on Botha's death in November 2006, as opposition leader I'd issued a careful statement of some equivocation, but then-president Thabo Mbeki had had no such qualms. He'd described Botha as ranking alongside ANC icon Oliver Tambo as 'partners in the creation of the peace of the brave'.[116] Mbeki had even, unlike me, attended Botha's funeral.

I'd noticed a similar pattern of behaviour in Nelson Mandela, who'd told me on several occasions how he distrusted De Klerk but admired Botha. I found this extraordinary – admiration for the man who'd kept him in prison and contempt for the other who'd released him – and queried it with him directly.

'Well,' said Mandela, 'at least you knew where you stood with Botha.'

I couldn't help but conclude that the animosity was in part because of the constitutional settlement that had obliged Mandela to share the stage with De Klerk, his mandated deputy president until 1996.

Perhaps in death De Klerk might, in the best South African tradition of arch-hypocrisy, receive some salutation from his opponents. Meantime, while still very much alive he provided an irresistible target for vilification. And he spurred on this process with an interview that aired just before the opening of Parliament on 13 February 2020 that was both clumsy and consequential.

Talking to the SABC, he said he did 'not fully agree' with the presenter who asked him to confirm that apartheid was 'a crime against humanity'. While he apologised profusely for his role in it, and for the crime of racial discrimination, he decided to get into a lawyerly parsing of words. He insisted that the system was responsible for few deaths and that it shouldn't be put in the same category as genocide or crimes against humanity.[117]

The interview itself received little traction or much adverse comment, until it was noticed by arch-opportunist and parliamentary vandal of note Julius Malema. Languishing in the polls and starved of the oxygen of publicity he craved, the leader of the EFF, with his exquisite sense of timing and penchant for hyperbole, found the perfect moment to strike.

Malema faced a dilemma on the night of Ramaphosa's State of the Nation address. He was deprived of the cartoon villain of a president in the form of Jacob Zuma, and was marooned in the political margins because Ramaphosa was effectively implementing a centrepiece of EFF policy in the form of land expropriation without compensation (EWC); he also faced uncomfortable questions on his party's receipts from the recently looted VBS Mutual Bank.[118] He needed a new target, and he needed to change the subject.

And so, before Ramaphosa could address Parliament, Malema attacked. De Klerk was seated in the gallery at the event, and Malema rose on a spurious point of order demanding that De Klerk be removed from the chamber. 'We have a murderer in the house,' he declared; 'we have a man who has got the blood of innocent people [on his hands] in this house.'[119]

A furious back-and-forth ensued, and bedlam in the chamber delayed Ramaphosa's address by one and a half hours – perhaps the original intention, since most of the country had either retired to bed or changed television channels by the time he commenced.

While De Klerk sat stoically in his seat during the melee, members of his foundation were formulating a fightback. The next day it issued a statement of blunt denialism and defiance. It described the original De Klerk comment as correct, since the UN General Assembly resolution branding the system as a crime against humanity was 'an "agitprop" project initiated by the Soviets and their ANC/SACP allies to stigmatise white South Africans by associating them with genuine crimes against humanity – which have generally included totalitarian repression and the slaughter of millions of people'.[120]

This led to an angry countering. Philippe Sands, an expert on international law, stated the obvious general point – 'It is unarguable and hopeless to claim today that apartheid is not, and never has been, "a crime against humanity".'[121] Not only had it been criminalised by the International Criminal Court but it hardly required certification by the UN for the subjects of apartheid's lash to be branded as victims of an inhumane system.

De Klerk realised the futility of his foundation's stance and withdrew its statement, with contrition, three days later.

A number of issues flowed from this episode, some reflecting on De Klerk and others on the environment in which he and the country, and indeed the world, found itself in at the beginning of the third decade of the new century.

INFLAMED WOUNDS, UNBURIED RESENTMENTS

Like any politician, De Klerk had the human instinct to seek memorialisation and affirmation for the one big thing he'd got right: the epoch of change his decisions, announced on 2 February 1990, had inaugurated. Yet history and many of his compatriots were determined to remind him and the world of the many things he'd done wrong in the decades before then.

His FW de Klerk Foundation made little or no mention of his eighteen years of parliamentary and ministerial duty, from 1972 to 1989, all in service to bolstering the apartheid state. But to criminalise apartheid, as his interrogators and critics goaded him to do, would not only have been a repudiation of most of his public career, it would have branded members of his close family (his father and uncle, for example) as purveyors of inhumanity.

The De Klerk fracas reminded me sharply of one of the most scintillating public conversations I'd ever witnessed, some six years before, in London at the Jewish Book Week. British novelist Ian McEwan observed to Israeli writer David Grossman that many of his writings emphasised the adverb of place 'there' as opposed to the adverb of time 'then'.

Describing the difference of emphasis between the words with reference to the Nazi Holocaust, which resulted in the murder of six million European Jews and led directly to the much-contested establishment of the State of Israel, Grossman explained that for Israeli Jews, the Holocaust was always about 'there' or 'over there' – it happened in Europe – but it 'is always with us … it is ever present'.

I realised that, inadvertently, Grossman had touched on a real difference in both the perception and the reality of the apartheid era back home, even three decades after its formal ending and our country's embrace of non-racial democracy. I suspect that for most black South Africans, apartheid is always about 'there' and not 'then'. It remains with the subjects, or the direct victims of the system, long after its formal ending, and even long past the point when the same group has attained full civil rights and even, for some, high levels of material prosperity.

On the other side of the divide, for most members of the white minority in South Africa, that system is more about 'then'. The reasoning goes something like this: it ended in 1994, and we can honour the past, even make reparation for it, but we can't live in it. If the country is to get ahead, it needs to get beyond the confines of its own history, terrible though it might be.

The difference, in my view, goes to the heart of the debate of the meaning of apartheid and how to overcome its legacy – something that continually trips up our ability to get some consensus on the way ahead.

My thoughtful contemplations of that London literary event found no following echo in the cacophony of name-calling and personal attacks that passed as debate in South Africa's public (and social media) square when De Klerk's complicity in a crime against humanity was being 'debated' in 2020.

It was impossible in an era of 'critical race theory' (which assumes that institutions are inherently racist, and that race is used by whites to further their interests at the expense of people of colour) and 'victimology' (where the status of 'victim' confers automatic innocence on the holder, and feeds the demand that any injustice entitles reparation) to have a discussion to reach some form of consensus, even if it was respectful disagreement. And this applied especially since the bona fides of participants, especially those from the 'suspect [white] class', were never accepted.

Yet another eminent novelist, Saul Bellow, had anticipated this. 'The more furious the political debate, the less tolerance [he had] for nuance, uncertainty, moral complexity,' observed writer Nathaniel Rich.[122] Into this fetid stew that inhibited discourse and debate arrived the concept of 'wokeness' – a demand for vigilant social awareness that led to a new culture of censoriousness and puritanical rectitude against any who dissented from politically correct norms. The right not to be offended rather than the right to express an opinion, even if unedifying, had become an almost universal norm by 2020. And the gatekeepers who zealously determined what thoughts or speech could pass through an ever-narrower intellectual isthmus were both self-regarding and self-appointed.

Complexity, nuance and tolerance were certainly not on the homeland agenda. Here, Twitter (often driven by fake accounts or 'bots') and other platforms provided a virtual sewer for outrage and insult, laced often with generous invective. The press – which had done so much to expose the horrors of apartheid, and the excesses of Zumaism more latterly – suffered from 'virtue-signalling' excesses. This meant that many journalists, and particularly those in white and other minority groups, felt the need to proclaim their fealty to the new South Africa by blowing up any comment and racial slur from a white person, and often giving a pass to equally or even worse racist comments from black South Africans; or they drew a specious and false equivalence between the serially corrupt ruling ANC and the far less ethically compromised DA.

There were many examples of this dispiriting trend, which effectively chilled the constitutional promises of free speech and academic freedom, and had the effect of closing a debate before it even got underway. And with race being the South African salient, and identity politics a proven vote winner, attacking the racial origins of a participant was far easier than challenging the merits of an argument.

OF LESSER SPARROWS AND BIGGER BEASTS

Of course, there were genuine white racists who transgressed basic norms of decency and threw more gelignite onto the home fires. The most egregious, although not sole, example of this was an obscure KwaZulu-Natal estate agent, Penny Sparrow. In a virulent Facebook post on New Year's Eve 2016 she compared black beach bathers to monkeys. She didn't remain long in obscurity thereafter – and a viral backlash saw her summonsed to the Equality Court, where she was charged with and convicted of crimen injuria.

But the opprobrium didn't end with Sparrow. In similar fashion, from the pomp of his State of the Nation address in February 2000, then President Thabo Mbeki used a hate-filled racist email from a white person to point the finger at whites generally,[123] there were larger forces at play in the Sparrow saga. James Myburgh went to the nub of the issue, likening the rapid and reckless wide dissemination of Sparrow's remarks as intended to deliberately inflame racial tensions. He wrote:

> One of the standard methods of racial propaganda ... is to focus obsessively on isolated but inexcusable actions by individuals from the targeted group. These are then used to foster a particular stereotype about the group as a whole and create a climate of moral panic whereby violent or arbitrary measures can ... be taken against members of the group as whole.[124]

While Sparrow proved to be a bird of little brain or empathy, others in the aviary of racial madness were busy at work, either as protagonists or as targets of moral panic. In the first category, Gauteng government employee Velaphi Khumalo posted on Facebook that whites 'deserve to be hacked and killed like Jews' as Hitler had done. He, too, was eventually indicted and convicted of hate speech in the Equality Court although, unlike Sparrow, he kept his job.[125]

No one suggested that Khumalo was representative of collective black opinion, as many claimed about Sparrow in terms of the white community. She was taken to court on charges brought by the ANC, which offered no comment or action on Khumalo. For example, Philip Dexter, one of the more offensive MPs of my time, who had defected from the ANC to opposition COPE, and was working his passage back to the ANC at the time of the Sparrow and Khumalo sagas, stamped Sparrow's views as unmitigated racism but defended Kumalo's more extreme invective as 'mere prejudice'. He held the peculiar view that 'the claim that black and white people can both be racist is simply, factually wrong'.[126]

The moral panic of which Myburgh warned was soon in overdrive. Respected senior Standard Bank economist Chris Hart was forced out of his job for the sin of offering on Twitter the comment, 'More than 25 years after apartheid ended, the victims are increasing along with a sense of entitlement and hatred toward minorities.'[127] He was roasted on social media and the ANC charged him criminally.

The bank didn't wait for the court process to proceed. It suspended Hart for his 'racist undertones' and 'factually incorrect' assumptions. Standard Bank never bothered to elaborate in public on these, and Hart subsequently announced his resignation, despite not having 'been found guilty of any wrongdoing'.[128]

The popular Gareth Cliff was fired as a judge from the talent show *Idols* by the broadcast network M-Net for disagreeing with Sparrow's views but defending her right to free speech.[129]

It was one thing to ostracise or even criminalise Sparrow (and Khumalo). But when a leading financial institution and a powerful privately owned broadcaster applied self-regulation verging on censorship, South Africa had veered into dangerous territory. Indeed, as 'cancel culture' – the popular practice of, via social media, withdrawing support for public figures or companies after they've done or said something considered objectionable or offensive – swept the world in 2020, American commentator Lance Morrow wrote:

> This fear to speak is a civic catastrophe and an affront to the Constitution. It induces silent rage in the silenced. It is impossible to exaggerate the corrupting effect that the terror of being called a 'racist' – even a whiff of the toxin, the slightest hint, the ghost of an imputation – has on freedom of discussion ...[130]

AN INCONVENIENT OPINION

There was always a disconnect between reality, on the one hand, and the preoccupations of the political elite and the chattering classes, on the other – especially those who drove their views or took their cues from the highly unrepresentative platforms of social media. But the real opinions of the population at large revealed another, more inconvenient truth for the ethnic entrepreneurs who flourished in latter-day South Africa.

The year following the Sparrow brouhaha, 2017, saw a number of disturbing racially charged incidents in the country. These included the relatively trivial – a black woman and a white man hurled abuse at each other in a Spur restaurant in Johannesburg, after which the man was banned from Spur restaurants, which in turn led to a consumer boycott by a large number of white patrons. But there were also far more deadly incidents, such as that at Coligny, a small farming town in the country's North West province. The place exploded into full-blown racial hatred and violence after two white farmworkers were accused of killing a 16-year-old black youth after allegedly throwing him off the back of a vehicle. They were both acquitted on appeal in 2020. (In late 2020, with the roles reversed, the Free State town of Senekal erupted in racial clashes after a 21-year-old white farm manager was murdered in the most brutal circumstances, allegedly by two black stock thieves.)

This hardly seemed a positive time for race relations. Yet when the Institute of Race Relations (IRR), appropriately, published a large national opinion survey at the end of 2018, the findings were striking: 77 percent of black respondents had 'never personally experienced racism directed against them', and the same percentage believed that 'with education and more jobs the differences between races will disappear'.[131]

Most noteworthy, perhaps, of black respondents only four percent believed 'fighting racism' should be the 'top priority of government' and only one percent chose 'speeding up affirmative action' as the number-one issue. By contrast, the three top issues identified were 'creating more jobs' (35 percent of South Africans; 38 percent of black respondents), 'improving education' (27 percent of all respondents; 26 percent of blacks) and 'fighting crime'

(26 percent of all respondents; 26 percent of blacks).[132]

Government's priorities were, of course, the exact reverse of this popular sentiment.

UNIVERSITIES RACE DOWNHILL

If the country were to have a fighting chance of turning its back on the racial divisions of the past and heading into a brave new world of technocratic excellence, its campuses needed to mould the new generation accordingly.

With perhaps the single exception of Wits under the leadership of Adam Habib, there wasn't a single university in the country by 2020 that had remotely demonstrated the sort of intellectual toughness exemplified by, for example, the University of Chicago. In 2016 its president, Robert Zimmer, sent a welcome letter to all incoming first years containing the following warning:

> Our commitment to academic freedom means we do not ... cancel invited speakers because their topics might prove controversial, and we do not condone the creation of intellectual 'safe spaces' where individuals can retreat from ideas and perspectives at odds with their own.[133]

This sort of no-nonsense approach (and its prodigious financial endowment) had seen the University of Chicago produce no fewer than ninety Nobel Prize winners in its storied history.

The best South African haul of Nobel laureates, a modest five, was from the UCT. But at the time of this writing it would be unlikely to produce any in the future. There was a financial reason for this: UCT had by 2018 around thirty-five A-rated researchers, the highest rank, but funding for their endeavours had been cut by ninety percent in order to meet the bill for free fees for students.

In the view of another administrator, Jonathan Jansen, it was likely that within the next ten years there would be no top-ranking universities left in the country, 'only teacher-training colleges'.[134]

When explanations are one day sought for the failure of universities to maintain themselves as centres of critical thought and intellectual excellence, a key answer, beyond crimped finances, will lie in the dismal abdication by its academic leaders.

Here, again, UCT led the pack. I witnessed this first-hand just a few months after reading the stirring letter of President Zimmer of Chicago. I'd attended the UCT annual Rabinowitz law lecture, and at the dinner afterwards I was seated next to the dean of the law faculty, Professor Penny Andrews.

At the time attention had focused on her faculty when – ventilated once again on social media – a notice had called a mass meeting of students to 'decolonise UCT Law'. Absurd, perhaps, but the restriction attached to the invitation was ominous: 'Blacks only. All oppressed, conquered, enslaved people of the African diaspora.'

I asked the professor whether her administration had received any blowback on this racist proscription, the very antithesis, on any reading, of the university's non-racial and inclusive credo. She said that her faculty was 'perfectly relaxed, since the event was not an official meeting … and anyway very few students attended'.

Intrigued by this line of argument that numbers and officialdom cured any violation of the university's professed principles, I responded with a hypothetical: 'What if a group of students called a whites-only meeting on campus. Would you be happy with that?'

Andrews countered that 'historical context' was the key differentiator in allowing discrimination, a slightly more elegant elevation of the Philip Dexter nostrum that blacks can never be racist.

By this time, the university administration had decided that acquiescence in the desecration of symbols and destruction of intellectual independence was the path of least resistance. And, like all such capitulations, it led downhill.

THE PRICE OF APPEASEMENT

The impeccably Marxist economist Paul Baran stated in 1961, 'The desire to tell the truth is … only one condition for being an intellectual. The other is courage, readiness to carry on rational enquiry to wherever it may lead', to avoid succumbing to 'comfortable and lucrative conformity'.[135] These conditions were in short supply at UCT during the time of my conversation with its law-faculty head; and the leadership – or, more precisely, the lack of it – flowed from the top in the form of its vice-chancellor and principal, Dr Max Price.

In 1977 Price, a medical student at the time, was elected president of the Wits Student Representative Council (SRC), heading a liberal 'Positive Action' ticket for which, as the local head of the 'Young Progressives', I arranged covert off-campus funding (since political parties were then banned at Wits) from the Progressive Federal Party (PFP). But by the time I'd joined the SRC a few months later via a by-election, Price had transferred his allegiance from the liberal camp to the hard left on the council. His ideological malleability was matched by an easy manner and ready charm.

At the time of my student politicking during those undergraduate years, I spent a lot of time in the Fellside, Johannesburg home of photographer David Goldblatt, whose son Steven was a close friend. Goldblatt senior was an ascetic and accomplished visual chronicler of South African life, from the devastation and dehumanisation of the migrant-labour system to everyday racially segregated life in obscure towns such as Boksburg on the East Rand of Johannesburg.

Back then he was well regarded locally, but not internationally famous. By 2017 he'd become one of the most acclaimed photographers in the world. Garlanded with international and South African awards for his achievements, he'd housed his impressive photographic archive at UCT – the wrong address, as it turned out.

In that year UCT, under the baton of Price, decided to take down or cover up some seventy-five works of art from the university's collection 'on the grounds of their vulnerability to potential damage' or because 'some members of the campus community have identified certain works of art as offensive to them – for cultural, religious or political reasons'.[136]

Price decreed that Goldblatt and other photographers' works 'might have intended to reveal the callousness of apartheid' but that they nevertheless depicted black people as desolate and dehumanised. By contrast, he contended, 'Photographs of white people, in the same collection, portray them as powerful, privileged overlords.'[137]

This dualism was a pretty perfect description of the system of racial supremacy itself, but such reasoning was entirely lost on Price. Goldblatt would have no truck with this thought-blocking nonsense and craven piffle, a violation of the core principles of freedom of expression and artistic integrity – the shaky foundations on which the university professed to stand – and promptly removed his collection. 'I completely disagree with the policy at UCT and to have left my work in the collection there would have been tantamount to endorsing that policy,' he said.[138]

His works were eagerly accepted and curated by Yale University in the USA.

Sadly, the covering up and removing of statuary and artworks at UCT was the culmination of a disfiguring process. 'Fallism', which started with the removal of the statue of colonial bad man and university benefactor Cecil Rhodes in 2015, had moved by then from statues to thought control: all education, from science to law, needed, according to student agitators, to be 'decolonised'.

There was nothing new in any of this. In 2001 the Taliban in Afghanistan had demolished the two monumental Buddha figures at Bamiyan as part of the drive to destroy all the country's pre-

Islamic 'icons'[139]; and hundreds of years before that in England demolition squads acting on the orders of Thomas Cromwell had, according to historian Simon Schama, removed all monuments 'of superstition and idolatry' offensive to the new Puritan order.[140]

By contrast, when I visited Saint Petersburg, Russia in 2017 I was struck by the lengths to which both the Soviet and Putin regimes had gone to preserve and restore to past glory all manner of artefacts and palaces of the less-than-glorious Romanoff empire, much despised by VI Lenin. He supplanted the Czars but insisted on the preservation of their iconography.

When Petersburg was in the grip of communism in 1985, and was still known as Leningrad, its deputy director of architecture, Vladimir Popov, advised the *Christian Science Monitor*, 'Why do we restore everything? We take an important historical principle into account: those who reject the past don't have a future.'[141]

So another feature of Sovietism at UCT was the Trotsky notion of 'the dustbin of history', into which historical art and 'offensive' thoughts were consigned. There, the university cancelled its lecture on academic freedom in 2016 because, ironically, the lecturer, Danish cultural editor Flemming Rose, may have offended some section of the campus audience. In September 2005 cartoons depicting the Prophet Muhammad were published by Danish newspaper *Jyllands-Posten* under the editorial direction of Rose. Price justified the ban by saying that the campus was 'in a fragile state'.[142]

In the same year university authorities signed an agreement with a group described as 'violent and law breaking' which had destroyed university property. Instead of being handed over for prosecution, they were offered an 'Institutional Reconciliation and Transformation Commission'.[143] (At Wits, by contrast, Principal Adam Habib called in the police to quell similar rampages.)

Cataloguing Price and UCT's capitulations, an article by a

dissenting senior lecturer in its department of philosophy, Dr Elisa Galgut, was aptly headlined 'When a university loses its mind'.[144]

Max Price departed his post at UCT in June 2018 but the mindlessness Dr Galgut had identified continued after his departure. Exhibit A of this dismal continuance occurred when the powerful fist exercised at UCT by a shadowy group named the Black Academic Caucus metaphorically hit highly respected professor Nicoli Nattrass, described by an academic peer as 'probably the country's leading academic economist'.[145]

In May 2020, Nattrass published a commentary in a scientific journal reporting results of a question-based study among the university's students entitled 'Why are black SA students less likely to consider studying biological sciences?' This flowed from her concern over the struggle to recruit black postgraduate students at UCT, which, beyond the merits of diversity, was a response to the constant pressures to 'transform' all disciplines.

She applied for, and was granted, ethics clearance by the university hierarchy to proceed with the survey. She presented her results to the relevant university review panel, and a panel member suggested she publish it, and the *South African Journal of Science* accepted it.[146]

The moment the article appeared, some months later, the Black Academic Caucus wrote to the university executive demanding the condemnation of the study. The executive duly issued a statement, ignoring that one of its number (a deputy vice-chancellor) had sanctioned the study, slamming Nattrass for producing a commentary with 'methodological and conceptual flaws that raise questions about the standards and ethics of research at UCT'.[147]

The university's appeasement of a secret group (the Black Academic Caucus operated, like the old Broederbond, furtively, and its constitution and membership list were never published) was most concerning. By pre-emptively censoring its scholars and scholarship – even those pre-cleared – the university had indicated that pacifying the outraged remained its default setting.

Nattrass herself underlined her worry about 'the rise of "thought police" in universities', commenting that had the *South African Journal of Science* been a book, the Black Academic Caucus 'would be burning it in the main avenue of the university'.[148]

From Nattrass's colleagues came only a 'deafening silence'.[149]

Max Price and his successors at UCT and at other South African universities would, and did, answer charges of appeasement, intellectual failure and their concessions to the loudest (and sometimes violent) protest groups, as the necessary cost for buying peace on campus and allowing university life to continue.

My intellectual hero, the late Clive James, provided a salutary warning from ancient history on the wisdom of buying peace by conceding principle. In his reflections on the reign of Tiberius, which James describes as the 'morphology of limitless power', the Roman philosopher Tacitus predicted the ruin of the Roman Empire because its elites had bowed down before various plundering and indeed mad emperors. They thought they were purchasing tranquillity in exchange. Tacitus warned, 'solitudinem faciunt, pacem appellant.'[150]

Since those seeking to 'decolonise' legal education had already succeeded in having Latin removed from the LLB syllabus, a translation is helpful.

'They make a desert and they call it peace.'

CHAPTER 7

___

Real money: Why the ANC is bad for business

Despite the magic of Mandela and the so-called 'rainbow miracle', 900 000 South Africans left the country between 1990 and 2018. Although this covers all eras from De Klerk through to Zuma, it gives a flavour of the size of the exodus. And the group with the greatest mobility and the easiest options were South Africa's super-rich.

In February 2016 the South Africa Wealth Report, the findings of a 2015 migration survey by New World Wealth, a Johannesburg-based consultancy, revealed that almost a thousand millionaires had left South Africa in 2015, and the country's dollar millionaires had declined from 46 800 in 2014 to 38 500 at the end of 2015, a fall of eighteen percent in one year.[151] By 2018 South Africa had around only two thousand multimillionaires (with assets worth US$10 million or more) and just five genuine billionaires (each with net assets of US$1 billion).[152]

In early 2020, on a visit to the town of Naples, Florida in the USA, a friend who's resident there told me, 'There are at least twelve billionaires who have second homes here.' So one small town on the US gulf coast with a resident population of around

22 000 has twice as many super-rich homeowners than the whole of South Africa, population 58 000 000.

Over the past few years, as the South African state has made ever more extravagant demands on its hard-pressed taxpayers to fund a dizzying array of government initiatives – personal taxes are the single largest component of state income – it has been sobering to be reminded of just how small the tax base in the country actually is. In 2020, there were over fourteen million people registered as taxpayers but, as financial journalist Bruce Whitfield indicated, just four percent of them (574 000 people) paid more than half of the R546.8 billion in revenue the state collected from individuals in 2019. An even tinier subgroup – 125 000 people, or 0.2 percent of the country's population – contributed a whopping R150 billion of this total. This small elite was, in Whitfield's words, 'a handful of globally mobile individuals'.[153]

TRIUMPHALISTS AND DECLINISTS

Even in the rarefied stratosphere inhabited by the country's uber-rich there was a sharp division on the country's prospects, at least as they chose to express it in public. The optimists among the elect were given voice by Adrian Gore, who had, with great determination, high intellect and actuarial wizardry, created the largest medical-insurance company in South Africa, Discovery.

Acknowledging and listing some of the major crises and unresolved issues confronting the country, he took on the doomsday 'declinists' who saw an Armageddon outcome for the beleaguered nation. His worldview was founded on what he termed a 'vision-based leadership approach' that saw South Africa's problems as 'real but solvable'.

It would have been easy to dismiss this as pie-in-the-sky management mumbo-jumbo, save for the fact that Gore is a data guy: he provided a welter of statistics, ranging from the decline in

HIV infections to a falling crime rate, a more-than-doubling of the country's economic size, huge increases in housing stock, the wealth of its pension-fund assets, and other metrics which had all moved upwards, and sometimes dramatically, since 1994.[154]

It wasn't so much that the country was in bad shape, Gore noted, but that bad attitudes shaped outcomes that tended to be negatively self-fulfilling: 'Attitude drives fundamentals, not the other way round,' he cautioned.

There was, at the same time, little sunshine from Johann Rupert, probably the wealthiest man in the country and by his estimation 'by far the highest individual taxpayer in this country for the past twenty years'.[155] Rupert, contra the norm that a small fortune is the result of the next generation squandering the large one they'd inherited, had vastly increased and extended his father Anton Rupert's tobacco and liquor empire, creating the global luxury-goods behemoth, Richemont.

But he'd become decidedly bearish on the country's prospects as the 2010s drew to a close and he certainly felt unloved by his own government. 'The French gave me the Légion d'honneur; I've created job opportunities; I pay my taxes; I give away money. You'd think people would say "thank you", not "eff you". I'm sick and tired ... My heart is here, but my body will be overseas. I don't want to hear day and night about what we, the Rupert family, allegedly did wrong. That's the main reason [for wanting to leave].'[156]

Doubtless, Rupert also seethed with fury at the recent memory of one of Jacob Zuma's wayward sons, Edward, charging him with 'corruption' at a local police station in March 2016,[157] and then later declaring that the Stellenbosch tycoon had the judiciary under his thumb.

The arrival of the global coronavirus pandemic on these shores in 2020 changed this narrative decisively in favour of the Ruperts – and of the Oppenheimers, another ultra-wealthy South African family that had been frequently fingered in the social-media sphere as exemplars of 'white monopoly capital'. This term of abuse had been popularised by the Zuma family and the Guptas, and their PR satraps at Bell Pottinger in the UK, which collapsed in 2017 because of this odious campaign and their role in developing it.

Rupert, whose counsel (like his father's) was sought by Nelson Mandela, had never had a single interaction with Ramaphosa since the latter became president in February 2018. Suddenly there was direct communication between the Ruperts, the Oppenheimers and Ramaphosa, who in his 23 March 2020 announcement of a national lockdown, stated that each family would donate R1 billion to mitigate the immediate economic impact of the pandemic by keeping companies in business and protecting jobs.[158]

Thus the weaponised attacks on white monopoly capital boomeranged. South Africa had few billionaires, but at least two of them (both white by birth, and 'monopoly capitalists' by slander) had come to the aid of the cash-strapped state.

The double irony was that the initiator of the outrage against them, the Zuma claque and its supporters, had emptied the treasury at the precise moment it was needed to right-size the economy and the state at the moment of its greatest peril.

BILLIONAIRES DISAGREE, MILLIONAIRES FLEE

But there was and remains a larger issue to hand: can any country with the ambitious developmental goals of South Africa and its huge needs afford to kiss its wealth class goodbye?

I'd come across Ruchir Sharma when I read several of his books, including *The Rise and Fall of Nations: Forces of change in the post-crisis world*, and had enjoyed his pithy observations from his perch as global strategist at Morgan Stanley Investment Management. There, he used his expertise to focus a lot of attention on emerging markets such as South Africa.

Back in 2012, when I was reporting back to South Africa and its international-relations department from my ambassadorial post in Argentina, I often used to flag, alongside my weekly reports, articles of interest relating to the country. One, penned by Sharma under the headline 'South Africa should forget the BRICS era' (BRICS being an acronym for developing-world economies Brazil, Russia, India, China and South Africa), noted the country's high levels of unemployment, low growth and investment, and overreliance on consumption spending. Sharma observed overall state malfunction on all fronts: 'The result is maximum government, minimum governance.'[159]

Five years later Sharma widened his gaze, in June 2018 noting the findings of the same Johannesburg-based research outfit, New World Wealth, that had provided the figures on the paucity of South African-based billionaires. He looked at the global trends used by New World Wealth to pen an article for *The New York Times* with the arresting headline 'The millionaires are fleeing. Maybe you should, too'.[160]

New World Wealth's global survey didn't deal with South Africa per se but its observations and Sharma's gloss on them could have been etched on a Pierneef canvas. He noted, 'When a country begins to fall into economic and political difficulty, wealthy people are often the first to ship their money to safer havens abroad. The rich don't always emigrate along with their money, but when they do, it is an even more telling sign of trouble.'

Tracking 'millionaire migrations', some 100 000 out of 15 million global US-dollar millionaires had changed their country of residence in the preceding year. The report, Sharma noted, awarded Turkey as the top country from which the super-rich flee, followed closely by failed state Venezuela. Some 12 percent of Turkey's millionaires had left and, Sharma noted, 'As if on cue, the Turkish lira is now in a free fall.'

Taking these figures into consideration, if in 2015 South Africa lost 950 millionaires to emigration, it's probable that 2017, given our cratering currency and that it was the final year of Jacob Zuma's misrule, was even worse. In fact, by the commencement of the third decade of this century, January 2020, the situation had indeed deteriorated considerably. 'Three years ago,' a local newspaper reported, 'SA had 7 500 taxpayers earning more than R5m annually, but this dropped by 1 000 in 2018. The figure for last year is not yet available.'[161]

Head of research at New World Wealth Andrew Amoils said the decline in numbers was due mainly to 'poor economic conditions', followed by 'the inability [presumably of leavers] to deal with changing social dynamics', 'concerns for their children's future', crime and BEE requirements, among other issues.[162]

In early 2020 veteran estate-agency head Herschel Jawitz advised that 'stock levels' (a euphemism for unsold homes on the market) 'at the upper end', such as in the tonier suburbs of northern Johannesburg, were 'the highest they've been in over 35 years' – that is, since 1985, during the apartheid state of emergency, when the country faced a full-blown civil war. He estimated the number of sellers emigrating (presumably if they could flog their homes) was as high as fifteen percent – one in seven sellers. 'The numbers are big,' he warned.[163]

BUSINESS AS USUAL?

So much for the factors pushing the rich out. What brings them in or attracts wealth creators?

According to the New World Wealth survey, topping the list are strong ownership rights, strong economic growth, a well-developed banking system, a free and independent media, low levels of government intervention and taxation, and ease of investment.

Other than the boisterous media space in South Africa, it's easy to see how we've slid ever further down the totem pole of attractive places to be for the well-heeled. South Africa's ranking for ease of doing business dropped from a respectable 28th position out of 155 countries surveyed in 2006 to a lowly 74th out of 190 countries on the 2017 list.[164] In his State of the Nation address in early 2018, President Cyril Ramaphosa promised to raise the country's standing in the rankings by 25 places, but since he and the government have missed practically every other target range since, from growth in GDP (gross domestic product – the total value of goods produced and services provided in the country during one year) to employment creation, the wish in this case is unlikely to father any dreams.

Hot on the heels of Sharma's article were the remarks of Investec global head of private banking Ciaran Whelan, whose clients disproportionately number the super-wealthy. I know Whelan quite well and his lilting Irish accent is matched only by his measured understatement: he is not, in other words, either a gloomster or an exaggerator. He told a video conference that South Africa 'is deemed to be a high-risk jurisdiction in terms of the compliance, and the amount of paperwork and the number of questions you have to answer is extremely high.'[165]

Another anomaly was government, even under supposed 'business-friendly' Cyril Ramaphosa. Beyond the chronic unanswered emails and telephones at various ministries, especially those tasked with promoting investment and industrial activity, and even outright hostility from many key quarters in the senior reaches of the ANC, there was often a studied indifference to the views of the country's wealth creators.

WAR ON WEALTH CREATORS

In early 2013, at the height of an enervating crime wave, First National Bank (FNB), one of the country's largest retail banks, ran an innocuous advertising campaign entitled 'You can help'. On its website and on other online platforms, the bank featured young South Africans commenting on their hopes for the country. One youngster opined, 'Stop voting for the same government in hope for change. Instead, change your hopes to a government that has the same hopes as us.'

In the campaign's 'live broadcast' segment expressing the younger generation's dissatisfaction with the government's failure to deliver on quality education and crime control, education minister Angie Motshekga was called 'brainless'.

This led to the bank being labelled 'treasonous' by the ANC Youth League, and the political party received an unctuous apology from the CEO of the bank's holding company, Sizwe Nxasana.

This was insufficient for the ruling-party panjandrums. Summoned to ANC headquarters, the contrite bosses of the bank issued a grovelling apology for the youth campaign 'and the CEO of Firstrand, Sizwe Nxasana, agreed that the research clippings posted online were regrettable', a triumphant ANC statement crowed.[166]

Former editor and commentator at *Business Day*, an old friend, Tim Cohen, reminded his readers that the FNB somersault induced courtesy of the ANC uncomfortably mirrored the fits of pique and paranoia meted out to FNB's predecessor, Barclays Bank, for allegedly funding – ironically – an advertisement for the banned ANC in the 1980s. This led President PW Botha to denounce the bank in Parliament and appoint a judicial commission to investigate. The CEO resigned and the bank buckled to the state. *Plus ça change* …

In March the following year, Dr Anthea Jeffery of the Institute of Race Relations (IRR) produced research that examined eleven items of legislation in immaculate detail.[167] These ranged from tightened rules for black empowerment and mandatory gender and racial quotas for the boardroom, to controls over mining and offshore gas and oil exploration, to reduced protection for foreign investors and property owners. (Six years later, most had either been written into legislation or were at an advanced stage in the legislative grinder.)

Jeffery's findings – she'd lectured me in public international law back in 1980 – were headlined 'The ANC govt's war on economic rationality', an apt and lapidary title. *The Economist* magazine, something of a bible for scarce foreign investors, pressed home the point: 'These ... business-bashing bills are part of an ominous trend ... a common thread is that "they weaken property rights, reduce private-sector autonomy, threaten business with draconian penalties and undermine investor confidence".'[168]

But far from being deterred by such warning voices, perhaps perversely being emboldened by criticism from 'the usual suspects', the government intensified the pressure on business and the private sector. By 2017, a state entity with a mouthful of a name, the Broad-Based Black Economic Empowerment Commission, announced, 'acting on a tip-off', that it was investigating a slew of listed companies, including private health group Netcare, cellphone manufacturer Nokia and telecoms company MTN, for alleged non-compliance with empowerment legislation. Fines of up to ten percent of annual turnover, a ban on doing business with the state for ten years and imprisonment of up to ten years for convicted individuals were among the business-friendly prescripts here.

Then, in 2018, the Department of Labour brought forth even stricter race percentages. Its Employment Equity Amendment Bill set compulsory targets, with massively increased penalties for non-compliance. Little dissent was heard from large business on this wheeze. And the voices of small business were, as always, ignored.

Although organised business rediscovered elements of its backbone during the final years of Zuma's state plunder, and some impressive dissent was conspicuously offered by Sipho Pityana, a former government insider who by then was chairman of a major gold-mining company and a leader in the umbrella lobby group, Business Leadership SA (BLSA), I was quite amazed at the passive approach of BLSA and other business groupings in the run-up to the 2019 election campaign.

Once again, the ANC didn't hide its future intentions under vague bromides. Its election manifesto explicitly called for expropriation of property without compensation, an issue that has been in the public domain and debate since first adopted by the ANC conference in 2017. It also dusted off from the NP siege economics playbook of the apartheid era an equally dangerous idea: prescribed assets. This, simply put, would oblige private pension funds to invest in state companies, the very sites of mismanagement, plunder and insolvency bequeathed from the locust years of Zuma Inc. Even the trade union Cosatu sounded a note of caution on this.

Yet, extraordinarily, BLSA announced that 'business welcomes the ANC manifesto'.[169] The statement was, bar one reservation on changing the mandate of the Reserve Bank, entirely laudatory on the governing party's economic aims. Even more extraordinary was the fact that four key members of the lobby were the largest fund and pension fund managers in the country – Alexander Forbes, Sanlam, Old Mutual and Coronation.

WHAT MIGHT HAVE BEEN

South Africa is the second-largest economy in Africa. The country is rich in natural resources and is a leading producer of platinum, gold, chromium and iron.

The economy recorded its fastest growth rates since the 1960s over the period 2004 to 2007, with real GDP growth averaging 5.2 percent per annum, although this coincided with both a booming commodities market and strong bull market on the stock exchange.[170]

However, the same government that for the first two decades of democracy practised fiscal restraint and prudence would soon throw out the rule book in funding expenditure beyond the country's means and imperilling both its hard-won sovereign credit rating and its capital programmes. Bringing debt within levels of sustainability, flagged so warmly in the Goldman Sachs report of 2013, would be disregarded in the hope of buying off a ballooning civil-servants' payroll and an ever-widening pool of social-grants recipients.

The failures to embark on promised reforms to make the labour-market model fit for the workers South Africa actually had, rather than the ones the government wished they had, meant simply that there would soon enough be more people receiving grants than actual salaries in paid employment. And this would be significantly worsened by the corrosive economic effects of the coronavirus crisis, which cost the country at least three million jobs.

In 2000, my parliamentary colleague and our finance spokesman Ken Andrew had warned the newly elected government, 'If you are passionate about alleviating poverty, you need to be passionate about economic growth.' He also offered that the only way to beat poverty and joblessness was 'not to dare settle for less than six percent GDP annual growth'.

Twenty-five years later this has been rendered moot, as growth has plunged below one percent, crumbling to minus-ten percent after the onset of the coronavirus crisis, its worst fall since the First World War. Successive governments have failed to address structural problems such as the widening gap between rich and poor, a low-skilled labour force, the high unemployment rate, deteriorating infrastructure, and high corruption and crime rates.

As these events have gathered pace, the government's culture of failure has been explained repeatedly, and to an ever more, often violently, disaffected citizenry, not by self-correction at the top, but by scapegoating racial minorities below. Short-term populist solutions and slogans have been offered in place of the longer-term policies that would realistically address the country's needs and provide a leg-up to a chronically undereducated and poorly skilled majority. The skilled, educated and more affluent minority have retreated into enclaves of first-world exclusion or simply emigrated.

It's an incontestable truth that before you can slice the pie, you need to grow it. And this in turn requires sustainable public finances, high levels of investment and business confidence as pre-conditions for job creation. But each of these was in the deep-red zone as, in 2020, the country tipped into its second recession in two years, the third since 1994.

Achieving the rate of growth offered by a step change in policy to reach the level outlined by Ken would have seen a starkly different country, having, one estimate suggested, almost 22 million people in work had jobs grown by just three percent per year since 2000. Instead, on the back of policies identified by Mbeki and others, there were just 16.3 million people in employment in 2019 and nearly 10 million either unemployed or 'discouraged work seekers' who had given up the search.[171]

David Maynier, who'd served as my chief of staff when I was leader of the opposition, was appointed member of the executive council (MEC) for finance in the Western Cape after the 2019 election. At one of our regular Saturday coffee sessions, he provided a telling statistical update on Ken's formulation: if South Africa had achieved the 5.4 percent GDP growth promised but never sighted by the National Development Plan (NDP), a broadly market-sensible approach to eliminate poverty and reduce inequality by 2030, then average GDP per capita – generally regarded as a good measurement of a country's standard of living, illustrating how prosperous each citizen feels – would have doubled in just thirteen years. Instead, the wrong policy path chosen had ensured a minuscule GDP growth, and meant it would take over seventy years before the same outcome could be achieved.

As RW Johnson put it, in his rollicking 2015 read of South Africa heading apparently down the red-flagged potholed road towards a head-on collision between its industrialised modernity and its corrupt attachment to a darker atavism, 'South Africa can either choose to have an ANC government or it can have a modern industrial economy. It cannot have both.'[172]

After the results of the May 2019 election confirmed (though with a reduced vote) that South Africa had chosen the ANC to govern it for a sixth term, Johnson analysed a national pre-election poll he and polling company Markdata had conducted for a local TV station. Of particular interest was its key finding: a large majority of voters believed the government 'doesn't care' about issues from job creation to reducing poverty. Johnson noted:

> Large majorities of black voters were quite happy to jettison affirmative action, BEE (Black Economic Empowerment), and expropriation without compensation, if the result would be to bring more investment and thus jobs. This straightforward disavowal of so many African nationalist articles of faith suggests that no amount of ideology is proof against twenty-five years of rising unemployment and five years of steadily falling real incomes.[173]

SCREECHING TO A HALT

In March 2020 South Africa was locked down to 'flatten the curve' of the deadly coronavirus – to delay the peak of the outbreak so the country's health system would be able to cope with the demand on its services. But even before the pathogens from China via Europe infected us, our very fragile economy and floundering currency were in intensive care.

And there was an extraordinary disconnect between the government's apparent pre-emptive public-health measures (which in time proved poorly conceived, and shockingly and corruptly implemented in certain provinces) to stop the pandemic in its tracks, and our lethargic non-reaction to the economic crisis that interdicts our ability to fight back against the virus – and to rebuild the economy after the plague passes.

It was profoundly ironic that at midnight on first day of the lock-down, 27 March 2020, Moody's Investors Service announced its downgrade to junk status of South Africa's sovereign bonds. This would send the government's borrowing costs into the stratosphere and discourage most international investors from funding the country's burgeoning current-account deficit except at exorbitant cost, creating a debt-trap in which repaying the borrowings of the state subsumes vital spending on core departments, or when the point is reached where the state can no longer meet its debt obligations, and it defaults.

Cyril Ramaphosa and the government had spent the three years since April 2017, when two other rating agencies, Fitch and Standard & Poor's (S&P), had downgraded the country to junk status, simply doing nothing to avert economic meltdown. In fact, they actually aggravated the possibility of our final exit from economic normalcy with vastly unaffordable and credit-ruinous gestures. These ranged from padding public servants' salaries by an estimated 40 percent above inflation for the past dozen years,[174] to the free-university-fees giveaway at a projected cost of R172.2 billion by 2022.[175] And the missteps on the Eskom and energy fronts are as long as they are depressing.

This failure on the economic front has also meant that government has simply ignored its most important inside counsel. Before he was exiled to social-media purdah in his home in Tzaneen (he was forbidden for a while to express his vehement views on

Twitter), finance minister Tito Mboweni tweeted in January 2020, 'If you cannot effect deep structural reforms, then game over! Stay as you are and you are downgraded to junk status! The consequences are dire.'[176]

Hobbled and disarmed fiscally in the most important fight of our lives, South Africa needs to alter course. Yet there is little sign of state shibboleths being changed. In fact, the responses of key ministers indicate that there will, pandemic economics notwithstanding, be a doubling down on some mistaken policy choices undertaken before the virus struck.

The economic peril was in plain sight at the early stages of the pandemic: the lengthened lockdown forced the Reserve Bank to slash the interest rate to its lowest point, 3.5 percent, in the post-apartheid era. This was good news for hard-pressed and retrenched consumers; not so much for pensioners and savers. Speedy action by the Reserve Bank was also required to calm turbulent local bond markets, where interest rates on government bonds spiked to more than 13 percent, representing the price government has to pay to borrow money. The intervention seems to have worked, for now, as markets have settled to a nervous 'wait and see' posture.

But the episode was an ominous portent. South Africa, with its low savings rate, depends on foreign funders. Higher bond rates would usually attract the kind of fast money that circles the globe looking for higher yields. Here, though, a becalmed economy, ruinous public finances and escalating political risk have sent foreign investors fleeing. Foreign funders spoke with the quiet but deadly click of the mouse: in the first quarter of 2020, numbers released by the Reserve Bank showed an outflow of R96 billion in bonds and shares, illustrating a sharp decline in confidence.

In the meantime the battered rand, one of the world's worst-performing and most volatile currencies, had in just four months of 2020 lost a fifth of its value against the US dollar, the safe-haven currency to which investors turned at a time of unfathomable crisis.[177] (The rand recovered towards the end of the year, but remained ever-volatile.)

Analysts Greg Mills and Ray Hartley of the thinktank the Brenthurst Foundation highlighted that these figures predated the strangulation of the economy by covid-19 regulations, indicating that the metrics for the succeeding quarters would be even worse. They offered the elegiac warning, 'A lesson from Zimbabwe … is that just when you have seemingly hit rock bottom, things can always get worse. And in South Africa, things are now about to get much worse.'[178]

PART II

PAST TENSE

CHAPTER 8

——

The two roads: Jews asking questions

I served with politician Harry Schwarz during my first term in Parliament after 1989. He'd been my political boss when I was elected as one of his Yeoville constituency councillors in Johannesburg three years before that. My predecessor as MP for Houghton, liberal icon Helen Suzman, and I shared a common trait with Schwarz, in addition to party affiliation. We were all members of the same tribe: South African Jews.

Both Schwarz and Suzman lived to a great age and both died in South Africa.

For me, the maxim of Margaret Thatcher's ideological mentor, British barrister and politician Sir Keith Joseph, is a perfect personal fit: 'minimally observing, but maximally acknowledging'. For Schwarz, a person of extreme sensitivity in most matters, religion and its observance weighed heavily on him. Suzman was far more irreverent and less believing; she once offered the throwaway line, 'When the Jews leave South Africa, it's time to go.'

Indeed, in 2019, when the Kaplan Centre at UCT unveiled the results of its first survey of the Jewish community in fifteen years, they indicated a dramatic decline in the number of South African Jews still living in the country. Reckoned to be 50 000 in strength, the number had weakened by more than 25 percent since the previous survey in 2004, and had more than halved since the heyday of the community in the 1970s, when it was estimated at 120 000.

Most had immigrated to the UK, Canada, Australia and New Zealand – 'the white Commonwealth', as Thabo Mbeki once sneeringly called it. But an increasing number were apparently seeking a new home in Israel, where being white and Jewish were positives, which certainly wasn't true of democratic South Africa as it entered the 2020s.[179]

There was a very cogent reason why most South African Jews identified and voted for liberal parties such as the DA – and why Suzman, Schwarz and I had been so involved in its politics, despite very different levels of observance of our common religion: Jews were a tiny minority in the body politic of the country. Liberal institutions such as the Constitution, the Bill of Rights and the rule of law made it far easier to enjoy a common citizenship than any ties based on blood and tribe – which defined nationalist movements such as the ANC, and its predecessor in power, the NP.

SUCCESS AND INSECURITY

Even by the sinking standards of the traditional fear-and-loathing style of campaigning, the 1987 white general-election campaign was a nadir. Schwarz, Suzman and I were involved in the campaign of the PFP, a previous version of today's DA. On the other side stood PW Botha and his lieutenants.

One of them, finance minister Barend du Plessis, took charge of the campaign against our party, which did very poorly in that election, losing ten seats. Du Plessis quipped, memorably, 'PFP? That means Packing for Perth.' Questioning your opponents' patriotism always helped close the argument – especially when embedded within the putdown is the ring of truth.

Raising this point of its being somehow 'un-South African',

about a party that enjoyed disproportionate support from the small South African Jewish population, was a step up from the crude antisemitism of Du Plessis' predecessors in office.

South African historian Milton Shain's 2015 book *A Perfect Storm: Anti-Semitism in South Africa 1930-1948* traced the two important decades between the world wars as a time when 'the South African Jewish community was under siege. This was because, for a great number of whites, the Jew was an unwelcome challenge and a disturbing addition to society.'

Many of the leading anti-Semites described in his pages were 'sincere' in their Jew-hatred and regarded the resolution of the 'Jewish question' as part of resolving the economic deprivation of the significant 'poor white' population. With the current political tropes suggesting that South African whites have, since their arrival on these shores over 370 years back, enjoyed great and unearned economic prosperity, the book was a reminder that this 'prosperity' simply did not exist as recently as 1932: then, both 'poor' and 'very poor' whites constituted 56 percent of the white population in South Africa.

Leading anti-Semites of that period married a strident anti-capitalism to a rising anti-Semitism. The 'Hoggenheimer' cartoons in *Die Burger* were one example, and the anti-Semitism of the leader of the Afrikaner nationalists of the day (and the editor of the newspaper) Dr DF Malan was another. He cynically noted in an interview in 1931, 'It is very easy to rouse a feeling of hate towards the Jew in the country.'[180]

Malan assiduously, as leader of the opposition, fanned these flames of enmity; yet on achieving power in 1948 he dropped anti-Semitism from his political repertoire and moved in the opposite direction: he switched from depicting Jews as 'unassimilable' to using their example as a model for Afrikaners to emulate in a rapidly decolonising world.

Back then, in 1948, when PW Botha was a mere provincial organiser for a party he would ultimately lead, 'Hoggenheimer' was identified with mining entrepreneur and founder of Anglo American Sir Ernest Oppenheimer. He was the personification of both the opposition (representing it in Parliament) and, more materially in the demonology of those times, prime evil as the face of much-despised 'British-Jewish capital', a double slur with the handy anti-Semitic trope fused to the alien nature of imperial (in this case, British) capital, which Anglo American in both its leadership and funding origins exemplified. Ironically, Oppenheimer was a converted Anglican, but his Jewish origins sufficed to stick the label, and the mud.

LESSONS LEARNT

An old friend now resident in Canada once joked that South African Jews 'are born wearing running shoes'. He wasn't suggesting that this group was cowardly; rather, he was nodding at the origins of the local community. It had been seared by the vicious hatreds and pogroms unleashed in greater Russia and Eastern Europe in the 19th and 20th centuries. Many had found refuge in South Africa.

By the time I was born into a very secular family on the eastern seaboard of Durban, a far worse catastrophe than the Russian pogroms had befallen the European Jews – the Nazi Holocaust. It was crisply defined and categorised by an eminent history scholar of that era, Richard J Evans: 'No crime in human history outdoes the genocidal extermination of six million Jews on the orders of the leader of Germany's self-styled third Reich.'

The lessons of the Holocaust were a stable and certain shadow that always reminded the community of the permanence of impermanence, no matter how propitious the local circumstances might appear. Masterful *New York Times* columnist Bret Stephens tapped into the well of ambivalence between even the most materially successful Jewish communities and a nagging depth of insecurity. 'There is an understanding, born of repeated exile, that everything that seems solid and valuable is ultimately perishable, while everything that is intangible – knowledge most of all – is potentially everlasting,' he wrote at the end of 2019, a year in the world noteworthy for the 'Jew hatred' that was making a rousing comeback in various forms.[181]

(In addition, echoes of the Jew-baiting of the 1930s in the race-coarsened discourse evident in South Africa today, with a change of targets, is very apparent and audible. The presumed power and wealth of the 1930s Jewish community finds contemporary expression in the attacks on several fronts in today's South Africa, on the white and Indian communities.)

In the heated run-up to the ANC's 2017 contest for the party presidency, frontrunner Cyril Ramaphosa was hit with a headline story in the *City Press* newspaper early in the campaign. An ally of Jacob Zuma expressed 'concern' that Ramaphosa would be a liability because of his closeness to 'the Jews' – presumably a reference to Stephen Kosseff, a banker, and Michael Katz, a leading lawyer (and my first boss), both of whom regularly advised him.[182]

But once in office, Ramaphosa felt that virtue-signalling against Israel was the best inoculation against his perceived sin. Shortly after his against-the-odds victory, he announced that he backed his party's motion to downgrade the South African embassy in Israel, although, like many government commitments, this pledge was honoured only in its breach.

Since Zionism – an ideology that espouses the re-establishment of a Jewish state in the territory defined as the historic Land of Israel (Palestine) – was a deeply held belief for perhaps ninety percent of South Africa's Jews, this could only further their discomfort and feeling of impermanence. The local noise generated by the local and hugely well-funded Palestinian-led Boycott,

Dinvestment, Sanctions (BDS) campaign, and attempts to sever ties between local academics and Israel, heightened anxiety.

NO TRACK IS INEVITABLE

In July 2013 I delivered a speech at the invitation of the Council of KwaZulu-Natal Jewry a few months after arriving back from my ambassadorial stint in South America. I was at the time reading a book that dealt with both the magnificence and the tragedy of Harry Schwarz's community of origin: *The Pity of It All: A history of the Jews in Germany, 1743-1933* by Amos Elon, published in 2002.

The book, which ended its account just after Adolf Hitler was installed as chancellor, explored whether two hundred years of German-Jewish life was inevitably headed for extinction. I chose to share with the audience Elon's key finding, which seemed worth retelling to any community spared such ravages but with uncertain thoughts on its own future and facing different existential challenges: that the ultimate outcome was neither predictable nor assured.

> Some claim to have discerned an inexorable pattern in German history preordained from Luther's days to culminate in the Nazi Holocaust. According to this theory, German Jews were doomed from the outset, their fate as immutable as a law of nature. Such absolute uncertainties have eluded me.[183]

He then contrasted the two historical currents that flowed through Germany before 1933:

> Alongside the Germany of anti-Semitism there was a Germany of enlightened liberalism, humane concern, civilised rule of law, good government, social security, and

thriving social democracy. Even Hitler's rise to power in January 1933 was not the result of electoral success (the Nazi share of the vote had seriously declined in the fall of 1932). Rather, Hitler's triumph was the product of backstage machinations by conservative politicians and industrialists who overcame the hesitations of a senile president by convincing him (and themselves) that they were 'hiring' Hitler to restore order and curb the trade unions.[184]

And, as he observed, the history of Jews in Germany was 'much more than the history of tragedy; it was also, for a long time, the story of an extraordinary success'.

Ultimately, the darker, violent torrent of race and blood overwhelmed the stream of liberal enlightenment, as the drumbeat of Germany's next phase proved. Still, to me what was most aptly contemporary and relevant to the lesser uncertainties confronting South Africa in 2013, and in the years after, was Elon's reminder that the most tragic historical earthquake, which destroyed a once-thriving community, did not unravel inexorably nor inevitably. Rather – and this was essential – it was preceded by 'a series of ups and downs and a succession of unforeseeable contingencies, none of which seem to have been inevitable'.

That 2013 evening in peaceful Durban, I offered the view that in one sense South Africa's future trajectory also ran on two tracks.

The 2010 FIFA World Cup had shown the world South Africa's very best face –peaceful, patriotic and united. And despite the horrendous costs of mostly white-elephant stadiums ordered up by the imperious and corrupt FIFA boss Sepp Blatter, hosting the event had also left behind at least one modern totem of practical modernity, the Gautrain.

This fifteen-minute fast ride in carriages of sleek comfort between the airport and Sandton and beyond was suggestive, to me at least, of the sort of rail network that could operate as a metaphor for a better future for all. South Africa was a fast-track country at peace with itself and the world, bolstered by an inclusive and growing economy, fortified by democratic practice, and inspired by committed and ethical leadership. And it was living up to its own best national aspiration – emblazoned on its coat of arms was the motto 'Diverse people unite!', written as *!ke e: /xarra //ke* in the Khoisan language of the /Xam people.

In fact, a few weeks before, a friend of mine from university days, my former Roman-law lecturer, Edwin Cameron, then sitting as a Constitutional Court justice, had offered his view in a speech in Johannesburg, signposting impressive evidence to fortify an optimistic outlook based on hard reality after almost two decades of living in a constitutional democracy:

Much has been achieved – perhaps more than those of us who tend to worry realise.

Almost all violent crime is down. Compared with 1994, the murder rate has almost halved. The government's housing programme has put many millions of South Africans in their own homes. In 1994, just more than half of households had electricity; now 85 percent do. In 1994, just more than a third of 6-year-old children were in school; now 85 percent are.

The income of the average black family has increased by about a third. And through the system of social grants totalling about R120 billion every year, the very poorest in our country are afforded some elements of a dignified material existence and access to a measure of social power.

… [A]fter nearly two decades, we have more freedom, more

debate, more robust and direct engagement with each other – and certainly more practically tangible social justice than twenty years ago.[185]

Many of the same metrics appeared a few months later in a report by American multinational investment bank Goldman Sachs entitled *Two Decades of Freedom*: the size of the economy had quadrupled since the end of apartheid, repairs had been effected in the post-apartheid sovereign balance sheet, inflation had been tamed, and there had been an overall rise in living standards.[186]

The bank, headed in South Africa by a former leftist of my university years, Colin Coleman – who certainly knew how to throw a good party – lived up to the company's informal moniker, 'Government Sachs'. Former minister (at that time) Tito Mboweni served on its advisory board; the finance minister of the day, Pravin Gordhan, attended the launch; and ANC treasurer Zweli Mkhize described the report as 'positive for the ANC'.[187]

But Goldman Sachs tiptoed around the robust choices needed to conquer the very 'challenges' it highlighted, a euphemism for the pressing and explosive issues of low growth and sky-high unemployment.

Cameron, by contrast, was honest and intellectually rigorous. And after listing the country's not-inconsiderable achievements, he went on to caution that all was not well. The political debate was 'divisive to the point of annihilation', the prevalence of race rhetoric 'still sometimes substitutes for performance' and 'the tide of corruption' was washing higher and higher – 'it threatens to engulf us'. Long before even the 'state capture' of the final years of Zuma's benighted misrule was fully sighted, this eminent jurist was prescient to warn, 'The shameless looting of our public assets by many politicians and government officials is a direct threat to our democracy and all we hope to achieve in it.'[188]

This was the other path, the dirt-track destination of a failed state. And the potholes on this road were quite apparent: economic redistribution trumping the growth imperative, adding in turn to ever-escalating unemployment and a spike in poverty levels; failing public institutions corroded by a metastasising culture of corruption led by uncivil servants taking their cues from a self-enriching political leadership.

At the same time I was reading Amos Elon, I came across the 2013 update on South Africa of Bill Keller, who'd been the Johannesburg bureau chief for *The New York Times* back in 1992, at the outset of the country's brave journey.

> If South Africa does not leave you full of ambivalence, you have not been paying attention ... It is a country where the ruling alliance includes the Communist Party, but the real economic power is capitalist; where corruption is rampant but a vigorous press copiously reports it; where the constitutional court legalized gay marriage and lesbians are gang-raped; where the malls are populated by a multiracial consumer class, and millions live in sheds. It is inspiring and dispiriting ...[189]

CHAPTER 9

The vexed question of race:
A zero-sum game

Back in 1981, when I was midway through my LLB degree at Wits in Johannesburg, the British punk-rock group The Clash produced its hot album *Combat Rock*. One song captured our collective imaginations: 'Should I Stay or Should I Go?'

The appeal of the song wasn't just about the rhythms and the hardcore lyrics. For many middle-class South Africans, especially the pampered variety of our mostly white postgraduate class then, that was a number-one theme as we contemplated our futures in the country of our birth.

Every young white South African male had call-up papers to serve in the army, and some in my class were less attracted to the rigours of legal study than using the LLB years to extend their university stay in order to postpone the clutches of compulsory military service, a dubious joy I'd already experienced after matriculating in 1975.

But by the mid-1980s, to the perils of serving along and even outside the country's borders was added army patrols and suppression in the very urban townships where most urban black South Africans lived. And by the time my classmates and I had left the groves of academe, or more accurately the confines of Braamfontein, Johannesburg, home of Wits, the 'people's war' mandated by the ANC-in-exile was being taken into the very heartlands of apartheid South Africa, especially the townships that ringed Johannesburg. So if you were going to depart for safer climes, then the mid-1980s were a good time to *vamos*.

If avoiding army service was one push factor accelerating the skills flight back then, there was no shortage of other motivations. One was a detestation of the system of institutionalised racial discrimination, which jarred with the more liberal and radical-left sensibilities of many English-speaking students.

Another was despair that the system, then being reformed hesitatingly by the government of PW Botha, would ever be dismantled root and branch.

An ever-more atavistic (though less articulated) fear was that a racial civil war would engulf the country and lead to a vengeful Mozambique-style Marxist regime being erected on the ashes of the vanquished embers of white-ruled South Africa.

And, finally, there was the real sense of deep isolation as South Africa receded ever further from the tides of international respectability and engagement, as its pariah status was measured by investor and financial sanctions, and the disinvestment by multi-national corporations that had been lodestars in the country's economic development.

So there were any number of reasons to leave South Africa, provided you had a skills set and a taste for adventure. Even the uncertainties and emotional wrench of departing trumped what then seemed the certainty of the South African story ending rather badly, if not bloodily, for its middle-class minorities.

I stayed.

I wanted to help my political cause achieve its improbable objective of founding a new non-racial constitutional order on the stony soil of our conflicted past. And once I had (by the narrowest margin) been elected in a by-election in February 1986 to the Johannesburg City Council, my course was set on a political destination which would rapidly engulf me in the founding of a new South Africa.

RADICAL CHIC

Ironically, among the earlier – and later, after a democratic all-race new order was founded in 1994 – white leavers to foreign destinations were members of the radical left with whom I'd had such furious disagreements across the table of the Wits Student Representative Council (SRC) meeting room. Their rallying cry was the NUSAS (National Union of South African Students) endorsed message 'African education for an African future'. (Thirty-five years later the almost entirely black 'Rhodes Must Fall' decolonisation movement provided an answering echo at Wits and similar institutions.)

But the real point of difference between the white-left and liberal-student movements of my day was in the matter of race. Our liberal viewpoint was that 'non-racialism' was the key to unburdening the country of its shameful past. Since race was the basis of past discrimination, in our view, a future prospectus could only be worthwhile if we recognised that fact and built a country anew on the firm ground of equal rights for every person, regardless of racial origin or group membership. Bridging the gap between black aspirations for an equal claim to full citizenship, and the political rights and minority fears of evisceration and dispossession, was the essential work of crafting a sustainable and just future for all.

But for the members of the white left, this was 'false consciousness'. In their analysis, race was simply a cover for class exploitation, and the real evil in South Africa wasn't simply the superimposition of colour discrimination but the problem of

capitalism, which co-opted a 'white working-class labour aris-
tocracy' to its mendacious cause of impoverishing the black working
class at cheap rates and in conditions of misery. Apartheid, they
believed, should be viewed not through the lens of race but via class
relations. Reset those, and a golden worker-led future beckoned.

In essence, and with some crudity, this gives a flavour of some of
the debates in which we then engaged with much fury and passion.
But what I didn't fully realise at the time was that the Marxist
worldview that enjoyed such a warm reception in the hearts and
minds of my student political rivals and many of my lecturers, also
gave its advocates a place in the future. Because if identity with an
oppressed class was the ticket to future engagement, then that was
something for which the unalterable condition of race posed no
exclusion. Problem then squared away for the white fellow travellers
of what was then, with a few exceptions, a struggle that pitted black
South Africans against the forces of the white status quo.

But of course this was also a crude caricature because, like
colonial India under the heel of the British Raj, apartheid South
Africa would never have endured as long as it did without an army
of black collaborators, from township councillors and bantustan
politicians and bureaucrats, to many in the ranks of the army and
the police.

Equally, on the other side of the barricades, four of the original
eleven accused in the country's most famous political case, the
Rivonia trial of 1963, were white South Africans. And others, such
as Ruth First and Neil Aggett, would pay the ultimate price for the
struggle they unwaveringly supported.

THE GREAT RACE CONUNDRUM

A few years after graduating from university I read one of the more
original accounts of South African reality. Rian Malan's *My Traitor's
Heart*, published in 1990, laid bare the lethal contradictions and

madcap caricatures that so informed my early adulthood, and the choices that many of its middle classes would make. Or, as the account in Malan's book made clear, the choices that might be forced on them in the very future world many on the white left aspired to help birth.

Describing a mass funeral in Cape Town – replete with flag-draped coffins, singing and speech making – of the 'Gugulethu Seven' shot by the police some days before in March 1986, Malan recorded a snapshot of the day:

> A column of black women rounded a corner and bore down on us, dancing and singing their way toward the funeral. This was the contingent of the United Women's Congress ... Running abreast of them was a gawky white girl, a student by the look of her, wearing jeans and thick glasses, hair tied back in a sensible bun. She was trying to insinuate herself into the packed black ranks. She was smiling nervously, waving her fist in the sky, and copying the black sisters' steps, but there was no room for her in the formation. [Veteran CBS journalist Allen] Pizzey and I turned to stare at her. 'Oh, baby,' chuckled the CBS news correspondent, 'when the day comes, you'll still be whitey.'[190]

'Baby' was a perfect indentikit for a legion of those earnest white radicals – 'the sack and sandal brigade', we called them – who populated the ranks of the various student formations of my time at Wits.

And just to underline the takeaway from his vivid observation, Malan added the coruscating putdown:

> Baby was a little ridiculous. Whatever her politics, Baby remained whitey when the chips were down, which is why

there were never any whites at the burning barricades. If you were white in the wrong place at the wrong time, you were a target.[191]

Yet barely four years after his searing bestseller was published, Malan would witness the extraordinary changes in and the explicit multiracial character of the new South Africa led by its revolutionary warrior-turned-rainbow-reconciler Nelson Mandela, inaugurated as its first democratic president in May 1994.

I was an engaged eyewitness to that splendid event amid the granite splendour and colonial architecture of Pretoria's Union Buildings, and I would participate in the new country's history-in-the-making for the next decade and a half. And while a lot of early things went wrong, many of the big matters went astonishingly right. Mandela used the power of his personal example, rather than the example of his presidential power, to allow even the most cynical and jaded to willingly suspend their disbelief.

A recruit to the ranks of these latter-day converts was Rian Malan. By early 2004, fully one decade into the brave new world of democracy South African style, the peace dividend was real enough and Malan wrote a public apology of sorts:

In my view, peace would never come. There was too much history, too much pain and anger for that. ... Ten days before the predicted apocalypse [27 April 1994, the date of the all-race elections] there came a miraculous reprieve. A reverent quiet settled upon the nation, and the election passed off entirely peacefully ...

I set out to discredit the outcome. The peace is illusory, I sneered, anarchy is still coming. Look at crime! Rape! Guns and mayhem! Decaying cities! Abandoned factories!

Incompetence and corruption everywhere! ... Hospitals that don't work any more! Surly nurses! Drunken teachers! A civil service where the phones just ring![192]

He concluded:

It is infinitely worse to receive than to give, especially if one is arrogant and the gift is forgiveness or mercy. The gift of 1994 was so huge that I choked on it and couldn't say thank you. But I am not too proud to say it now.

MBEKI'S MIXED BAG

A fortnight later, on 6 February 2004, President Thabo Mbeki quoted Malan's story with strong approval in his State of the Nation address in the Houses of Parliament in Cape Town. For him it was a counterpoint to supposed gloombuckets such as me, then leader of the opposition, who 'opened their doors to despair'.[193]

Mbeki, as Mandela's deputy president between 1994 and 1999, and then his successor as president, could certainly take credit for the peaceful attainment and relatively benign first decade of full-blown democratic rule in the country. But he was famously sensitive to any form of criticism or opposition, essential weaves of the democratic quilt knitted at Kempton Park where the interim constitution had been fashioned.[194]

Mbeki would also unstitch its delicate threads in many areas. He abandoned reconciliation in favour of racial entitlement, his deep suspicion of any internal or external opponent proving anew the old saw that even the paranoid have enemies; and his lack of the common touch jarred with the ease and warmth of his predecessor, Nelson Mandela (and, for that matter, his successor, Jacob Zuma).

Then there was the infamy, and the hundreds of thousands of needless deaths (over 330 000, according to at least one authoritative study),[195] occasioned by his Aids denialism. He publicly challenged the scientific consensus that HIV causes Aids, and delayed launching an antiretroviral (ARV) drug programme, charging that the drugs were 'poison' and an effort by the west to weaken his country. His health minister, Manto Tshabalala-Msimang, promoted herbal remedies, including beetroot, garlic and lemon, as alternatives for ARVs.

Mbeki parsed his words on both the origins and treatment of this pandemic, and gave voice to his own racial insecurities on its genesis and spread. This exact toxic combination – personal insecurity and misplaced racial solidarity – disallowed him from confronting the tyranny playing out with full destructive force on the country's northern border in Robert Mugabe's Zimbabwe.

Since Mbeki's presidency opened at the same time, and courtesy of the same election, as my being elected leader of the official opposition in Parliament, I would, theoretically at least, clash with him on these life-and-death matters and a clutch of other issues. But in practice, given Mbeki's icy contempt for opposition, this often amounted to a debate with a ghost. Rather than direct confrontation, he usually vented his passionate furies in letters (I received an inordinately long and angry series of them, justifying his decision to disallow ARVs for HIV-positive and Aids patients) and midnight ramblings produced in his weekly online newsletter.

That said, in the realm of the economy, in terms of investor attractiveness, respectable growth levels and repairing the sovereign balance sheet, Mbeki acted deftly and sensitively. The tangled politics of his own movement, and especially its alignment with the South African Communist Party (SACP) and the Congress of South African Trade Unions (Cosatu), prevented him from introducing a full raft of Thatcherite reforms[196] but many South Africans could thank him for the dividends, including workers enjoying the fruits of an expanded economy (even though unemployment remained high), and an expanding safety net of social grants, and new investment and offshore options for the capitalists.

The record 69.69 percent poll achieved by the ANC in the next election, in 2004, seemed to affirm a sentiment once captured in a British election slogan, for one of Margaret Thatcher's predecessors, Harold Macmillan: 'You've never had it so good.'

By the mid-2000s, and just before Mbeki's growing ranks of party opponents encircled him in 2007 when he famously lost his bid to retain the party presidency against his surging opponent Jacob Zuma, there was increasing justification for both the 1994 fears and 2004 recantation-apologia of Rian Malan.

THINGS WERE BOTH BAD AND BETTER ...[197]

The Mbeki administration did little, however, to shorten the unemployment lines and to reset the economic fundamentals to create more work opportunities for an ever-rising number of those who would later be dubbed the NEETs (not in employment, education or training), especially in the country's bulging youth cohort.

It also aggressively used race both as the measurement for expanding the ownership elite at the top and for ridding the civil service of its expertise at all levels. This rapidly 'embourgeoisified' those historically excluded from the public and private sectors, but the manner in which it was undertaken focused far more on redistributing the wealth base than either adding to it or training new workers with scalable and relevant skills.

In addition, big-ticket items such as the notorious 'Arms Deal' (the Strategic Defence Package, which ended up costing the state over R70 billion, with millions of rands of public money lost to bribery and other irregularities) and his obsessive determination to create a new elite via Black Economic Empowerment (BEE), opened the floodgates to corruption through public procurement.

And in the matter of personal wealth and its warehousing, the admittedly somewhat leaky (since billions had flowed out of the country illegally) apartheid exchange-control regime was relaxed, enabling millionaires in the middle and upper economic reaches of South Africa to prudently, and legally, invest offshore. Even the hitherto prohibited listing of South African corporates on foreign bourses and locations was greenlighted by Mbeki and his finance minister, Trevor Manuel.

In the meantime, the public service, while correctly covering those excluded by apartheid, rapidly began to resemble the caricature that Rian Malan had painted in self-mockery: angry (often striking) nurses, drunken (or worse) teachers, and unanswered (or broken or stolen) telephones. On Mbeki's watch, corruption – soon to be the most persistent feature of the successor administration – loomed across the landscape in matters large (such as the Arms Deal) and small (MPs enriching themselves through fraudulent air-travel claims).

Mbeki's sonorous affirmation of 'a developmental state' – referring to collective economic and human development, but also the state's essential role in harnessing national resources and directing incentives through a specific policy-making process[198] – allowed the government to use the inefficient and cash-guzzling state-owned companies (soon enough to number over 700) as vehicles for party patronage.

Hence, on several sets of figures and, more pertinently, in the lived reality of the people, the toss could be argued in both directions simultaneously. Growth was up from its apartheid (1990-1993) low average of 1.4 percent to an average 4.3 percent in the period 2001 to 2007. (Thereafter, post the global financial crisis and the locust years of Jacob Zuma, it would go rapidly downhill.)[199] But the unemployment rate crested under Mbeki at 29.3 percent in

March 2003, a record not even his economically challenged successor would match.[200]

GLOOM UNDER SUNNY SKIES

For all this, for those with work, skills, security walls and the lifestyles of suburban 'braaivleis, rugby, sunny skies and Chevrolet' (or, to update the 1974 radio jingle, now driving Range Rovers), the view looked fair – that is, if you could survive the terrors of urban crime, including often-violent home invasions, and murder. And in the rural areas, where farmers and their workers were often killed with a brutal intensity, matters were much worse.

The dysfunctionality of the government actually began on Mandela's watch, and continued in the benign years of Mbeki. The acceleration, though, gathered frightening speed after the forced exit of Mbeki at the very moment when the state's functioning had all but seized up, and it would be expected to perform lifesaving services.

The truism uttered by General Jan Smuts, whose political defeat in 1948 ushered in the extremity of National Party (NP) rule and the intensification of the struggle against it, applies. He observed, with a remarkable equanimity which foretold the tide of eventual events, 'The worst, like the best, never happens [in South Africa].'[201]

More earthily, and honestly, a good friend who immigrated to Sydney, Australia a decade ago and initially found the going hard and unfamiliar, told a wonderfully South African-only tale to describe the difference between the two places. 'When I went to work in Johannesburg and took the mince out of the deep freeze, I would come home at night to a dish of lasagne for the family. When I do the same in Sydney, I come home from work in the evening and all there is is defrosted mince.'

However, the same friend offered this: 'But the other difference is that here in Sydney my children have a real future, and we have a better chance of being bitten by a dangerous spider than being robbed, raped or killed in our home.'

Just how bad things had become on the crime front, for example, was relayed in a raft of bleak statistics: between April 2017 and March 2018 over twenty thousand people were murdered in South Africa, a seven percent increase on the previous year, with around fifty-seven people dying in brutal circumstances *every single day*. This made the country the fifth-highest killing field in the world, eclipsed only by war zones such as Syria, Iraq, Afghanistan and Yemen.[202]

Of the hundreds of thousands of mourning victims left in the bloodied path hacked out by this local killing spree, one death in particular caught my attention, in June 2019. Over forty-five years before I had shared a dormitory with Warwick Hultzer at Kearsney College, the boarding school I attended atop KwaZulu-Natal's rolling green Valley of a Thousand Hills, near Hillcrest. I hadn't seen Hultzer since leaving school although I'd occasionally wondered what had become of him.

On a crisp, winterish mid-2019 day, sitting in my relatively secure Cape Town suburban home, I checked in on Facebook on my old matric-class page. It flagged a truly awful report, a story that day from the *Daily News* of Durban. Headlined 'Hillcrest businessman bludgeoned to death', it provided the gristly detail of my former schoolmate's terrible end. Hultzer, then 62 years old and the owner of a construction company, living alone, had been found lying on the floor of his home with his hands and legs bound, and his throat slit.'[203]

A POOR PROGNOSIS

News of Warwick Hultzer's terrible end was more devastating than the intimations of mortality that came unbidden each time I heard the sad news of other schoolfriends who'd succumbed to the dread diseases that kick in with gathering frequency in the over-60 cohort in which I uncomfortably found myself. But as future healthcare needs became the preoccupation of the late-middle-aged, it was clear enough that for middle-class South Africans, the public hospitals – with some noteworthy exceptions – were no place for anyone who could remotely afford private health care.

The difference was often a literal distinction between survival and death. The terrible stories of negligence, ill-treatment and worse in government hospitals was sharply different from the mostly well run private clinics, and would be one of the aggravating factors limiting the response to the 2020 coronavirus disaster in the country.

Long before the arrival of the pandemic, however, an extreme example of this collapse in government healthcare was the 2015 Life Esidimeni scandal in Gauteng. A 'precipitous and shambolic decision' by the local MEC for health, Qedani Mahlangu, to place mental-health patients in the 'care' of ill-equipped and unregulated non-government organisations had catastrophic and lethal results: 143 people died at sub-par so-called psychiatric facilities used in the name of 'cost saving'.

This was as a direct result of the instructions of a provincial government known for its lavish and reckless spending on perks for its provincial ministers, and the normal dose of corruption and rigged tenders that had become the depressing norm in Zumafied South Africa.[204] At the time of writing in 2020, not a single politician or official had been prosecuted for these deaths.

But if the callous 'care' provided was appalling, it appeared that the funds had at least been spent as intended. What if the funds were diverted entirely? For this, we need to switch attention from Gauteng to the Eastern Cape – one of the worst-governed provinces in a highly competitive field.

William Safire, a *New York Times* columnist and former speech writer for Richard Nixon, coined the memorable acronym 'mego' (my eyes glaze over), shorthand for what happens when too much information, particularly of the negative and detailed sort, is consumed by even the most intrepid observer. This would soon enough, in the Zuma era, become the depressing and daily norm of news ingestion in South Africa: overcome by 'mego', you simply turned the page or changed the channel.

Little surprise, then, that only one newspaper, the *Mail & Guardian*, reported in late April 2019 that desperately needed funds in the whopping amount of R111 million had been diverted from a budget for hospitals and clinics in the blighted Eastern Cape and, according to the report, had apparently 'found its way into the pockets of senior officials in the province'.[205]

But in an only-in-South-Africa twist in this miserable and mego-inducing tale, it was noted that the heroic blower of the whistle on this saga had himself been dismissed from the province's employ for 'soliciting a bribe, arranging a R30 000 salary for a friend in exchange for tenders and paying one company exorbitant rates to change light bulbs at health facilities in the province'.

How many people it takes to change a light bulb then, in corroded South Africa, depends on the amount and number of bribes being paid for the service.

The malign neglect and corruption in the Eastern Cape health services was revealed again amid the coronavirus storm engulfing the province and country in mid-2020. In a BBC special report, Livingstone Hospital, the main covid-19 health facility in Port Elizabeth, was described by doctors there as 'like a war situation': blood and waste on the floors, lack of personal protective equipment for health personnel, oxygen shortages, a severe shortage of ambulances, and patients 'sleeping under newspapers'.[206]

Extraordinarily, perhaps, for foreign viewers, the Eastern Cape Health department director general, Dr Thobile Mbengashe, blamed the crisis on 'historic issues dating back to white minority rule'. South African viewers were more familiar with this ruse – it was hardwired into the default responses of every government spokesman and neatly elided the fact that the ANC had enjoyed a monopoly of political and fiscal power for fully twenty-six years.

You also needed, if you were a member of a minority community, to drown out the background noise on 'white privilege'. For other minorities – coloureds and Indians – you also had to ignore the fact that your working-class dispossession under apartheid still largely disqualified your preferment under stringent race-based appointment and promotion prospects in the public sector, and increasingly, via ever-tightening employment-equity regulations, in the private sector as well.

BAD EDUCATION

For all South Africans, of all races and classes, a decent education is imperative for their children's future. Under apartheid, as the ANC government reminded us constantly, education was designed to keep blacks out of skills, training and upward advancement. But it was clear that after more than two decades of ANC rule, the trend had continued almost without interruption and certainly without improvement.

In 2008 I was a participant in a debate organised by the *Sunday Times* on Constitution Hill, Johannesburg, on the state of the country. Two of my fellow panellists, both black women of eminence, businesswoman Wendy Luhabe and educationist Mamphela Ramphele, surprised me and the audience by declaring that the dreaded 'Bantu education' had been better than the current schools system, a claim repeated by Ramphele in 2012.[207]

Just how bad the situation in state schools had become was revealed in perhaps the most shocking report ever tabled in post-apartheid South Africa. The Progress in International Reading

Literacy Study, published in December 2017, found that eight out of ten children in Grade 4 across South Africa 'could not read for meaning' – in other words, while they could 'sound the words', they didn't understand them.[208] Out of fifty countries surveyed for the study, South Africa came last, behind such war-zone areas as Iraq and the Gaza Strip.

If you were privileged to live in the so-called leafy suburbs, then the neighbourhood government schools, semi-private hangovers from the apartheid government's early-1990s restructuring of the white education system in anticipation of democracy, offered pretty good educational outcomes at more affordable fees than the full-blown private-school alternatives. But even at these enclaves of multiracial achievement at the scholar level, the race-warriors in our midst had launched a full-scale assault on the demographics in the staffroom.

The binary racial bean-counting which by the second decade of the 21st century had become the most, perhaps only, public policy around which both government and much of the commentariat class could unite, now assailed schools not for their admissions policy but for the lack of black teachers in the classroom. Just what the parents, or the pupils, thought about the quality of their teachers was irrelevant. Race trumped all other considerations, and the interests of the child – always the basis of the law in any dispute – were the last thing on the mind of the virtue signallers and those who measured every goal by quantitative pigment, not on results, achievement, personal commitment or educational outcome.

When I was elected in 1989 to represent one of the most affluent areas in Johannesburg, Houghton and the surrounding suburbs, I made a typical speech in Parliament pointing out the iniquities of apartheid, then on its political deathbed. I received a withering res-ponse from a backbench National Party MP who represented a white working-class constituency. He said, 'It's easy for you and your voters: you can just buy your own apartheid while denouncing it.'

That may indeed have been a reasonable description of the new, multiracial elite as it walled itself off from the vast underclass populating the townships and squatter camps only kilometres away from their suburban fastness. But the outlook, even from the rarefied heights of privilege and prosperity, remained cloudy.

CHAPTER 10

———

Last visit to the New Dawn:
The problem of cadre deployment

There were several ironies, both known and at the time unknown, when I arrived at the official presidential residence in Bryntirion, Pretoria back in November 2012.

The most paradoxical was in the original name of this grand Cape Dutch sentinel, as home to a succession of segregationist and apartheid leaders who had denied its essence to the bulk of their citizens: 'Libertas'. No less haunting for the man I was about to visit was the new name emblazoned on the gates of his presidential home – 'Mahlamba Ndlopfu', Xitsonga for 'New Dawn'. That would become the winning slogan for his successor, Cyril Ramaphosa, who would be the next inhabitant of this grand home, as a rallying counterpoint against the road to ruin charted by Zuma.

But those events lay in the future. That night, I'd just returned from my stint as ambassador to Argentina and had arrived there to report back to the man who'd appointed me to that post. I'd lived for three years in that South American country, an even more cautionary tale of a nation with matchless natural and human resources unable to escape low-growth snares and entrapped by chronic failures of governance gifted to it by reckless, populist leaders.

Brazil, to the north, was doing just enough to avoid hurtling off the cliff edge but never realise its golden potential; and since Brazil in size and scale was the moon that lifted all South American tides, I knew only too well its huge but unrealised, perhaps unrealisable, potential.

TAKING NOTE OF THE YELLOW CARDS

On Zuma's enquiry on my experience as his appointed emissary in Argentina, I joked, 'It's far more corrupt and worse governed than we are.'

He laughed heartily, then said that he'd recently been at the United Nations with Argentine president Cristina Fernández de Kirchner, whose eccentric economic policies and distortion of financial figures – such as grossly manipulating the statistics on runaway inflation – had recently earned the rebuke of Christine Lagarde, the head of the International Monetary Fund (IMF), which had threatened to red-card Argentina.

Kirchner, at the UN General Assembly, had thundered back at the IMF, announcing that despite bequeathing to the world such football gods as Maradona and Lionel Messi, Argentina was 'not a player in a soccer game'; it was a sovereign nation, which made its decisions on a sovereign basis, she said.[209]

I indicated to Zuma, with whom I shared tales of how the 2010 World Cup had boosted our standing in South America, that we could not defy or ignore the red and yellow cards from these pesky (to the presidents) but hugely influential (to the markets) international arbiters. I also noted that South Africa and Argentina had much in common. Our economies and populations were almost identical in size, and we were both extractors of natural resources.

Until 2012, or for the bulk of his first term, Zuma had never really had a governing philosophy to speak of. He'd salted few clues in advance of his presidential ascent as to what he'd do when he entered the Union Buildings; not being the aloof and imperious Thabo Mbeki seemed enough for the party faithful. He had promised, however, to continue the economic and fiscal policies of his predecessors, Mandela and Mbeki, and had offered vague bromides on how he would go 'with the majority of the ANC' and stick to its stated policies.

That evening, when I asked Zuma how he wanted to anchor his likely second term as party president, and thereafter his next term as state president following the 2014 election, he told me it would be based firmly on the principles and detail embedded in the National Development Plan (NDP), which Parliament had adopted in August.

Indeed, a few weeks later, when Zuma was re-elected ANC president, he tied his term of office to the NDP. Entirely absent in both the document and the party conference at Mangaung in Bloemfontein was any reference to 'radical economic trans-formation' (RET); it also contained an acceptance of the property rights enshrined in the Constitution.

Of course, Zuma had a very outdated idea of what the presidency was really about. Not only had the ANC smothered most distinctions between party and state, but at the apex of its power, in the opinion of one insider quoted by *The Economist*, 'Zuma [had] a pre-capitalist notion of power ... He just [couldn't] understand why he [couldn't] have access to state resources.'[210]

And until December 2015, when he fired the first of two finance ministers in five days, Zuma had more or less allowed technocrats, applying expertise and learning to problem-solving, to run the Treasury, which was headed by an economically competent and financially literate minister. He'd also seemed until then to have some regard for the 'amorphous markets' – in Trevor Manuel's phrase[211] – which quite easily at the first hint of local turmoil could yank their funds out of the country. These monies were much needed to fund the country's rising import bills and pay for the generous public servants' wage increases cited previously.

But when Zuma pulled down the pillars of the Treasury temple, over the head of finance minister Nhlanhla Nene, in December 2015, the markets rebelled and went into freefall. The always-volatile rand dropped a staggering nine percent in four days and a record slump in sovereign bonds forced up the cost of government borrowing by about fifteen percent. This was a consequence of Zuma's appointment of an obscure parliamentary backbencher, Des van Rooyen, as the new minister of finance.

The market and investor reaction was so strong and sharp that for once Zuma did an embarrassing U-turn. Van Rooyen was sidelined after just four days in office (he was moved to a lesser portfolio) and, despite their mutual antipathy, Zuma obliged the markets by installing Pravin Gordhan at the Treasury. (As things unravelled further, however, Gordhan would be removed in eighteen months.)

LITIGATING THE PAST

There was, to me at least, little that distinguished Zuma's private comments from his public utterances. He, less than Mandela, but far more in the mould of his successor, Cyril Ramaphosa, litigated the past: rather than accept blame and interrogate a course correction for the glaring failures of state policies, comfort and victimhood were sought in the appalling legacy and privations of apartheid.

This was victimology on steroids: it was far easier to cast back to an epoch when the leadership of current government was in exile or imprisoned. It also provided a reminder of the so-called 'liberation dividend': however bad the current situation might be, and whatever mistakes had been made by the extant administration, always remember the regime before was more mendacious.

Paradoxically, the NDP to which Zuma had pledged such fealty pointed in the opposite direction. Its concluding premise was clear enough:

> Successful countries have what is called a 'future orientation'. Their policy bias is to take decisions that lead to long-term benefits, as opposed to short-run solutions that could have negative effects later on. Such countries generally prefer investment over consumption, have high savings rates, sound fiscal policy, high levels of fixed investment, a high degree of policy certainty and clear rules of engagement for the private sector. A clear and predictable policy environment enables businesses to take a long-term perspective on growth and development.[212]

Events and the deliberate (or careless) acts of the South African government almost before the ink had dried on the parliamentary resolution affirming the NDP would mock both the essence and the essential detail of this commitment, and the distillation of what demarcated 'successful countries'.

The other nugget offered to me during my conversation with Zuma was his determination, in his words, to be 'an education president'. Refreshingly unembarrassed by his own lack of formal education, he used his paucity of qualifications to urge others to accomplish what he lacked.

When I politely enquired how he intended to achieve this outcome, given the iron grip the recalcitrant South African Democratic Teachers Union (SADTU) had on the government school system, he answered immediately and with great emphasis: 'We have created two departments, one for basic education and the other for higher education.'

In the pause that followed, I expected him to explain how increasing, or doubling, the bureaucracy would lead to better-educated and more skilled scholars and graduates; he offered none.

Long after Zuma had been forced from office, and into the second year of the Ramaphosa administration, anything but certainty prevailed in government policy-making and its erratic execution. A new mining charter was mired in court challenges. A promised auction of the telecommunications spectrum was bogged down by delay. The much-touted restructuring of flailing Eskom announced by Ramaphosa in February 2019 had yet to commence by the end of that year; and the implementation of energy alternatives to add power to the national grid had been stymied by a recalcitrant minister. Fast-tracking visas for skilled workers was much touted but never quite sighted. And threatening property rights and the independence of the admired Reserve Bank, and tearing up protection codes for international investors, featured in rhetoric and, in some cases, were implemented. Again, the list was long and disheartening.

Zuma and the entire apparat of the ANC reminded me of the apocryphal tale of the outgoing president handing over three envelopes to his successor. 'When the going gets rough,' he advises the new head of state, 'open an envelope.'

As an early crisis hits the new president, he opens the first envelope. In the note inside it, his predecessor has written, 'Blame the global financial crisis.'

This buys some time for the new man until a new problem confronts him. So he opens the second envelope. The note in it from the former president advises, 'Blame me.'

This also works for a good while, until yet another crunch point threatens his administration. With rising panic he reaches into his desk for the third envelope prepared for him by his predecessor. The note inside it says, 'Prepare three envelopes.'

IN THE BELLY OF THE BEAST

Some months after my one-on-one with the president, he gave an interview to the *Financial Times*. Zuma, metaphorically, opened the first and second envelopes when he blamed both the Eurozone crisis and the legacy of apartheid for the flatlining of the South African economy and our coruscating failure to create growth and employment.[213]

But just a few weeks later, planning minister Trevor Manuel actually threw away the second envelope entirely with his headline-grabbing speech to a government leadership summit. 'Nineteen years into democracy, our government has run out of excuses,' he said. 'We cannot continue to blame apartheid for our failings as a state.'[214]

Such brutal candour was both unusual and refreshing, and led to suggestions that Manuel was preparing to leave government – which he duly did, the following year. It was a serious loss. Manuel had created an enclave of excellence in his many years at National Treasury, and had bequeathed the country an impressive roadmap to a sustainable and inclusive future in the form of the NDP.

In addition to his various government roles, in 2008 he'd served on the Spence Commission on Growth and Development, a global conclave of the economically grand and financially literate. Doubtless he was also in agreement with its fundamental conclusion (quoting Brian Lee Crowley in his introduction to Fred McMahon's *Road to Growth: How lagging economies become prosperous*), although he then served in a government that utterly violated the proposition.

> Economic growth is not a mysterious force that strikes unpredictably or whose absence is inexplicable. On the contrary, growth is the fruit of two forces: the ability of people to recognise opportunities, on the one hand, and the creation by government of a legal, fiscal and regulatory

framework in which it is worthwhile for people to exploit those opportunities.[215]

Noting that there was no shortage of energetic and entrepreneurial people 'wherever human beings are to be found', Crowley found a key difference between successful high-growth countries and their depressing counterparts in the field of public policy. As he rather sensibly observed, with a hint of obviousness, 'That key is simply to put sensible policies in place, and then let the intelligence, industriousness and ingenuity of people do the rest.'[216]

In my last discussion with Jacob Zuma, I shared some of my frustration after three years in the belly of the beast as a chief director and ambassador in the public service. I'd experienced first hand and would readily identify with Manuel's later observation about a 'risk-averse public service that thrives on passing the buck'.[217]

I recounted to Zuma some of the lurid tales of missed opportunities and hair-raising bureaucratic obstacles placed in the path of the public servants who did actually arrive at work on time and display a conscientious application to their tasks. One of the stories was a small experience with much larger meaning.

In 2012, when our embassy was planning to use the Freedom Day celebrations in Argentina to showcase a gifted emerging South African artist to art-loving Argentines, I obtained the buy-in of the South African director-general of arts and culture. He promptly sent us the details of a programme by the department to showcase emerging artistic talent abroad, and we selected an artist from the approved list. However, the problems and obstacles emerged the moment the matter left the desk of the director-general and went down into the lower reaches of his department.

In short – and it is a very long and sad tale – John Vusi Mfupi was eventually flown from Johannesburg to Buenos Aires, but due to a combination of incompetence and lethargy, he arrived without his excellent portfolio of works to display to the audience of more than 200 high-end locals we'd gathered together. The artworks had been erroneously sent to Amsterdam, and arrived four days after the scheduled event.

The net result of this botch-up is that I have a large Mfupi collage on display in my lounge in Cape Town, since I both appreciate his art, and felt so bad about his missed opportunity that I purchased it for my own account.

South Africa, of course, had more pressing issues than showcasing its artistic talent. But the same malady in the middle and lower reaches of arts and culture is evident in health, education and the police, to name just three frontline services where the state has the essential role in provisioning public goods.

Zuma expressed considerable interest in this tale of artistic woe and advised me to send him a short memo highlighting the essence of the problem with a recalcitrant and underperforming civil service. I duly despatched it a few days afterwards, and never heard another word from him.

RUNNING ON EMPTY

The biggest threat to national solvency had become the public-sector wage bill. Over-promoted, pampered in permanent employment as many government servants were, by 2019 they were simply unaffordable: nearly 60 percent of the budget was consumed by civil servants' wages, constituting 14 percent of the nation's GDP, figures *The Economist* described as 'jaw dropping'.[218]

And their pay rises outstripped those in the private sector, despite overall low productivity and ballooning numbers (the number of state employees rose by 25 percent in ten years). Numbering more than 1.3 million, public servants constituted just 2.2 percent of the population – a veritable elite consuming most of the revenues of the state.

In the low-growth economy that both policy choices and reform inaction had created, the interest on debt, accumulated in part to fund state workers, had by 2019 soared to around R1 billion per working day.[219] Little wonder, then – except to the financially illiterate – that debt-to-GDP ratio had touched 70 percent, a world away from the 22 percent it had been in the Mbeki-Manuel years.

Since the workforce was almost entirely unionised, and the Cosatu trade-union federation had an effective veto as the third pillar (along with the SA Communist Party) of the so-called 'triple alliance' with the ruling ANC, the chance of change here was close to zero. But with revenue-collection shortfalls reckoned to be north of R285 billion for the first year of the new decade (2020), the music fuelling this jig was about to end.[220] Just as the apartheid regime had been felled by an investor strike against it, it was likely that, as the funding ran dry, some sort of change in this unsustainable number might happen.

It wouldn't be due, however, to government's reading the financial tea leaves in time – it's hard to give up largesse, especially when it's funded by hard-pressed taxpayers. And, indeed, extraordinarily, despite the masses of red ink on the public finances and the collapsed growth rate, Cyril Ramaphosa in October 2020 decided that more public servants and ever greater cost were the answer. He announced that the government intended to create 800 000 public-sector jobs over the following three years.[221]

Of all the dire and depressing statistics on display in 2019, two sets of figures stood out for the contradictions they offered of a vampire state in practice: an administration that simultaneously sucked the lifeblood from economic activity and effectiveness, and was hugely enriched for doing so.

On the one hand, the civil-service mandarins charged with guarding the public purse and spending it with prudence clocked up 'irregular spending' of a whopping R62.8 billion in 2018

(21 percent higher than the previous year), according a report released by the auditor-general in late 2019. Another accounting term of art covering a multitude of sins and thievery, 'fruitless and wasted expenditure' had ballooned to a five-year running total of R4.1 billion. In fact, only about a quarter of all national and provincial entities audited achieved a clean bill of financial health.

Strikingly, the opposition-governed Western Cape, which had been under the political control of the DA, obtained 100-percent clean audits. By contrast, the domain of the corruption-accused ANC secretary-general Ace Magashule (a key ally of Zuma and chief opponent of Ramaphosa, who had targeted state corruption early on), the Free State province, 'recorded the highest fruitless and wasteful expenditure' – 69 percent of the entities there required, according to the auditor-general, 'urgent intervention'.[222]

On the other hand, 29 000 civil servants, many at the top who were clearly delinquent in their core task, earned over R1 million per year, and dozens earned three times that amount - which in some large way explained why the wage bill of the state had risen 70 percent in a decade.[223]

SHORT SHELF LIFE
Zuma had also mastered the art of removing, replacing and reshuffling the administration, both for his own allegedly corrupt purposes and to reward personal loyalty. A study in mid-2017, authored by Gareth van Onselen on behalf of the IRR, revealed that the average life of a cabinet minister was nine months: 'In total, since 10 May 2009, Zuma has made 126 changes to the national executive [including] 62 changes to ministerial positions [and] 63 changes to deputy ministerial positions,' Van Onselen wrote.[224]

The churn in the administration was even worse: 60 percent of all directors-general had lasted in their posts less than a year, and more than a third of them less than six months.

(The national ministers were the political heads, responsible for policy direction, oversight and communication, while the directors-general were the administrative heads, responsible for implementation, procurement, staff performance and financial management.)

'This is not how you manage a national government, it is how to sow chaos, uncertainty and disorder and, it would seem, Jacob Zuma has perfected that particular art,' Van Onselen concluded.[225]

And, of course, a number of the civil servants further down the food chain, plus their political overlords, could also not perform their functions. This became glaringly apparent during the coronavirus crisis in 2020, when a range of state interventions seized up, from delivering unemployment relief via the sclerotic and corrupted Unemployment Insurance Fund (UIF) to actually getting food parcels to hungry citizens.

One of the core needs for all communities in the face of the invisible microscopic and contagious pathogen was hand sanitation. But washing hands with soap and water – a key curb of infection offered by the World Health Organization (WHO) – was difficult or impossible for poorer communities reliant on creaking, inadequate or nonexistent infrastructure.

The Constitution promised that 'everyone has the right to have access to sufficient food and water'. So much for the theory. A detailed study by the IRR in March 2020 found epic failures in the supply of reliable water and disposal of sewage, and these were primarily attributable to 'the disintegration of local government'. As the report pointed out, you didn't need to be an apartheid supporter to note that the water system of South Africa was once, like Eskom and its electricity supply, the finest in the world – even if the administration which purposed them was racist or worse.[226]

The local-government situation was compounded by both ineptitude and crass corruption. Another study revealed in 2019 that to plug the gap left by mismanagement and a shortage of skilled workers (many of whom exited due to employment-equity targets), over R3.4 billion had been spent by the 23 largest municipalities on 'consultants', yet this was largely wasted since the same local governments had managed to *not* spend R44 billion of their budgets in one financial year (2017-2018), and much of that was earmarked for infrastructure such as water. As governance expert, associate professor William Gumede, noted, 'The more patronage there is, the more consultants are used.'[227]

Manuel, in his speech to the government leadership summit, had clearly had an eye on the both the Spence report and the NDP 2030 plan which he had helped birth. He'd correctly diagnosed state dysfunction, attributing the problems to the high turnover of staff and the critical shortage of technical skills, and a fondness for blaming the past for present maladies.

He was right in his diagnosis, except on one essential point. He stated, 'South Africa has not suffered ... from having incorrect policies.'[228] Actually, one of the roots of the problem he so fearlessly dissected was just such a policy. It's called 'cadre deployment', and it explicitly requires party loyalists to be deployed into all 'centres of power' and 'to transform their institutions ... to ensure that the goals of the national revolution [are] pursued with the necessary vigour'.[229]

In 1996 the ANC removed the power of the independent Public Service Commission to promote the careers of public servants, gifting this privilege to the political heads of department. By 1997, the merit-based system of appointment and promotion of public servants had been scrapped.

CHAPTER 11

———

Men of zeal: How state control has shuttered the state

The National Democratic Revolution (NDR) is a Soviet model for the advance of a developing country towards socialism through incremental reforms and without a bloody revolution. 'The fact that this model died with the USSR and is ridiculed by today's Russians has had no impact on the ANC,' notes RW Johnson, who also points out that it 'included no precise programme of what exactly was to be done or by when'.[230]

The NDR, together with the Freedom Charter (a collection of slogans and aspirations), was the animating idea and corrosive ideal that begat the breaking of the back of the state and opened the floodgates to the corruption that followed.

But how did South Africa, such a hopeful entrant into the new world of dynamic and forward-looking democracies in 1994, choose policies and practices that placed it in the column of countries heading in the opposite direction?

The answer? Ideology.

WELL-MEANING MEN
In 1928 US Justice Louis Brandeis wrote a famous dissenting

judgment that contained a warning that applies in spades to contemporary South Africa. 'Experience should teach us to be most on our guard to protect liberty when the government's purposes are beneficent,' he wrote. 'Men born to freedom are naturally alert to repel invasion of their liberty by evil-minded rulers. The greatest dangers to liberty lurk in insidious encroachment by men of zeal, well-meaning but with little understanding.'[231]

Trevor Manuel, whose bombast toward the opposition in Parliament and later in the boardroom was offset by personal charm in private and an almost romantic ability to lace the dry text of budget speeches with literary allusions, was a pragmatic minister of finance – the right man for his country's times. But his sincere belief that the ANC's policies were right, and that the error lay only in their erratic, poor or even dishonest implementation, was, in my view, wrong.

The failure of the public service and government to provide the bare bones of a 'capable' and 'developmental' state – a core of ANC catechism – lay in a bundle of other policies to which the ANC leadership, from its most decent leaders to the bad and corrupt, all subscribed. The more development and action by the state was demanded by the developmental-state nostrum, the less, in fact, the state could deliver. This was precisely because a raft of other policies and prescripts preferenced party loyalty, race and political connectivity for key appointments of those mandated to do the implementing.

In January 2015 I led a company group to a meeting with a government minister whom I'd known since the early 1990s. As we waited in the sparsely furnished anteroom outside his Pretoria office, one of our party enquired, 'What's the minister like to deal with?'

'I'll give you the good news first,' I half-joked. 'He's honest, so there'll be no question of anything improper. He's also intelligent and industrious. You can rest assured he'll be properly briefed and able to engage fully on topic.

'The bad news is that he's totally ideological. If your request aligns with his ideology, you'll be fine. If not, forget about it.'

EVIL-MINDED RULERS

In a post-Jacob Zuma, traumatised nation, many were on guard against the villains of state capture. But in excavating the ideological foundations that had fast-tracked this capture and slow-tracked the economy, there was less enquiry and little vigilance.

During the 2019 festive season, the newspapers headlined a series of imminent arrests, including those of Brian Molefe and two of his fellow alleged plunderers, Anoj Singh (who, like Molefe, had done stints at both Transnet and Eskom, and who faced eighteen charges of misconduct and gross negligence) and Siyabonga Gama, one-time head of the rail monolith Transnet, from which he was fired.

The Transnet chairman, ANC heavyweight Popo Molefe, called the trio 'the key protagonists or architects of state capture at Transnet', telling the Judicial Commission of Inquiry into Allegations of State Capture (Zondo Commission) headed by Justice Raymond Zondo that this unholy trinity had 'siphoned off' money; 'it represented what I call a horror show'.[232] (Some months later Popo Molefe charged that the ANC's top leadership, including Cyril Ramaphosa, had been made aware of the Transnet money heist five years before but had done nothing about it.)[233]

But a similar tale of ransacking institutions and removing capable and incorruptible investigators was at play in the National Prosecuting Authority (NPA), whose mandate is to institute and conduct criminal proceedings on behalf of the state, but where investigations were either not undertaken or delayed, or dockets implicating the powerful and the corrupt were simply 'lost'.

Another arm of state capture stretched into the South African

Revenue Service (SARS), headed by key Zuma enabler, prisons boss Tom Moyane, who closed down investigations into politically powerful people, of whom the most powerful, Zuma himself, was revealed in Jacques Pauw's book, *The President's Keepers*, to be a 'delinquent taxpayer'.[234]

Thus, the alleged misdeeds of Brian Molefe, Anoj Sigh and Siyabonga Gama, and others who charted the road to ruin of the state-owned entities, had become so infamous, the detail of their apparent self-enrichment so glaring, and any judicial consequences so absent, that a sort of 'mego' effect dulled even the senses of the most alert. This led CNN personality Richard Quest, once a cheer-leader for South Africa, to address the country in January 2020 with, 'Actually, the entire economy was hijacked! … How many people have gone to prison so far?'[235]

Two years after Ramaphosa had promised to take swift action on the corruption front, the answer to that was zero.

The new head of the NPA, Shamila Batohi, while untainted, unlike her Zuma-stained predecessor, appeared over-cautious and ineffective to the point of inertia: she failed in her first year and a half on the job to advance a single arrest or prosecution.

Finally, in September 2020, the first arrests happened. Busi-nessmen Thoshan Panday of KwaZulu-Natal, Bosasa executive Angelo Agrizzi and three business types implicated in an asbestos-cleanup scam, most notably Edwin Sodi, were charged with various crimes. These spanned the gamut of 'state capture' offences from fraud and corruption to illegal tender procurements and money laundering. A few retired politicians were also arrested, notably former ANC MP Vincent Smith.[236]

However, it remains an open question whether and when the far more senior politicians and ministers who facilitated the looting of the state would be arrested, indicted and charged and convicted, if ever. Some hope on this score emerged in late 2020: ANC secretary-general Ace Magashule was arrested for corruption in the Free State related to an asbestos-eradication project there – but would the charges go anywhere? After all, the highest-profile of the lot, Jacob Zuma, had since 2007 managed to delay and filibuster his own criminal trial, which at the time of writing was still in process. Eminent people such as former and admired public protector Thuli Madonsela had begun to moot the appalling idea of a blanket amnesty for the political looters.

AN ECONOMICALLY DUBIOUS SCAFFOLD

Trevor Manuel, Popo Molefe, Cyril Ramaphosa et al would, justifiably, be branded 'the good guys' in the fractured and ferocious cockpit of ANC politics. But their clinging to the carcass of failed policies was also due to their collectivist belief in the purity of high purpose and Struggle in which they'd cut their political teeth.

Men of this stripe, for the most part, didn't countenance illegality or flouting of process and procedure – but at key moments since South Africa's democratic journey had begun in 1994, they'd provided the intellectual cover and moral armour for the plunder that followed.

It's easy to lose sight of the fact that an essential enabler of the blatant illegalities birthed by what was termed 'state capture' had its origins in crucial decisions taken during the presidency of Nelson Mandela. The intellectual cement for it was cast during those benign years. Alongside Mandela's rainbow nation, the men of zeal were constructing a scaffold that was far more mono-chromatic and economically dubious.

In early 2004, some months after the country went about celebrating 'the first decade of freedom', I and my brains trust of strategist Ryan Coetzee, researchers James Myburgh and Gareth van Onselen, and speech writer Joel Pollak examined a series of documents which, in our view, unpacked the real agenda of the ruling party. We packaged this into a speech that I delivered in June 2004 at the Joburg Press Club, in which I pointed out that beyond and below the fine words inked in the Constitution and mouthed in the national slogan ('Diverse people unite'), another entirely contradictory, arguably injurious, agenda lurked in plain sight.[237]

I advised my audience that the key to the future actually lay as much in 1997 as it did in 1994. The year 1997 was when the ANC and its alliance partners endorsed a key document, 'The State, Property Relations and Social Transformation',[238] authored by Joel Netshitenzhe, which explicitly rejected the concept of a politically unaligned and merit-driven civil service. It also mandated that the state – and, crucially, parastatal companies – was an instrument in the hands of the liberation movement. All areas in its remit were deemed 'crucial for the transformation project'. The 'national liberation movement' was tasked with 'extending [its] power ... over all levers of power', and state-owned companies featured high on this list.

As early as 1996, the party had made plain that the NDR had intentions and scope far beyond electoral wins: '[it] is a process of struggle that seeks the transfer of power to the people ... When we talk of power we mean political, social and economic control'.[239]

If South Africans were surprised decades later that a rogue president and his backers stole the country's patrimony, it had been preordained back in the late 1990s that the party, the people, the whole of society and all activities in it, were one and the same.

The devil lay in the detail of another ANC seminal document, *Nation Formation and Nation Building*, which offered this insight: 'The main content of the National Democratic Revolution [NDR] should find expression in the leadership structures of the ANC, and indeed in the country as whole. This is usually referred to as "African leadership".'[240]

Thus, even if the 'African leadership' after Zuma's election in

2009 was an economically ignorant, morally challenged and legally delinquent president, then toppling the top man would be a negation of the very essence and personification of the revolution itself. Hence the durability of Zuma – through seven failed votes of no confidence against him in Parliament, he hung on with finger-wrenching intensity, until just a few months before the expiry of his second term of office in 2018.

THE TRANSFORMATION FABLE

In 1994 the ANC inherited a racially unequal society, and it had a moral mission, on paper at least: to use the state to perform its core functions aimed at advantaging the most disadvantaged, overwhelmingly black, South Africans. That was a moral non-negotiable, which largely had support from all sides of politics and society.

But the party had a choice in how to tackle this key task: it could use the tools of experience and the very beneficiaries of past discrimination to create, through excellent public education and well-run hospitals, the 'better life for all' proclaimed in its election manifesto. It could define 'transformation' as a commitment, indeed an imperative, to implement the constitutional guarantees of equality, non-racialism and human dignity, in which there were many takers from all communities.

Instead, it chose, quite deliberately if not heedlessly, to narrow the definition and reduce the sum of all aspirations to a racial zero-sum game.

A core assumption of the ANC analysis, around which an entire edifice of legislation and regulatory regimes was fashioned, was that the state should play a central and even domineering role in the economy. To enable it to do so, the concept of 'transformation' – which soon enough became a weasel word from which all true meaning was sucked – was promoted as the essence of all state policy and rammed down the throats of a mostly compliant private sector.

Indeed, as far back as 1999, the ANC signalled that its enormous electoral majority and its control of the machinery of state were insufficient. It complained in another key party document, '[E]ven though we may have made progress in material terms, unless the forces for change are able to exercise hegemony, it will impact on our capacity to mobilize society.'[241]

The same paper, noting with approval the 'transformation of the SABC' – which in reality was the independence of the state broadcaster having been flattened – hungered for more control. 'The movement also needs to look at other elements of the ideological apparatus in society,' it noted, listing 'universities, research and policy institutes, culture, etc'.[242] Thus the road to state control over the intellectual fortresses, those bastions of inde- pendent enquiry and dissent in an open society, was opened by those determined to close the South African mind.

The fellow traveller along this road was 'demographic representivity', which ultimately became not just a mantra, but about the only policy which, despite the ruinous results of using racial percentages as the basis for all public-sector (and increasingly private-sector) appointments, was pursued with a grim relent- lessness – even if whole swathes of the country's economy and state institutions, from the electricity provider to the statistical service, were shuttered in the process.

There was an impeccable backdrop of racial exclusions and far worse under apartheid to justify a form of affirmative action to level the playing field and give everyone a fighting chance to get ahead. This was both reasonable and morally just. But in the grand designs of the ANC, this was insufficient. 'Demographic representivity' went far beyond a levelling, or the 'colourblindness' offered by Nelson Mandela.

On his path to power back in 1991, Mandela had said, 'The

primary aims of affirmative action must be to redress the imbalances created by apartheid. We are not … asking for handouts for anyone, nor are we saying that, just as a white skin was a passport to privilege in the past, so a black skin should be a privilege in the future. Nor … is it our aim to do away with qualifications … [T]he special measures that we envisage to overcome the legacy of past discrimination are not intended to ensure the advancement of unqualified persons but to see that those who have been denied access in the past can become qualified now … affirmative action must be rooted in principles of justice and equality.'[243]

In August 1998, to catcalls and jeers from the serried ranks of the ANC MPs, I quoted his fine words in Parliament when opposing the first Employment Equity Bill, the essential legislative edifice of the transformation project. I described it then as a 'pious in intention and destructive in effect'.[244]

Just how pernicious and destructive it actually was would become apparent in the years that followed. The legislation required all firms of more than fifty people to categorise their workforce along racial lines, and provide for an 'empowerment plan' to the satisfaction of government, and mandated stiff criminal penalties for non-compliance. An army of state enforcers, coupled with an immense burden of compliance obligations for private companies, made sure the fiat and fist of government was felt across the whole of the economy.

Both the mother legislation and later iterations made it impossible without a certificate of high compliance to do business with the state, which increasingly controlled ever larger swathes of economic activity.

THE BEE PATHOGEN

Five years later, in 2002, came the next stage in 'the revolution': an attack on the 'racial imbalances in the economy'. Black Economic

Empowerment (BEE) was the lynchpin, and the unruly nature of the private sector was suborned through government control over tenders, policy and legislation, crucially for mining and other licences, such as for banking, oil and gas, and radio and television stations.

In 2007, just before the ascent of Zuma, ANC secretary-general Kgalema Motlanthe, who served briefly as president after Thabo Mbeki was ousted, saw the situation plainly enough, and the consequences of such policies. 'This rot is across the board. It is not confined to any level or any area of the country. Almost every project is conceived because it offers opportunities for certain people to make money.'[245]

He was writing the perfect preface to the Zuma presidency. In the years that followed, the rot would spread wide and far; it infested the foundations of a functioning economy and paralysed much of the machinery of state.

The propulsive thrust for these policies was the assumption by the ruling-party mandarins that only compulsion and prescription on both citizens and corporates would compel the achievement of more integrated, racially diverse public and private sectors. This, in turn, did violence to the demographic realities and spoke of a dirigiste party's deep distrust of both markets and human motivation – both of which fuelled the success of high-growth, labour-absorbing economies, as the record proved elsewhere.

Through various charters mandated by government, the private sector was obliged to transfer shares to BEE partners, and by 2010 it was estimated that some R500 billion in shares had been extracted from the private sector by the stringent BEE requirements – although, as Myburgh noted, the 'huge sums [were] not going to the historically deprived black majority, as was the stated intention, but [to] by now already privileged ANC insiders'.[246]

There were hundreds of examples, and the reports arrived thick and fast on how this rent-seeking or cronyism was destroying the economy, fuelling corruption and perverting the normal rules of economics and 'moral hazard' – the understanding that you'll be exposed to the consequences of risk if you indulge in reckless conduct.

One such was my former nemesis, the Parliamentary speaker of my day, Baleka Mbete, a person with serious conflicts of interest: she doubled as speaker of the National Assembly and ANC chairperson, and was a ferocious protector of Zuma and not the legislature. It emerged in 2013 that she'd received around R25 million after being 'invited' to join Gold Fields Ltd as a new shareholder in a local mining operation. Similar jackpots were extended to others in the same Invictus consortium, including a daughter of Nelson Mandela, a lawyer who represented Jacob Zuma in his 2006 rape trial, and the infamous Aids denialist, one-time minister of health Dr Manto Tshabalala-Msimang.

The chairperson at the time of the transaction in 2010 was another Struggle activist turned tycoon, Mamphela Ramphele, who told the media in 2013, 'The South African government had shoved the list of some of Invictus Gold's black economic empowerment shareholders down Gold Fields' throat, with an ultimatum that if the preferred names were not taken on board it would be denied a mining licence,' a claim that was denied by a former department official. [247]

It was certainly questionable behaviour, morally problematic and economically hazardous – but it wasn't illegal.

'PERSON ZERO'

In 2009 the South African Police Service (SAPS) advertised for applicants for the positions of cluster commander in the Gauteng region. Experienced Indian woman police officer Jennila Naidoo applied for one of them.

She should have been, in crime ravaged and race-focused South Africa, just the ticket, and indeed she placed second in terms of her overall mark. However, and despite the provincial selection panel recommending her appointment, the national panel declined her application on the basis that it wouldn't enhance employment equity. A black man was appointed instead, despite his lower total mark.

Naidoo took the case to the Labour Court and won. Interestingly, what emerged during the case was that her fate had been determined by the application of a demographic grid that showed that the number of posts at such a senior level were so few that Indians, who comprise less than three percent of the country's population, could never meet the threshold for appointment. In other words, the ideal number of Indians to be appointed as cluster commanders under the blunt-instrument used by the SAPS to measure affirmative action was zero.[248]

The manifestation of this version of the apartheid pencil test, applied with different degrees of severity, and leavened by occasional instances of sanity, across all government departments, explains a lot about the incapacitation of the state.

When the coronavirus hit South Africa big-time in March 2020, and Cyril Ramaphosa, with commendable speed, placed the entire country in enforced lockdown and won many local and international plaudits, he did in one predictable respect allow his own message to be trodden on. In his initial television broadcast he reminded the nation that 'we're all in this together' and emphasised that the viral pathogen was heedless of the race or circumstance of its victims – but it didn't take long for his ministers to shoehorn any state (taxpayer-funded) relief into racial compartments.

The most egregious, but not isolated, example of this was in the tourism sector, traditionally one of the job-richest economic zones in the country, and one of the hardest hit by the lockdown, with all international and local travel suspended. Heedless of the fact that most employees working in the sector were black, even if many owners of hotels, B&Bs and game lodges were not, the minister insisted that BEE would prevail when it came to financial assistance.

Only finance minister Tito Mboweni dared to oppose the racial measures mandated for business relief efforts, pointing out that the white owner of a local hotel near his farm in Magoebaskloof had gone out of business, and 300 black workers had lost their jobs, because the white owner wasn't entitled to access government recovery funds.

Minister of tourism Mmamoloko Kubayi-Ngubane may have had little in her resumé to suggest any keen understanding of this vital private-sector-led industry but on the ruling party's cardinal policy choice she had perfect understanding. And her racial criterion for disaster relief was soon copycatted by other ministers charged with disbursing relief funds.

Her energetic counterpart in the DA, Dean Macpherson, indicated that BEE was legislatively confined to doing business with the state, and wasn't legally required to access disaster-funding – 'This is a lifeline, not a business transaction,' he correctly noted.[249]

So the minister doubled down. She improperly compared the BEE element to the legal and universal strictures of taxation compliance, in my view a complete misunderstanding. But the Gauteng courts ruled in her favour on the issue, and so racial categorising and penalisation continued under covid-19. It was an uncomfortable posture for the country's constitutional guardians to adopt, which I believe is eerily reminiscent of how under PW Botha's state of emergency in the 1980s the courts had kowtowed to the government.

Missteps as the lockdown continued saw early affirmation of it by South Africa's citizenry curdle into resentment. Beyond perfecting racial quotas, there was heavy-handed policing, and bizarre extremes and exclusions in the lockdown rules – no exercise outside the home, and no sale of cigarettes or booze or cooked food, for example. Ramaphosa himself seemed adrift, content to ride the initial high ratings he'd received and unable to command his government to implement rational measures and to break the culture of inept implementation.

In an only-in-South-Africa twist, the delivery of food-relief parcels to communities in need was, in several provinces, 'hampered as opportunists – mainly local [ANC] councillors – allegedly divert[ed the aid] to themselves and their supporters, and in some instances, [sold it] on'.[250]

Other funds running into millions were simply stolen. Tenders for lifesaving equipment were padded and diverted to ANC-connected cadres, including the husband of Ramaphosa's spokeswoman, Khusela Diko, spawning the nickname 'covidtrepeneurs'.

'The thieves were waiting at the door,' lamented finance minister Tito Mboweni.[251] No sign of ubuntu or common humanity here.

The real and callous failure of government during the lockdown was revealed when the minister of basic education and all but the DA-controlled Western Cape provincial governments suspended school-feeding schemes, which provided nine million pupils with a daily meal. The minister and eight provincial MECs were subsequently found by the North Gauteng Court to be in 'breach of their constitutional duties' for having halted this 'life-saving programme for the poorest of the poor child'.[252]

The fact that the recalcitrant ministry and provincial departments had to be dragged to court by two NGOs was noteworthy, and the judge's observation that 'there is administrative chaos and confusion in the provinces' pointed to much of the state's response to the crisis beyond just the scheme in question. All over the country, ordinary South Africans quickly realised that the ANC wasn't going to help, that they were on their own, and they stepped in, using their own time, money and resources to help each other.

RACIAL PURGES, THIN SUPPLY LINES

The policies that sought to cleanse the public service of its 'racial imbalances' encouraged a mass exodus of its most senior and skilled members. Within the first years of the new policy (1996–1997), 22 449 mostly white civil servants rushed to accept severance packages, and at a provincial level – where teachers and nurses were the core, and many were coloured and Indian – the figure rose to 25 805.

Yet it was these teachers, this core of public servants, who, by dint of their previous years of service and learnt experience, could have provided a pipeline of well-educated and skilled school and university graduates fit for the job market of the future. And, in simple demographic terms, the beneficiaries of such experience would be black.

The effects of this 'de-skilling' were glaring and everywhere, and the rot began at the top. For example, a Zuma-Gupta favourite minister Mosebenzi Zwane, who controversially served as minister of mineral resources, advised the Zondo Commission of Inquiry into state capture of an alarming feature of his tenure as MEC for housing in the Free State. He told an incredulous commission that he was 'unaware' of the provisions of the Housing Act (specifying his duties relating to a R1-billion housing scandal) as he had 'never read the Act'.[253]

Then there was the egregious Nomvula Mokonyane, the erstwhile minister of water and sanitation, who, when then president Zuma sacked key cabinet ministers in April 2017, leading to two credit downgrades, airily proclaimed, 'Let the rand fall. We will pick it up.'[254] Precisely three years later, in April 2020, the credit-rating agencies and markets had ignored her advice and the third and final credit-rating agency, Moody's, downgraded South Africa to junk status.

Venezuelan national Ricardo Hausmann is one of the most

engaged economists of this age and a leading light on developing economies such as our own. I'd got to know him during a stint as a Fellow at the Institute of Politics at Harvard University in 2007, and his keen and lucid mind had been tapped by South Africa's National Treasury on several occasions (although many of his useful and intellectually penetrating observations were ignored by its political overlords).

In South Africa in March 2017 at the invitation of the Centre for Development and Enterprise, giving a series of lectures to various audiences both in government and out, he offered the following observation: 'Know-how can be quickly hired, but it cannot be quickly transferred from one person to another ... [it] certainly can't be extracted, like teeth, from the brains that possess it.'[255]

His observation was coupled with a warning: that South Africa risked following countries like Zimbabwe, Venezuela and Algeria, where new governments had inherited a stock of know-how located in the brains of people 'the new leaders may not have liked'.

One glaring example of this was a forced removal of knowledge at Eskom, which in February 2019 was instructed, according to media reports, to remove 1 308 whites including 336 engineers from its books by March 2020.[256] This was in the context of a predictably crimped budget in a practically zero-growth economy – a year later it tipped into its second recession, which was caused in no small way by the state's inability to provide uninterrupted electricity.

(Amazingly, a leading DA MP dismissed concern about this forced removal of knowledge and technical expertise as 'racist'.[257] But by then, just weeks before its 2019 electoral setback, the party was driving blindly into an intellectual cul de sac.)

Eskom was indeed overstaffed. Trade unions were understandably incensed that more than two hundred of its managers received over R1.5 million each in annual salaries and bonuses[258] – the average salary package at the power utility was in the order of

R800 000 per annum. Across all state companies, economic ruin marched in lockstep with ever-larger bonus payouts to the inept and often corrupt management and boards.

To sacrifice qualified and scarce skills on the altar of preordained racial targets constituted a form of actual insanity. But the real de-skilling, of course, begins with poor educational outcomes, and in this regard a very telling view was offered by a key South African business and financial leader.

In October 2019, Gerrie Fourie, CEO of Capitec Bank – one of the very few companies in the country, in the face of a severe economic turndown, that added both jobs and bottom-line expansion to its already impressive growth trajectory – called out government on its crashing failure on the education front. Out of 1.2 million children who'd started school in 2005, only about 55 000 of them, or 4.5 percent, had achieved a matric pass rate of 50 percent or higher in mathematics, and only 13 percent of the starters had qualified to get into university.

Not only is such a thin supply line a problem if you're running a modern bank, but good education outcomes are fundamental to sustaining long-term growth, Fourie pointed out: 'We are looking to hire engineers, data architects, business architects, chartered accountants and lawyers. But there is a shortage of these skills.'[259]

A SINCERE AND LUCID 'MARKET LENINIST'

It was the papers and prescriptions of ANC national executive committee (NEC) member Joel Netshitenzhe, enthusiastically endorsed by his party, that explicitly called for the state to be an instrument in the hands of the national liberation movement and the extension of its tentacles everywhere 'over all levers of power.' Later, after the Democratic Party became the official opposition in 1999, he even warned that our staunchly law-abiding party was 'undermining the state'.[260]

What Netshitenzhe voiced here was pretty much common cause in his movement: the ANC wasn't in favour of 'pluralism' in the modern sense that all viewpoints jostled for public favour. He and his party were 'purists' – they alone held the monopoly on correct thinking, and those outside its political orbit were heretics or underminers of the state itself.

Doubtless he was convinced of his movement's moral righteousness, and equally doubtless he didn't envisage the extreme outcomes of the policies he authored. But, as *The Economist* observed of another democratic socialist, US presidential candidate Bernie Sanders, 'He has a dangerous tendency to put ends before means … Mr Sanders displays the intolerance of a Righteous Man. He embraces perfectly reasonable causes like reducing poverty … and then insists on the most unreasonable extremes in the policies he sets out to achieve them.'[261]

I doubt Netshitenzhe envisioned twenty years ago that the endpoint of cadre deployment, for which he provided the intellectual cover, would be to allow the infamous gang at Transnet to run riot. He wouldn't have thought it reasonable for the electricity supply to be shuttered through poor maintenance and human error.

But that's precisely what happens when political loyalty and demographic determinism trump all else. Or when ideology overpowers common sense. He and other party intellectuals had drunk too deeply from the well of creed and dogma to reverse course.

Observing the failure of communist intellectuals and reformers in the Soviet Union and Europe in the 1960s, where many in the ANC had cut their teeth, to grasp the scale of the economic catastrophe in the economic realm, historian Tony Judt concluded, 'They were neither stupid nor operating in bad faith. But their logical reasoning was subordinated to dogmatic first principles.'[262]

This analysis holds true in 2020s South Africa. Undeterred by a graveyard of policy failures and a broken-backed state, the government ploughs on with the idea that it alone knows best and will command the whole of society. Having illustrated how state control has shuttered electricity, seized up the railways and bottlenecked the ports, it now wants to turn its hand to leisure and sport. A new Bill agreed by cabinet and released by the minister of sport and recreation just before Christmas 2019 detailed 'government's plans to "nationalise" all sports, clubs and gyms in SA'.[263]

And an ANC policy document published in July 2020 proposed even further reaches for the state, from a state-owned bank to a government-owned pharmaceutical company.[264]

CHAPTER 12

———

How to steal a country: Hoodlums at the helm

By 2019 Joel Netshitenzhe was, ironically, a director of Nedbank Limited. Only in South Africa could the author of Leninist documents of the kind he wrote serve on the board of one of the country's largest private banks.

There was a further paradox at play: Nedbank was one of the key deciders in throwing bankrupt government-owned South African Airways (SAA) into business rescue in late 2019. This was despite the national carrier having received over R30 billion in government financial support between 2008 and 2017, with a couple more billion having been gifted to it before the banks declined to roll over more loans.[265]

And – irony of ironies – the cadre deployed at SAA had much to do with the airline's crash-landing into effective bankruptcy. Dudu Myeni was its key director from 2009 until 2017, and for some of that tenure its chairperson.

And the crowning – almost farcical – outcome of two decades of the ANC's BEE policy, high minded in motivation and ruinous in application, was that by 2020 a middle-aged white business-rescue practitioner, Les Matuson, had co-dominion over SAA. But the

ANC insisted that a black business-rescue practitioner be appointed alongside Matuson.

FLYING TROUBLED SKIES

As ambassador, I worked very closely with SAA in Argentina from 2009 to 2012, keeping the air route open to Johannesburg and energetically promoting tourist arrivals from South America. The route was discontinued after my return, in 2014, notwithstanding the more than 100 percent increase in arrivals to South Africa.

Years before, in 2000, some disturbing details emerged on murky goings-on at SAA, then under the baton of fast-talking American Coleman Andrews. He was paying his former company, Bain, some R208.9 million for consulting work;[266] he'd also decided to purchase Boeing aircraft, in an even more controversial arrangement, which in turn were sold to a leasing company for hundreds of millions of rands. This allowed SAA to claim a profit of R350 million for the year 2000 when in fact, stripped of the 'sale', the company had posted a loss. The 'profit' was significant since Andrews' pay package was linked in large measure to profitability, and a bonus provision in his package meant he earned around R200 million in just twenty months with the airline.[267]

During our parliamentary enquiries about all this, I visited Andrews at his sumptuous office at Jet Park, alongside Johannesburg airport. He was a beguiling character, filled with political stories about his business partner, Mitt Romney. But on his bid to get the DA to cease its parliamentary questions, I was totally unpersuaded.

It was during my time sorting out SAA's problems in South America – which included the cost of the landing fees for SAA at Ezeiza Airport, Buenos Aires and the high taxes and other charges levied by the Argentinian government on foreign airlines operating and selling tickets in Argentina – that an old schoolfriend, Chris

Smyth, took the controls of SAA as one of several acting CEOs of the troubled airline.

He was a chartered accountant and qualified pilot, and he had a great deal of aviation experience, at Kenya Airways and elsewhere. He was also the cleverest boy in our Kearsney College matric class, and was dux of the school in 1974. But his attempt to secure the top job on a permanent basis, for which he was well qualified, was quickly rebuffed, and he exited SAA in deep disappointment. Smyth lacked two essential non-aviation requirements which by that stage were de rigueur: political connectivity, and not being a member of a 'suspect class', in his case, a white male South African.

Three years later, when Dudu Myeni arrived at SAA, she was – for the very reasons that had disqualified Smyth – excellently credentialled. She was, however, woefully unqualified: as a primary-school teacher, she 'arguably should never have been allowed to serve on a school governing body, let alone the board of a state airline'.[268]

It was at that time very difficult, with so many competing needs on the state purse in the 21st century, to justify the existence and expense of the government owning an airline at all. But like so many other examples, from rail to electricity, the very idea of privatisation was taboo for a government that gloried in the idea that the state should command and control all sectors of the economy.

But the price tag for this indulgence was, literally, sky high: it was estimated that government, or, more accurately, the taxpayer, had from 1997 to 2020 pumped R50 billion into the airline. In the final two years (2018–2019) before it went into business rescue, the airline racked up a loss of R10 billion. Adding these figures together, analysts suggested that for the same price, the government could have purchased one of the most successful and cash-rich airlines, Emirates.[269] SAA, by contrast, was insolvent.

Elsewhere, Africans were making a fair fist of running airlines (at least until covid-19 grounded global aviation). Ethiopian Airways had replaced SAA by 2017 as the largest carrier on the continent: as SAA shed two million passengers between 2007 and 2019, Ethiopian increased its number from two million to twelve million. Two standout features of the new African aviation giant were that its management had a combined 421 years of airline and aviation experience, and it didn't expect a cent from government.[270]

By contrast, in just three months of the year 2020, between mid-February and mid-April, SAA burnt through anywhere between R500 million and R1 billion per month. The February 2020 budget revealed that a whopping R16.5 billion had already been handed over by the Treasury to pay the debt and debt-service costs of the airline. In a last-gasp effort to save the airline from insolvency, the state persuaded the Development Bank to hand over R3.5 billion, although aviation loans fell outside its mandate.

In April 2020 the business-rescue practitioners signalled that the state would need to transfer a further R10.5 billion to keep the airline flying[271] – and, indeed, in late October, finance minister Tito Mboweni announced in his budget statement that this sum would be supplied. But this was at the cost of stripping essential government departments, such as police, health and education, of their existing budgets[272] – it was, in the words of columnist Peter Bruce, 'going to be scrounged from school children and sick people'.[273]

PROXIMITY TO THE TOP

For six crucial years in SAA's descent, 2012 to 2017, Dudu Myeni chaired the board of the national carrier. And her pre-eminence there owed everything to her closeness to Zuma. Described as the queen on former president Zuma's chessboard, her relationship with him went, on many accounts, to the intimate and the personal. Ace legal journalist Karyn Maughan summarised Myeni as 'a powerful figure who had untrammelled access to law-enforcement investigators and evidence, the protection of the State Security Agency, and the ability to neutralise at least one finance minister'.[274]

During her tenure at SAA, Myeni, according to uncontradicted court evidence, 'created a climate of fear, as executives who crossed her were subjected to disciplinary procedures and victimisation';[275] she also ran through six CEOs[276] during her benighted tenure. She meddled – improperly, as a non-executive director – in operational issues and convened irregular meetings with executives, including one crucial conclave with senior officials, at which she arrived 'with unidentified armed guards' who confiscated the cellphones of other participants and, at the meeting's conclusion, 'all the written notes taken by the attendees, except the company secretary'.[277]

One of the alleged victims of her machinations was someone I knew from working with his association: John Harty, a veteran pilot who was chairman of the SAA Pilots Association (SAAPA). In 2015 he was advised by the Hawks, the state priority-crimes investigative arm, that they had received intelligence that he and other pilots were involved in a plot 'to recruit SAA technicians to tamper with the rudder system of an aircraft in a racist attempt to discredit the black pilot who would be flying the plane'.[278] The allegation was absurd and, indeed, the probe went nowhere. But, as Maughan noted, this 'intelligence' had emerged after SAAPA gave a vote of no confidence in the SAA board and in Myeni.[279]

Myeni's proximity to state power wasn't limited to one allegation. In November 2020, at the Zondo Commission, evidence was led that as recently as October 2019, Myeni was 'seemingly able to stop a Hawks search of her home as part of the Bosasa corruption probe' (Bosasa was a corrupt tender-facilitating company); that she received unlawful and improper protection by the State Security Agency; and that she provided the then CEO of Bosasa, Gavin Watson, and company COO Angelo Agrizzi with 'confidential NPA documents' about a potential corruption case against the company.[280]

Her response to the Commission was, improperly, to invoke the right to silence on the basis (with no foundation in laws governing such judicial enquiries) that her responses could incriminate her.[281]

The Zondo Commission did press criminal charges against Myeni for one item she offered it: the identity of a witness whose identity Zondo had expressly ordered 'should not be disclosed'.[282] The named secret witness had proffered evidence that his company bank accounts had been used to launder money to Myeni from a board she chaired, Mhlathuze Water in KwaZulu-Natal.[283]

These myriad investigations and allegations provided gory detail of profound alleged wrongdoing and impunity of action, and included testimony, which Myeni initially vigorously contested and denied, that Agrizzi of Bosasa had given her 'a Louis Vuitton handbag … stuffed with R300 000 cash'.[284] While they remained, at the time of writing, allegations and accusations, their breadth was extraordinary.

And even before Zondo's Commission aimed its sights at Myeni, back in late 2017 a parliamentary committee heard evidence from former chairman of ailing and indebted Eskom, Zola Tsotsi, that her interference in government went from aviation to electricity. He told MPs that on the eve of the first meeting of the new board he then chaired, Myeni summoned him to meeting at the presidential residence with the chief himself, President Zuma, at which both she and her son Thalente were present. The purpose of the meeting, he said, was to instruct him to suspend and discipline key executives – all to be facilitated by a Myeni-appointed lawyer who was also at the meeting.[285]

Tsotsi was allegedly later instructed by another I view as a Zuma toady, minister Lynne Brown, and Gupta trusty Salim Essa to facilitate the dislodgement of Eskom senior executives, 'opening the way for the appointment of Brian Molefe as CEO and Anoj Singh as chief financial officer of Eskom'. And, as the report noted, 'SAA chairperson Dudu Myeni had played a key role'.[286] Quite what the chair of an airline was doing in such intrigues was left unexplained.

'TO THE BRINK OF DISASTER'

Ultimately, it wasn't the criminal courts, nor one of four commissions of enquiry investigating elements of state capture, but the determined action of civil-society group OUTA (Organisation Undoing Tax Abuse) and the SAA pilots that laid bare in a court challenge, and in excruciating detail, evidence of the rule of error and ruin and malignancy of Myeni. The judgment of the Gauteng North High court by Judge Ronel Tolmay also constitutes, in all probability, the most damning and searing indictment ever delivered in the past 25 years by a judicial officer against a senior state official.

The essence of the case centred on two transactions, both in 2015: first, the so-called Emirates deal, which would have added over R2 billion to the beleaguered airline's finances and delivered other significant strategic benefits; and, second, the Airbus 'swap deal', which would have converted an onerous and costly agreement to purchase A320 aircraft into a leasing arrangement, allowing the 'technically insolvent' airline to claw back R1.4 billion in payments and obtain more fuel-efficient planes.

No fewer than six current and former SAA executives testified on behalf of the applicants, as did one official from the National Treasury. In defence of her case, Myeni offered only herself. Her solo starring role proved ill-fated and self-immolating, and the court branded her 'a dishonest and unreliable witness'.[287]

The court found that Myeni, despite approval for the Emirates arrangement from the board, the senior management of SAA and indeed the minister of transport, 'acted recklessly and broke her fiduciary duty in sabotaging this deal'.[288] And in her determined sabotage she scuppered the Emirates arrangement too, for unfathomable reasons, by telephoning then CEO Nico Bezuidenhout, who was on the verge of signing it, and telling him 'that there was an instruction from President Zuma not to sign the Emirates MOU [Memorandum of Understanding]'.[289]

The judge noted that the price of Myeni's actions was being paid by 'the people of South Africa and SAA's employees'.[290]

Myeni's defence amounted largely to a by-now-familiar claim that 'she was not afforded due respect by' three SAA white executives 'because she is a black woman'. The court dismissed this as being without basis and substantiation, and it collapsed on itself, since one of the key executives and witnesses against her was, in fact, a black woman.[291]

And, to the extent that Myeni offered any evidence beyond the racial claim, the court found it 'confusing', noted that 'in instances [it] contradicted her pleadings', and overall that 'her own evidence constituted two mutually destructive versions'.[292]

The Airbus-swap deal was far more serious in its reach. Although it was finally secured in December 2015, this was only because of the tenacious fightback for its survival by the National Treasury. It pitted Myeni against then finance minister Nhlanhla Nene, who was fired on 9 December after rejecting Myeni's attempt to alter the terms of the arrangement to insert an unknown 'African leasing company' into the arrangement.

An exasperated Nene had presciently advised his ANC colleagues, 'Either Ms Myeni leaves or I leave.'[293] He was fired; she stayed. Only the subsequent forced appointment of Pravin Gordhan saved the situation.

The costs of Myeni's determination to alter the arrangement by allowing an unknown leasing company to buy the aircraft and lease them back to SAA would have been ruinous. As the court expressed it, 'The evidence established that Ms Myeni knowingly took SAA and the country to the brink of disaster by delaying the conclusion of the swap transaction. Were it not for the intervention of the minister of finance and the efforts of Treasury officials in December 2015, SAA would have ... faced almost certain ruin.'[294]

Finally, the court held Myeni to be 'a director gone rogue' who 'was not a credible witness', and that her baleful actions 'did not constitute mere negligence but were reckless and wilful'.[295]

Unsurprisingly, the court found her to be a 'delinquent director' and slapped a lifetime ban on her serving as a director of any other company – not that any sane company would ever appoint her to any board, in the private sector at least.

To express its extreme displeasure at her conduct and her obfuscatory legal tactics, the court also handed her a punitive costs order in favour of OUTA and the SAA Pilots.

Judge Tolmay in her landmark ruling took 'judicial notice' of other related issues beyond the personal delinquencies of the defendant. She noted the 'immense harm that was done to the country and its people in the last years, due to the mismanagement, not only of SAA, but also other SOEs (state-owned enterprises), and the suffering that it brought and continues to bring to millions of South Africans'.[296] She also reminded the government, the appointing authority, that service on the boards of state enterprises 'should not be a privilege of the politically connected'.[297]

SAA had been in the skies for an uninterrupted 86 years and spanned the modern history of aviation; it had survived the Second World War, apartheid and sanctions. But it had taken just half a dozen years of Dudu Myeni to finish it off.

Judge Tolmay invited the NPA to investigate the evidence presented for possible criminal prosecution. At the time of writing, no criminal charges had been preferred against Myeni.

EMPIRE OF ROTTENNESS

Details first emerged of the pre-eminence of the arriviste Gupta family and their enablers in government in 2013. Soon, courtesy of an enquiring media and some exceptional whistleblowers, it became clear that their influence was pervasive and malignant, and that it sat at the heart of the government and the state. Impunity, shamelessness and wholesale lawlessness were its leitmotifs.

The process of state capture was assisted by a range of outside actors, such as the disgraced PR firm Bell Pottinger, the accountants KPMG, and the global advisory firm McKinsey.

The *Financial Times* reported at the end of 2017, which coincided with the curtain being drawn on the Zuma era, that the Guptas and their companies, which ranged from mining and media to armaments and dairy farms, and as middlemen across a range of enterprises from railways to electricity, had 'earned R30bn ... from their various lines of business facilitated by connections to the state'.[298] The detail and depth of it were extraordinary: for example, the Guptas had earned R5.6 billion in kickbacks for a locomotive deal with a Chinese company and Transnet via one of their front companies, Regiments Capital.

It had been a Gupta family wedding at Sun City, attended by four cabinet ministers, that had first put the family in the public gaze, when they took over a military airport, with state connivance, for the convenience of their imported guests. But it was the spinoff from that story that exposed the rotting carcass at the heart of the state. A Gupta company was awarded, without proper tender process and with no track record, a whopping R340 million by the Free State government (headed by Ace Magashule, today party secretary-general) for a model dairy project to uplift black farmers in the town of Vrede.

Deal done, the Guptas, aided by their accountants and the MEC for agriculture, Mosebenzi Zwane (whom they would allegedly soon handpick as minerals minister where he would do their bidding on the mining front), simply wired the money out of the country to various shell companies abroad, and used part of the proceeds to pay for the Sun City bling extravaganza. So the Free State government landed up paying for most of the wedding costs. The accountants, KPMG, wrote off the amount as a 'business expense'. The dairy farm never saw a cow milked, but the fiscus and the state were well and truly milched.

A half-baked prosecution on the scandalous misuse of provincial monies collapsed, due in no small measure to Zuma crony Shaun Abrahams, who headed the NPA at the time. Another Zuma toady, public protector Busisiwe Mkhwebane, whom the ANC shoehorned into position in late 2017, issued a report – later described by a judge as 'lamentable'[299] – that whitewashed the political figures involved.

(Mkhwebane in the Ramaphosa era seems to have attempted, with mendacity and maladroitness, to use her office as a club of attack against the new president and as a shield of defence for the old one and his coterie of enablers. Parliament is currently considering impeaching her.)

The costs of state capture, corruption and maladministration were difficult to quantify – Ramaphosa at a speech in London in late 2019 suggested the figure could be close to R1 trillion.[300] This represents no less than twenty percent of the country's GDP.

He was far better at quantifying this loss than explaining his passivity during the heyday of the process, when he sat at Zuma's shoulder for four years as his deputy president.

But the number went beyond pillage and plunder. Economist Chris Hart, for example, suggested that the add-on cost was the severe underperformance of the economy in the Zuma years, which amounted to an additional R1.6 trillion in 'lost GDP'. This included the country's slide downwards on the league tables that matter in the world, from global competitiveness to ease of doing business, economic freedom and – of course – 'perceptions of corruption'.[301]

In other words, absent the corruption, the investment strike and the ratings downgrades that followed, the South African economy would have been, by 2017, R344 billion larger. A similar figure was offered by economist David Fowkes, who estimated the growth rate absent state capture at four percent higher per year.[302]

VILLAINS AND HEROES

The Gupta family were by all accounts the lead villains in the state-capture horror show, but a clutch of Zuma trustees who served in his ever-revolving cabinet – Mosebenzi Zwane (at minerals), Malusi Gigaba (an under-talented apparatchik who held many important offices of state, including in the ministries of public enterprises and finance, and then home affairs) and Lynne Brown (also public enterprises) – were no doubt facilitators of the orgy of corruption, ransacking and maladministration that became the depressing benchmarks of the age.

But there were in Jacob Zuma's own ranks some genuine heroes who pushed back, against both him and the looters and plunderers he enabled and nurtured. One of the courageous few in the ANC hierarchy was deputy minister of finance Mcebisi Jonas. He revealed that shortly before Zuma fired well-regarded finance minister Nhlanhla Nene in December 2015 (sending the rand into a tailspin and wiping billions off the equity and bond markets), he (Jonas) had been offered the job at a meeting with the Guptas. Not only did he spurn the appointment (which went to obscure backbencher Des van Rooyen for all of four days, before Zuma was obliged to instal the incorruptible Pravin Gordhan) but he later blew the lid off the scandal and distilled the essence of the capture project: 'The pattern [of state capture] is a simple one: you remove management, and put in compliant management. You remove boards and put in boards that are compliant. The rest is very easy.

That has been the scenario at state-owned enterprises.'[303]

A similarly lucid description of the modus operandi that facilitated the project was offered by Sipho Pityana, chair of Anglo Gold Ashanti, who became the private sector's most voluble critic of Zuma Inc. He highlighted how all the nefarious networks of corruption ran through one person, right at the top – 'the personification of this nation's constitutional project', in the words of Chief Justice Mogoeng Mogoeng.[304]

'The essence of this is that you compromise the head of state, that you have the head of state in your pocket,' Pityana stated.[305] Well, the head of state and his family: Bongi Ngema-Zuma, one of the president's wives, worked for Gupta-controlled JIC Mining Services as a communications officer; his son Duduzane and daughter Duduzile were both employed by Gupta company Sahara; and Duduzane was a director and shareholder in various other Gupta enterprises.

Pityana, the public protector and crusading journalists revealed that the state-capture playbook followed a predictable path downwards: the law-enforcement and taxation authorities were disabled; pliant and ethically hobbled nonentities or mendacious enablers were placed in commanding positions; and the president himself had extraordinary power to hire and fire the key office bearers of the state.

For the Guptas and others, this was where they hit paydirt: credible evidence emerged that their home in Saxonwold, Johannesburg was the ground zero of the hijack project. It was there, according to ANC senior officials who later joined the ranks of whistleblowers, that they achieved unfettered access to people who owed their position in office to the pleasure of the president: cabinet ministers, intelligence officers, state-owned company board members – as Pityana put it, 'All key strategic appointments that you think would obstruct or enable your way into the state coffers.'[306]

THE VIRULENCE OF KAKONOMICS

Dudu Myeni in my view personified the idea of 'kakonomics' – not the rude Afrikaans term, but defined as 'the economics of rottenness', where mediocrity rules and low-quality – and far worse – work is regarded by its originators as excellent.[307]

She also practised, when cornered, what has been described as the 'dead cat strategy' – when confronted with inarguable facts, throw a dead cat on the table, and everyone will immediately shout, 'There's a dead cat on the table!' In other words, they will be distracted by the dead cat and will stop talking about the issue that has been causing the difficulties.[308]

The problem for Myeni was that too many rotten and compromised cadres had already used this tactic. Indeed, in this corner of cadre deployment, Myeni wasn't alone: it was an overcrowded field. Financial journalist Alec Hogg suggested that when 'Zumanomics' was historically archived, it would be the 'ruinous policy of rewarding loyal cadres with well paid jobs at state-owned enterprises', resulting in wastage of tens of billions in taxpayers' money, that would be a standout feature.[309]

In 2015, years before various commissions of enquiry had opened the sluice gates to revelations of the corruption and cadre despoliation of the country and its institutions, Hogg revealed one glimpse of the policy in practice. He cited the example of a now largely forgotten deployee in all her ruinous garb: Nonhlanhla Jiyane. As he retold her kakonomic road to ruin at state-owned enterprise, the story was at once familiar and eye-popping in its detail: 'A three-year spell in the early 1990s as a lab technician at Shell and BP was sufficient expertise for the ANC to appoint Nonhlanhla Jiyane chairman at PetroSA [the state oil and exploration company]. ... [A]long with her top executives, Jiyane was firmly in control of industrial-scale wastage leading to the relatively small SOE reporting a staggering R15bn loss last year [2014].'[310]

The rot in PetroSA apparently predated the Zuma era. In the 2004 general-election campaign, the taxpayer – via PetroSA – allegedly stumped up R18 million as a contribution to the ANC election coffers when the SOE, then chaired by ANC politician Popo Molefe, paid in advance for oil concentrate (for which it later had to pay again) to an ANC middleman, Sandi Matjila, who reportedly promptly transferred the full amount to the ANC election fund.[311]

I reported the matter to the public protector, but the president of the day, Thabo Mbeki, had appointed another ANC politician, Lawrence Mushwana, to that post. He incorrectly claimed he was not entitled to investigate any allegations of gross impropriety in the matter, for which he was later hauled over the coals by a High Court Judge.[312]

A lab technician is, perhaps, better qualified than a failed matriculant who falsified his school-leaving certificate – such were the 'qualifications' of the delusional SABC head Hlaudi Motsoeneng. He held sway at the public broadcaster from 2009 until he was finally fired for a host of issues in 2017. Having started life as an apparatchik for a bantustan homeland leader, he befriended Zuma. During his tenure, he instructed the broadcaster to not screen negative stories on the president; and, notwithstanding an adverse finding against him by the public protector, he was reappointed as SABC acting chief operating officer by the board on the instruction of Zuma minister Faith Muthambi.

His salary ballooned from R3.78 million to R4.197 million during the 2015/16 financial year. In 2016 the SABC racked up losses of R411 million but its executives flew themselves, at the corporation's expense, to a spa resort in Mauritius.[313]

The February 2020 budget review contained a laconic but terrifying one-liner buried in its text: National Treasury had expended R162 billion over the previous twelve years on 'financially distressed state-owned enterprises'. A staggering eighty percent-plus had been spent on Eskom alone.[314] Six months later the finance minister updated the figure to R187 billion over twenty years. Given the parlous state of many of them, it was money largely wasted.

Within weeks of the publication of that sobering statistic, word arrived that the Land Bank, a veritable South African institution founded in 1912 and which held 28 percent of all loans in agriculture, and was the largest credit provider to farmers, had hit the skids: it was set to default on its huge R50-billion debt pile and land the government with another R5-billion guarantee obligation.[315]

The Land Bank was even older than SAA. It had survived two world wars, civil insurrections, the Great Depression and the myriad political, economic and weather-related upheavals of more than a century. But it couldn't survive the ANC's revolving door of weak, poorly qualified and often temporary leadership, serial mismanagement and dodgy loans.

Myeni might have flown closest to the sun before she crashed the airline – but the South African skies were now crowded with other chickens coming home to roost, failed and bankrupt state-owned companies, many exhibiting similar pathologies. The key of these was that parastatals were treated as 'bottomless cookie jars rather than viable and ethically operated businesses'.[316]

And, of course, they were dumping grounds for the endless deployment of party-approved cadres.

FLOGGING A DEAD PHOENIX

In May 2020, the government announced the birth of a new airline, poised to rise 'like a phoenix' from the ashes of SAA after the coronavirus had passed.[317] Not surprisingly, great scepticism greeted this claim. As journalist Claire Bisseker wrote, with deadly accuracy, 'The pandemic has smashed the economy and ignited a fiscal crisis. Soon there will be no money for the basics, let alone airlines. If the government can't see this, then not even the IMF, as the global lender of last resort, can help us.'[318]

A month later, in a country where kakonomics coupled with ideological obstinacy now ruled supreme, President Cyril Ramaphosa announced that going forward there would be a new council to reform state owned companies – the Presidential State Owned Enterprise Council.[319]

Its chairman? None other than Joel Netshitenzhe, the intellectual father of cadre deployment.

CHAPTER 13

―――

Rewriting history: Truth and lies

In the summer of 2014 my wife Michal and I sat on the veranda of Fugitives Drift lodge in northern KwaZulu-Natal, looking out over the Buffalo River, G&Ts in hand. It was a tranquil scene, with only birdsong, the clink of ice in glasses, and murmured conversation to break the quiet.

The staff advised that just before our arrival, this idyll had been shattered by the *whup-whup-whup* of an approaching helicopter. Kicking up dust and scattering the resting dogs, it landed right in front of the gracious stone building. I wondered what great state potentate or super-wealthy business titan had descended among us.

My wonderment was soon answered: a slightly squat, bespectacled man and a tall, slender woman soon headed towards us. It was Brian Molefe, then the CEO of Transnet, the state monopoly behemoth in charge of most of the country's creaking infrastructure of ports, railways and pipelines. His companion, who turned out to be a member of the US military, was for this weekend the consort to one of the more economically powerful and politically connected members of South Africa's elite.

'You can bet that Transnet is picking up this tab,' I said to my wife.

Michal and I were there to celebrate my 58th birthday. We'd cherished the prospect of a few days of battlefield tourism ever since, a decade or so before, I'd been absorbed and unexpectedly touched by the heroic retelling of the epic back-to-back battles of Isandlwana and Rorke's Drift by master historian and raconteur David Rattray, the founder of Fugitives Drift lodge.

Michal and I wouldn't be lucky enough to meet Rattray this time: he'd been shot dead here at Fugitives Drift in January 2007, aged just 48, during an armed-robbery attempt by a gang of men. The intruders hadn't harmed his wife Nicky or any of the domestic staff who were on the premises at the time, and Nicky and Dave's family and guides had continued in his tradition, enthralling visitors with stories of the area's epic battles and giving them a hearing across the world.

On that December day in 2014, Brian Molefe appeared to be master of all he surveyed, and his dramatic and luxurious mode of arrival captured with some accuracy his role in Zuma's South Africa as one of the biggest of big men in the truly African sense. Handpicked for the top job as CEO of the Public Investment Corporation (PIC) in 2003, Molefe took charge of the state-owned R3-billion-plus investor of public servants' pension funds, the largest fund manager in the country and biggest single player on the stock exchange. His benefactor, Jacob Zuma, pressed for an extension of his term of office, allegedly to ensure a PIC investment in a uranium-mining venture in which both the president's son Duduzane and the Gupta family's Oakbay Resources and Energy company (which would soon be front and centre of the worst ravages of so-called 'state capture') were the direct beneficiaries.

A press expose of this manoeuvre apparently led to the abandonment of PIC interest in the project, but by 2011 Molefe had moved on, anyway, to Transnet, the post he was occupying at the time of our Fugitives Drift encounter.

ALTERNATIVE FACTS

The following day, in the pouring rain, Molefe and his companion joined Michal and me, and a small tour group, on a trip to the tiny mission station at Rorke's Drift, scene of one of the more epic and literal back-against-the-wall defences and turnarounds in the annals of 19th-century British military campaigns. In January 1879, just over 150 British troops, including the walking wounded pulled from their beds in the infirmary, successfully defended their garrison against an army of more than 3 000 Zulu warriors. This detachment of young soldiers had been held in reserve when the Zulus inflicted a shattering loss the day before on the British forces at nearby Isandlwana, whose battlefield our group had also walked around.

The details of the fightback at Rorke's Drift, which saw a record eleven Victoria Crosses awarded by a relieved British regent, anxious to offset the humiliations of Isandlwana, were hardly unknown. American historian Donald Morris had written a definitive text about it, *The Washing of the Spears*, in 1965. Decades later, Mangosuthu Buthelezi, no slouch in matters of honour and the history of his Zulu nation and its regal line, had advised me that the Zulu wars had no finer chronicler.

David Rattray, acclaimed across the world for his accurate and empathetic storytelling, had added precise and unforgettable detail, which was communicated to our small group by the expert Fugitives Drift guide that day. We all listened very closely to the narration.

Then Brian Molefe spoke. 'I have a different version of events,' he said. 'I have read other versions of this history, and as I understand it, the Zulu detachment allowed the British at Rorke's Drift to win in order to save face after their large defeat at Isandlwana.'

There was a somewhat embarrassed shuffling of feet and I poked Michal in the ribs at this phantasm. Our guide, schooled in both good history and good manners, listened politely to Molefe's ramblings, before saying quietly, 'I am not aware of this version but please send me the references and we will certainly look to incorporate this narrative ...'

I'm confident that Molefe never sent any such history to the Lodge, but he wouldn't have deemed it necessary, anyway, whether it existed or not. He had his own 'facts'.

Molefe's role at Transnet would be starkly revealed a few years later. By June 2018 a forensic report surfaced, heralded by banner headlines in the *Sunday Times*, that Molefe was a liar who between 2011 and 2015 had misled his board into approving costs and concluding financial transactions behind their backs. This, in turn, related to another Gupta-benefiting deal to the eye-watering tune of R19 billion which, according to the same report, was misused to purchase 1 064 rail locomotives for an inflated amount at the cost of the taxpayer.[320]

Allegations of even more corrupt conduct on his part at his later perch at Eskom would surface explosively in a report of the public protector, 'The State of Capture', in late 2016, which fingered Molefe for allegedly bending the rules and then some to privilege yet another Gupta-Oakbay company, Tegeta Exploration and Resources. Oakbay/Tegeta – and, once again, Zuma's son Duduzane, who was a major shareholder – allegedly paid for its acquisition of coal company Optimum Holdings, only because Eskom had facilitated 'an unbelievable turnaround for the once struggling coal mine'.[321]

Broker, banker, facilitator of suspect deals – there was apparently no end to the roles Molefe would perform to enrich the most egregious of the state capturers, the president and his family, while allegedly pocketing some useful cash for himself along the way. And he showed himself to be shameless in chasing financial opportunities.

After resigning his post at Eskom, he was appointed as an MP – but only briefly, as even the ANC recoiled from Zuma's idea of naming him minister of finance. Then he was reappointed to Eskom, as group CEO, in May 2017, by serial enabler of the Zuma looting spree, public enterprises minister Lynne Brown. News then emerged that Molefe had been paid out a massive pension, despite being only 50 years old at the time, and having been employed by Eskom for just eleven months.

His appointment to a second term at the utility was held by the courts to have been 'at variance with the principle of legality' and thus 'invalid and false'. The court also ordered him to pay back the R11 million that Eskom had already advanced him out of the promised R30-million bonanza.[322]

Brian Molefe was hardly alone in the ranks of the vastly overpaid, ethically hobbled and economically destructive heads of more than 700 state-owned state enterprises But even by the scale of the shocking depths of mismanagement and thievery across much of the state's business empire, Molefe's suzerainty, first of the national railways and then of the electricity network, left deficits in two of the most essential pillars of infrastructure. He also stretched the trust gap between government and citizen to breaking point.

BAD COMPANY

Creative not only in accounting to his own advantage, Brian Molefe also invented history – and in this he occupied a crowded patch.

Almost five years after he'd provided our intimate audience with his revisionist history of Rorke's Drift, a far larger figure, both physically and politically, offered his own invented history of another feature of the bloodied palimpsest on which South African fables have been etched.

A hundred kilometres or so from Fugitives Drift, nestling below the mighty Drakensberg mountain range, is the small town of Bergville. It was here, commemorating Reconciliation Day in 2019, that President Cyril Ramaphosa launched forth with a version of the Battle of Blood River of 1838 which was both contestable and seemed designed to inflame rather than reconcile the ever more restive descendants of the warring parties.

He called the Zulu warriors who perished that day in the Ncome River – bloodied with so many bodies of the dead impis that it was renamed Blood River – 'freedom fighters'. For the Boer Trekkers who'd avenged the murder of Voortrekker leader Piet Retief, his son and his confederates at the hands of Zulu king Dingane, Ramaphosa, the great new hope for a reconciled South Africa, offered the term 'invaders'.[323]

Then, retreating into a kind of doublespeak, Ramaphosa noted that South Africans are 'a people prepared to see each other as equals' and said, 'We have reached across the divide and embraced each other, and … we must continue to do so.'[324]

Unimpressed with the president's intellectual double-dealing and rhetorical sleights of hand, the Afrikanerbond, the latter-day successors of the Broederbond – which, during the heyday of apartheid, had offered its own extremist version of nationalist history as gospel – sent a short correction to the president. Its chairman, Jaco Schoeman, wrote that Ramaphosa had made 'no mention of the context of history at the time, the brutal murders of Voortrekkers and their leaders and treason … No mention of the bloody history and massacre between black tribes during tribal wars at the time.' Schoeman also offered the observation that 'the present government … is rarely bothered by the truth'.[325]

That the same observation could be offered of most of South Africa's past governments, especially the administrations the Broederbond had mostly supported and intellectually propped up, offered only the empty consolation that the current South Africa was simply in so many unfortunate ways and traditions mimicking its past.

Of course, the reason for Ramaphosa's swipe at historical

revisionism at Bergville had little to do with either history or reconciliation. He probably was by the time of his address simply desperate to change the subject, and to target the handy catch-all for the nation's misery, its shrinking white population. And the immediate context was the thunderous sound of ideological chickens and policy failures coming home to roost.

It also pointed, sadly, to the fact that when it came to rigging the past and knowledge control, the well-educated new president was in the same mould as his ill-educated predecessor. English-American historian Tony Judt understood why this historical manipulation was necessary to both the left and right: 'If you have power over the interpretation of what went before (or can simply lie about it), the present and the future are at your disposal'.[326]

Brian Molefe's plunder of Eskom and Cyril Ramaphosa's inability to right-size the state monopoly electricity provider had seen the country a few days before plunge into literal darkness during unprecedented stage-six 'loadshedding' (South Africa's euphemism for rolling electricity blackouts): with the national power grid on the verge of collapse, the blackouts lasted for an alarming four hours at a time for a scheduled four days.

This came some months after Ramaphosa had promised Parliament that loadshedding was in the past and – unfortunately for him – just days after he'd written a newsletter praising the country's newest power station, Medupi, as 'a fitting symbol of the importance of our state-owned enterprises'.[327] (He'd visited Medupi for the first time ever in November 2019, although he'd been appointed to head the so-called 'Eskom war room' five years before.)

In fact, Medupi was a ruinous white elephant of gargantuan proportions: together with its sister power station, Kusile, it was – correctly, in my view – labelled by academic Rod Crompton of Wits Business School as 'probably the largest single disaster in South Africa's economic history'.[328] Both had huge cost overruns and continuous breakdowns – and had provided the ANC with a funding piggybank. Perhaps they were indeed fitting symbols of state enterprise – but in ways Ramaphosa had never intended.

Ramaphosa had staunchly promised that there would be no loadshedding during Christmas-New Year 2019/20, so, that December, when South Africa was plunged into darkness of unprecedented proportions, with the fear and anxiety of knowing that only two stages down the failing road of loadshedding would mean a total blackout for an indeterminate time, a psychological boundary was crossed. The circumstances certainly provided a counterfactual to the credulous who believed that the ascent of Ramaphosa to the presidency, under his self-proclaimed slogan of 'a new dawn', would be a cure-all to the plunder and prejudicial policy choices of his predecessor.

But it was also a reminder that the malaise gripping the country had not commenced from a standing start.

Of course, the counterpoint to this spiral would have been to change direction, and ditch policy and personnel to meet the challenges of change. Instead, South Africa doubled down on a depressing diet of 'more of the same': more black elite empow-erment, more state interference in the economy, more spending, more ideology, more corruption, more minority targeting, more anti-western histrionics; and, at the same time, less investment and infrastructure, and fewer revenues.

This led, ineluctably, towards a final credit downgrade, which happened in March 2020, just as the deadly pandemic coronavirus struck our shores, sending the country into lockdown and the economy into the slammer. Two further downgrades were to follow in November 2020.

PART III

FUTURE TENSE

CHAPTER 14

——

Revenge economics: A recipe for failure

The same year I voted in Parliament for the passage of the Constitution, 1996, I attended an address at a conference in Israel by the elderly (he was then over 80) but remarkable historian Bernard Lewis. He pointed out there were two ways of viewing the world, and how nations respond to adversity and decline. The first, he said, is to ask, 'Who did this to us?' The second is 'What did *we* do wrong?'

The columnist Bret Stephens indicated in a later gloss on Lewis that the first question leads to self-pity, the other to self-help. 'One disavows personal responsibility and moral agency; the other commands them.' And in the circumstances in which economically imperilled South Africa found itself 24 years later, on the back of the policies of revenge analysis, 'one is a recipe for economic failure and political squalor; the other for success'.[329]

A cogent theme uniting a century of politics in South Africa and the nationalists who bestride it was the blame game.

The Boers blamed the Brits, but built an infrastructure for the minority. The ANC leadership blamed the whites and the west, but its miasma blinded it from expanding its inheritance to improve the lot of the majority. And it didn't like the property regime it had agreed to in 1996.

THE CURSE OF NATIONALISMS

Moeletsi Mbeki, younger brother of Thabo, is a sharp analyst of the political economy and author of the aptly named *Architects of Poverty*, a sweeping antidote to the paraphernalia of the elite-centred redistribution and the men and women of zeal who'd authored the policies and benefited from them. He was one of the people who appeared before the panel on which I served in August 2019 interrogating what had gone wrong for the DA in that year's elections.

But beyond his warm charm and useful views on what ailed the official opposition party, he shared with the panel his essential take on the unity of purpose between the past decades of Afrikaner nationalism and the epoch of African nationalism of the present and indeterminate future. It was a discouraging account.

'You can make a meal of the similarities,' he said, noting that both nationalisms were grounded in the politics of resentment – or, in his words, 'the demand for reparations'. It was this motivating force, not growth or redistribution, that lay at the essence of current and likely future policy-making and practice.

The two nationalisms, whatever their similarities, did differ in one crucial respect. The National Party of apartheid had advanced and practised an immoral policy – a crime against humanity – but had been deeply serious-minded in terms of administration and governance. Eskom was a key example of this.

Not so the current administration. As South Africa continued to endure endless electricity blackouts, a lightbulb reminder in early 2020 was offered by energy expert Professor Anton Eberhard: Eskom had been founded in 1923, less than two decades after the Union of South Africa. For 85 years, until 2008, it got no taxpayer bailouts. By contrast, over the preceding decade it had received a 'life-stealing' R83-billion in state support.[330]

Trevor Manuel, at the same time and on topic, chimed in with another reminder of the difference between a capable state and an incapacitated one. He told an audience that 'for some years after 1994 [Eskom] had a credit rating better than the sovereign ... and could borrow from capital markets against its own balance sheet without state guarantees'.[331] Manuel and the elder Mbeki's economic sensibility had had something to do with that, but it was also due to the inheritance from the detested past regime.

The ANC had commenced governing in 1994 with the winds of history and moral righteousness at its back, and had squandered its opportunity – or, if Moeletsi Mbeki and others were correct, it had never intended the 'better life for all' of its campaign slogan to move from rhetoric to reality.

So why couldn't the new nationalists build on the inheritance of the old? An ancient warning echoed Moeletsi's contemporary view. In 1790, reflecting on the French Revolution and its bloody men of zeal, Irish statesman Edmund Burke wrote, 'You had all these advantages ... but you chose to act as if you had never been moulded into civil society and had everything to begin anew. You began ill, because you began by despising everything that belonged to you. You set up your trade without a capital.'[332]

In the run-up to the 2019 polls, Moeletsi Mbeki had warned that the ANC and its 'little son', the EFF, were using the divisive issue of property rights as 'camouflage' to attack the white population. He confirmed, as did the polls cited by eNCA, a television station, and the Institute of Race Relations (IRR), that black voters were 'far more economically literate' than given credit for. 'They're not interested in race issues, they're interested in what is happening in the economy. The reason they're abandoning the ANC is precisely because its economic policies have failed,' Mbeki said.[333]

Indeed, one survey showed only one percent of black respondents declared 'more land reform' as the 'best way to improve lives'; by contrast 73 percent of black South Africans in the survey saw 'more jobs and better education' (two of the major failures of two and half decades of ANC rule) as the best enablers of their futures.[334]

Yet at the time of our meeting with Moeletsi Mbeki, most of the political oxygen in the country and public space was being sucked up by a state-sponsored roadshow whipping up sentiment to gut the Constitution of its property clause, section 25.

The real and unchanged narrative, and the connection between the two nationalisms, was all about payback for the past, hence the demand for ever more aggressive redistributions despite the very low growth rate.

'Both nationalisms,' Moeletsi Mbeki said, 'are driven by grievance for past exclusion.' Neither had any interest in changing the essential structure of the colonial economic model. 'They simply want to change the beneficiaries at the top of the system.'

THE TWO ANCS

At the time of Moeletsi Mbeki's chat with us, there was much in the media about the war between 'the good' and 'the bad' ANC – two versions of a ruling party, shadows of light (constitutionalists, sane economists and corruption fighters) versus the forces of darkness (the corrupt state capturers who masqueraded under slogans such as 'white monopoly capital' and 'radical economic transformation'), according to many versions on the same binary narrative.

But both factions – and any muddlers in between – were united in one essential regard: according to Mbeki, and undergirded by a huge weight of supporting evidence he produced, there was a doubling-down on failed policies.

He also pointed out that BEE, which Ramaphosa (one of its most conspicuous beneficiaries) had weeks before vowed to 'intensify', conferred random and rich benefits on its recipients. 'It was designed by the old elite as a means to hold on to their wealth,' he said.

Indeed, it was mining giant Anglo American and Afrikaans insurance behemoth Sanlam that had first conceived the policy and chosen the recipients for largesse from the new elite. As Mbeki wrote in 2009, 'Big business ... offered to transfer a small part of its assets to individual leaders of the black resistance movement in return for them leaving the business environment as they found it. The leaders found this offer of instant wealth hard to resist. ... Overnight the politicians were transformed into multi-millionaires without having had to lift a finger.'[335]

Sanlam was soon followed by Anglo American. 'The conglomerates took their marginal assets, and gave them to politically influential black people, with the purpose, in my view, not to transform the economy but to create a black political class that is in alliance with the conglomerates and therefore wants to maintain the status quo of our economy and the way in which it operates.'[336]

Mbeki had pencilled in 2020, 'give or take a couple of years', as the year when 'the bomb explodes'.[337] He suggested that the fiscal squeeze would force the government to cut back on the social grants 'which it uses to placate the black poor and to get their votes'. In fact, the 2020/21 budget squeezed some more funds for the 17 million social-grant recipients, but only at fearsome cost: a spiral of borrowing and spending on the back of little growth and low revenue collections.

And, of course, barely had the ink dried on this budget than the coronavirus was sweeping across the world and hitting global economies and shuttering output, factories and borders. South Africa's already frail economy was in line to be truly decimated.

According to Mbeki, at the explosion point, whether now or in the near future, we will know who to call to account: 'ANC leaders are like a group of children playing with a hand grenade. One day one of them will figure out how to pull out the pin and everyone will be killed.'[338]

One of the hand grenades already lobbed into the country's health system, ground zero for the campaign against the coronavirus, was the mooted National Health Insurance (NHI), described in June 2018 by President Ramaphosa as 'coming to you whether you like it or not',[339] and as recently as March 2020 by health minister Dr Zweli Mkhize (a medical doctor and former party treasurer) as 'one of the best things that ever happened to South Africa'.[340]

Experts disagree. Wits professor Alex van den Heever pointed out the key peril in the proposed National Health Insurance Fund, the core of the mooted NHI. It proposed collapsing public and private health systems into a single organisation under the full discretion (in terms of appointments) and funds disposal (estimated to be R450 billion in procurement of services) of a politician, the minister of health.

In launching the idea in 2019, the government blithely ignored its own pilot projects, which had failed; the costs to the economy to provide universal coverage, which were estimated to require a 31 percent increase in personal taxes or a 63 percent increase in corporate taxes; and the crisis already evident in public health facilities across the country (bar the opposition-controlled Western Cape).

Van den Heever concluded his assessment with the observation that what was being attempted in South Africa – on paper, at least, since there was practically no provision for it in the hairshirt budget the next year – 'has no equivalent in any setting in the world … Only a failing health department could generate a proposal like this and take it seriously – let alone expect everyone else to join them in their fantasy.'[341]

The pathogens that flew into the country in March 2020 would confront the ANC's magical thinking with new grim but practical realities: were there enough ICU beds, enough ventilators? The answer, a hundred days into the mid-2020 lockdown, was no; and the worst-prepared provinces, such as the Eastern Cape, where covid-19 patients were fighting over scarce oxygen, were those where the ANC had enjoyed uninterrupted power since 1994.

AN UNCHANGED IDEOLOGY

It was obviously important that the 'better side' of the ANC should prevail, but would even the so-called Ramaphosa faction actually change course from the doubling-down on failed policy? The available evidence wasn't reassuring.

For example, back in 2012, then ANC policy chief Jeff Radebe – Ramaphosa's brother-in-law, and until 2019 the longest-serving member of cabinet – announced the arrival of the second, more radical phase of the revolution. This suggested that the appetite of the NDR was far from sated; it had just tired of the restraints of the constitutional settlement of 1996. According to Radebe, changes in the balance of forces locally and globally had made it possible for the ANC to dispense with some of the 'constitutional compromises on which the "first transition" [ie, the Constitution] was based'.[342]

You didn't need a degree in Kremlinology to know what this meant. And there was enough evidence in plain sight. The 2019 Expropriation Bill, for example, tabled a full year after Cyril Ramaphosa assumed the presidency, and gazetted again in October 2020 in slightly revised terms, was, according to the IRR, 'the single culmination of the ideological, policy and stigmatisation processes of the past decade'.[343] The IRR had identified 'more than 30 separate legislative, policy, and regulatory attempts since 2008 to undermine [property] rights'.[344]

But, according to their expert Dr Anthea Jeffery, this was the big bazooka: both the 2019 Bill and its 2020 successor list various circumstances in which 'nil' compensation may be paid, for example, where land has been 'abandoned', or is 'unused' and is being held solely in the hope of its value appreciating. But the Bill also, alarmingly, states that the circumstances meriting 'nil' compensation are 'not limited' to those it lists. In addition, the Bill has a narrow definition of 'expropriation', which could allow government to take custodianship over all land (as it has over mineral and water resources) without any compensation being paid.

The same IRR analysis laundry-listed how policy planning in South Africa after Jacob Zuma assumed power, and running right through the early Ramaphosa years, 'turned the policy clock back to the socialist dogma of 1969' (when the ANC first adopted the concept of the NDR): cancelling more than ten bilateral investment treaties, introducing the NHI, restrictive immigration rules, hiking minimum-wage levels, the contested mining charter, and 'turning the screws on ever more onerous racial edicts'.[345]

President Zuma had called it 'radical economic transformation'. Ramaphosa, without the corruption stain, more emollient and more financially literate, spoke of a 'new dawn', and set his sights on the looters of the state whom Zuma had encouraged and enabled, and from whom he'd profited. But on ideology there was no discernible change: even with the coronavirus putting the country's finances on life support, Ramaphosa suggested that 'radical economic transformation' would be the ideal template to reset the economy.

HOW TO ACE A CONSTITUTION

To an extent, within the fractures of the ruling party, a discernible thread bound them together along the lines of grievance and reparation evinced by Moeletsi Mbeki. No clearer voice could be heard than the ethically hobbled but hugely powerful party secretary-general, Ace Magashule. He announced in July 2018 that the struggle not only continued, but wouldn't end until the Constitution itself was unstitched:

[It's] a false view that our democratic breakthrough was in itself the end of the struggle for the liberation of our country … The living truth is that … the democratic breakthrough was not at all the end of our revolution, but only the beginning of a more protracted struggle for transformation.[346]

Eighteen months later, and citing this desire by the ANC to unravel the constitutional settlement of which he was a co-architect, FW de Klerk lamented that 'it is now abundantly clear that the crossroads are behind us; that we took the wrong turning several years ago and that we are now rapidly heading away from the high road of non-racial constitutional democracy.'[347]

In July 2019 Magashule had the South African Reserve Bank in his sights when he questioned its constitutionally defined mandate and sought to expand it, doubtless to get it to print money and inflate away the problems caused by the policy choices he'd defined the year before.[348] This was the road to financial ruin I'd seen in Argentina.

Magashule was also at the forefront of demanding the enactment of all party policy, including the amendment of the Constitution, to greenlight expropriation of property without compensation as the law of the land.

All this gave me pause to wonder about how the Constitution, in drafting which many of us had invested some years, and which the government had for the past two decades heralded as a wonder to the world, had been rendered so susceptible to party diktat – especially at the hands of such a dodgy character as the ANC secretary-general.

Political theorist Hannah Arendt (of 'the banality of evil' fame) gifted to posterity a useful guide to 'the second phase of the revolution' here on our southern shores. Her study, *The Origins of Totalitarianism*,[349] published just after the Second World War, was hardly a working description of 21st-century South Africa which, warts (including Mr Magashule) and all, was more democratic than authoritarian. But there was one concept from it that somewhat approximates one of the crowning paradoxes of the state South Africa finds itself in right now.

Drilling into the malignancy of Stalin's Soviet Union, Arendt noted the 'absurdity' of that country's fine constitution and the grim realities of life and suffering under its tyrant's heel. This led her to a striking observation on the totalitarian regime: the coexistence and the conflict between the state and the party. She described this difference between ostensible and real power – the latter always residing in the party or in its leader – as 'dual authority'.

A version of 'dual authority' is at play right now in South Africa. Its existence under the framework of a constitutional democracy means the final word on whether the party or the other instruments of state prevail in the many contests of wills is less predictable than under conditions of totalitarianism. But there can be no doubt that we've reached a fork in the road between the limits imposed by our Constitution and the expansive needs of the ruling party.

In *The President's Keepers*, Jacques Pauw added an essential twist to the concept of dual authority and its perversions under a way-ward president: South Africa had become a 'shadow mafia state', he wrote. 'Under [Zuma's] rule South Africa [became] a two-government country. There is an elected government and there is a shadow government – a state within the state.'[350]

But while the essence of Zuma (tax evasion, suborning the security and prosecution authorities, et al, for personal, family and associates' advantage) had evaporated after his ousting from power in 2018, the party remained front and centre of it all. This was well illustrated by a comment just before the 2019 election by well-informed economic analyst Peter Attard Montalto. He suggested the results of the looming poll were essentially irrelevant: that the post-election environment would largely be the same, regardless of the share of the vote the ANC received.[351]

The real deciders on what mattered were the 109-odd members of the ANC national executive, not the millions of voters and, least of all, perhaps, the 400 MPs elected to serve them.

THE AMBUSH

Early in 2020, in a last-minute ambush of the draft amendment to section 25 (the 'property clause') of the Constitution agreed by a majority in the Parliamentary ad hoc committee, the ANC decided to remove a crucial brake against arbitrary dispossession of property. That there would be an amendment to the Constitution to enable EWC was common cause; but now the ANC let slip that it intended that the executive (ie, the government), and not the courts, would decide on whether or not the state would pay for the land it expropriated, and on the quantum.

(It is worth emphasising that the constitutional amendment process for section 25 went beyond the limits of the Expropriation Bill cited above. This constitutional amendment, whatever its final form, has no intention of amending the current Constitution's definition of property, which is 'not limited to land' – in other words, it includes the whole gamut of ownership, including homes, equities and even movable property.)

This indeed was a nod to, a grim replication, in fact, of the apartheid past against which the ANC sets its face: for that legal regime was infamous for systematically ousting the jurisdiction of the courts from controversial and rights-delinquent parliamentary acts and regulations. Once again, it was confirmation of an essential link between the two nationalisms.

Some months before, an inconvenient truth about the government's competence in dealing with land reform was given short shrift by the country's most senior jurists, the Constitutional

Court. In August 2019, in his valedictory judgment on behalf of a unanimous bench, Edwin Cameron (who retired from the bench on the day of this ruling) wasted no words in skewering the government's failure to make land restitution a reality for poor black farmers.

While the case concerned, narrowly, the betterment of the lives of labour tenants, the contentions were far larger. In the judgment Cameron wrote, 'At issue is the entire project of land reform and restitution that our country promised to fulfil when first the interim constitution came into effect, in 1994, and afterward in the final constitution in 1997.'[352]

He then noted the failure of the department of rural development and land reform to manage its basic mandate – something of urgent relevance, given that the ANC wishes to saddle up the same department (and others that are equally incompetent) with enormous power over the entire edifice of property dispossession and compensation. The court held that its failure 'to practically manage and expedite land reform measures in accordance with constitutional and statutory promises has profoundly exacerbated the intensity and bitterness of our national debate about land reform'.[353]

The ruling party then decided to throw in a full-scale assault on the judiciary. In the *Sunday Times*, ANC parliamentarian Mathole Motshekga – armed, ironically, with a doctorate of law – blamed the courts and not the state as responsible for 'the slow pace of land reform'. His view was that leaving the decision on expropriation to the courts would mean 'it will take another 25 or 50 years to sort out land reform'. Better, he thought, to hand this arduous task to the same government that had presided over the looting of R1 trillion via state capture, switched the lights off at Eskom, etc.

Presciently, in August 2019 the Constitutional Court had anticipated precisely this line of attack. In its judgment it held that 'it is not the constitution, nor the courts, nor the laws of the country that are at fault in this. It is the institutional capacity of the department to do what the statute and the constitution require of it that lies at the heart of this colossal crisis.'

BIRTH CERTIFICATE OR DRIVING LICENCE?

In the debate on the passage of the Constitution in Parliament in May 1996, Ramaphosa had described the new instrument – which included the right for any dispute to be determined by the courts, or 'another independent and impartial forum', and, crucially, the right to property – as the country's 'birth certificate'.[354]

In the same debate, Kader Asmal, a key ANC constitutional negotiator and member of both Nelson Mandela's and Thabo Mbeki's cabinets, reminded the Constitutional Assembly, 'The constitution is a modus vivendi, a means of living together for a whole nation, and not a party manifesto … It is not the exclusive property of one or the other party.'[355]

A few days after the adoption of the Constitution by Parliament, I was a guest, along with Cyril Ramaphosa, at a celebratory function. He dealt at some length with the property clause itself, advising the gathering that it was 'from the outset a difficult issue. How does one guarantee property rights in a society where the vast majority of people have had their right to property systematically denied to them since 1913?'

In answering the question he pointed correctly to the conundrum of balancing 'the twin imperatives of redress and land reform on the one hand, and current and future guarantees on the other'. He concluded that the new Constitution 'answers that question quite ably' and reassured his audience that 'the Constitution ensures that that no South African may ever again be arbitrarily deprived of property'.

Sceptics of the time warned that the ANC would simply use the

Constitution as an instrument to achieve power and, once secure in office, would begin to unravel the tapestry woven at Kempton Park. It now appears they glimpsed the future more clearly than I did.

And, given that the latest version of the amendment, produced apparently at a party meeting in January 2020 over which Ramaphosa presided, does precisely that, we may legitimately wonder what the worth is of Ramaphosa's guarantee. And does he profoundly believe still in the Constitution he heralded as the country's birth certificate? In the desire to tear down a key pillar of the entire democratic project, it is perhaps seen today by its key architect as more of a driver's licence, to be removed or altered according to changed circumstances.

STORMY DAYS AHEAD

Of course, it is possible that the entire proposal, along with many others flying out of the party conclaves (such as another wheeze borrowed from the old NP, namely prescribed assets, or forcing private pension funds to invest in bankrupt state companies), may be a bluff or feint to please one or other faction of the ANC. But as a weather vane of current thinking in the ruling party, it pointed to stormy days ahead.

The appetite for ever greater control of both society and the economy revved into overdrive at the precise period when the limitations of this approach had been so comprehensively revealed by the country's impaired finances and multiplicity of implementation failures.

For the zealots and the crooks – often interchangeable labels for the same comrades – who adorn the ANC national executive, there was every indication that the 'command and control' model foisted on the country during the covid-19 crisis was not just for public-health purposes. In their view, and ably driven by a slew of ministers who worshipped at the altar of a state-centric economy buttressed by an army of enforcers, the pandemic provided forward cover to perfect their utopian ideas. Reducing the economy to ashes would allow a new order, congenial to their distorted worldview.

CHAPTER 15

The league of losers: Friends without benefits

Dissipating, and often simply robbing, the depleted coffers of the state had become commonplace in Jacob Zuma's South Africa. It was a pattern that continued apace under the management of Cyril Ramaphosa.

In an overcrowded field of contenders for the crown of excrescent expenditure, the annual gathering for all South African heads of diplomatic missions, flown in from around the world, and fed and watered at state expense in Pretoria to hear often rambling discourses from the president, ministers and a clutch of state officials, was a top contender.

During my ambassadorship abroad, attendance at these gatherings added very little to my store of knowledge on the diplomatic function – in fact, nothing that couldn't be gleaned from the reams of documents that poured in daily to the South African embassy in Buenos Aires.

But these knees-ups did provide insight into the unvarnished views of some of my diplomatic colleagues, who, relieved of the necessity of mouthing platitudes abroad, often gave full vent at home to their prejudices in the comradely confines of the global heads of mission conference of the Department of International Relations and Co-operation (Dirco), the 2009 mouthful rebranding of the department of foreign affairs.

At one such conclave, in 2011, our man in Damascus – the South African chargé d'affaires – denounced the abuse of social media by Syrian pro-democracy activists for presenting, in his myopic opinion, 'the world with a distorted view of the position on the ground'. Clearly, our diplomat thought such a pro-Bashar al-Assad view would find favour with his government – because while Assad energetically slaughtered his own population as they revolted against his dictatorship and rule of fear, no word of criticism was to be heard about it from Pretoria.

By 2020 it was estimated that over 380 000 people, many of them civilians, had been killed in the Syrian civil war.[356] South Africa's offer was simply a hideous platitude suggesting 'negotiation and dialogue'[357] for the parties to the war – like an invitation to a lamb from a butcher.

A DIM LIGHT

Twenty-six years in power had seen the ANC government energetically, and across the world, extinguish Nelson Mandela's promise in 1993 that human rights would be the 'light that guides our foreign affairs'.[358]

In my own diplomatic hinterland of South America, the case of Venezuela provided no end of idiocy for words of immoderate mendaciousness uttered with apparent seriousness by South African diplomats and indeed their masters.

While president Hugo Chávez was lionised for his staunch anti-Americanism and his populist giveaways, there was at least on his watch some measure of basic governance and a vestige of democracy. But after his death in 2013, his successor, Nicolás Maduro, attempted to recreate Chávez's legacy (once dismissed by

The Economist as a 'gaseous concoction of authoritarianism, socialism and populism'), with dismal and bloody results.

A great deal of state-sponsored violence and impoverishment forced the migration of an estimated four million starving Venezuelans to neighbouring countries, since the plummeting oil price and runaway inflation had seen, according to economists, the largest economic collapse of any country outside of war in at least 45 years. In its heyday, Venezuela had been the richest country in the region; by 2018, it was reduced to beggary.[359]

Maduro closed down the opposition and ruled through violent military oppression, propped up by Moscow and Beijing. There wasn't the slightest hint of basic rights for its citizens, only their denial and impoverishment.

Into this mix, in July 2018, arrived Ambassador Joseph Nkosi, our man in Caracas. Putting the 'moron' into 'oxymoron' – ironically, at a commemorative function for Nelson Mandela – he expressed solidarity with the Maduro regime under economic blockade by the US, adding, 'If it is necessary that we bring our soldiers to fight against the Americans we will do it, we cannot allow ourselves to be dominated by the American administration … The days of the US dominating the world are numbered.'[360]

Nkosi was rebuked by Pretoria and recanted. Tellingly, however, Nkosi was neither recalled nor relieved of his duties – and remains in post as of this writing.

A few months later, ANC secretary-general Ace Magashule – no slouch in the corrupt-governance stakes himself – led a top-heavy ANC delegation to Caracas in support of the beleaguered and ever more tyrannous Maduro regime. On the weekend of the ANC's arrival, regime troops killed two and injured several people who were attempting to deliver a convoy of food into the starving country.[361]

This visceral anti-Americanism and placing South Africa as

'an instinctive supporter of tyrannical leaders hated by their own populations' – as *Business Day* in Johannesburg editorialised[362] – obtained the imprimatur later from Cyril Ramaphosa himself. In April 2020, while hungry residents of Caracas were eating their own pets to stay alive, he posted a warm tweet on his phonecall with 'my brother President Nicolas Maduro of Venezuela yesterday', noting 'Our two countries share a close and deep historical bond based on friendship, solidarity and cooperation.'[363]

There was a grim consistency to all this, in a long roll call across the globe of the South African government violating its own constitutional promises of human decency and democracy and temporising with tyranny. In 2015 the minister of international relations, Maite Nkoana-Mashabane, bundled out of the country Sudan's tyrant-president Omar al-Bashir, 'the butcher of Darfur', in defiance of a court order to arrest him.

The state had also granted spurious – arguably illegal – diplomatic immunity to Grace Mugabe after she assaulted a local citizen. It had propped up for more than two decades the continuing authoritarianism in neighbour Zimbabwe, and had greenlighted stolen elections across the continent.

And it had, infamously, denied a visa to South Africa for Nobel Peace laureate the Dalai Lama.

There was no difference, and every meeting of the UN Security Council and its dictator-coddling Human Rights Council confirmed it, between Russia and China and South Africa on a slew of foreign issues and interventions.

And should the assertive cold war between the US and China – whose 'hide [your capacities] and bide [your time]' foreign policy had, under emperor-for-life Xi Jinping, morphed into an aggressive push for global dominance – go hot, there was no doubt with which side South Africa would align.

THE CORE OF BELIEFS

Strangely enough, it wasn't South Africa's betrayal abroad of its human-rights commitments and the tossing aside of its moral compass that provided the best one-paragraph explanation for the animating impulse behind the country's foreign policy. It was in describing the worldview of British Labour leader, the far-left Jeremy Corbyn, that *The Economist* summarised matters with pinpoint precision and cynicism:

> The core of his beliefs is not opposition to war but opposition to 'Western imperialism'. His hostility to 'imperial powers' (most notably America and Israel) is so fierce that he is willing to make excuses for 'anti-imperial powers' such as Russia and Syria, as well as terrorist organisations like Hezbollah and Hamas. His support for national liberation movements stops short of support for the people of Crimea, Georgia or Ukraine. His sympathy for victims of oppression turns cold when the countries doing the oppressing are Vladimir Putin's Russia [or] Nicolás Maduro's Venezuela ...[364]

That was a perfect facsimile, with the addition of Cuba and Zimbabwe, of the past 26 years of ANC foreign policy. It rested, beyond prejudice and hypocrisy, on the faulty and mediocre pillar of a warped and outdated worldview: America and the west are very bad; their opponents always and everywhere are very good.

The results of the last cold war, between the west and the USSR, are well known – the communist bloc disappeared behind the rubble of the Berlin Wall. But for the ANC it was – childishly, simplistically – never over.

South Africa practises a version of foreign policy similar to Corbyn's from its position of regional pre-eminence. But because of the country's reduced economic significance and in the absence of the huge moral authority of Nelson Mandela, it has less clout in the world today.

South Africa's now predictable and consistent relitigating the struggles of the past and dressing them up in garbs not fit for purpose in the hyper-competitive and often ruthlessly self-interested world in which it operates might not count for much in the forums that matter internationally. Joining the overcrowded balcony of third-world countries is a comfortable zone for an also-ran nation. The price of admission might be cheap, along with the rhetoric; but the problem is that it is a far view from the front-rank places reserved for more serious and engaged players in the world – the place South Africa seemed destined to occupy after 1994, but from which it has slid in succeeding years.

BITING THE HAND

Some years back, I had an engaging evening with Gideon Rachman, the influential chief foreign affairs commentator of the *Financial Times*, when he was on a visit to Cape Town. During our dinner I discovered that his parents were South African, and that he'd spent some of his childhood years in the country. So behind his polemics there was a background of personal identification.

In February 2018, just days before Cyril Ramaphosa was elected president, Rachman wrote a major op-ed for his newspaper entitled 'Why South Africa matters to the world'.[365] Rachman noted that the continent of Africa could either tip into atrophy and induce mass migration into Europe, on the one hand, or, on the other, 'if things go really well', could 'become a new pole of growth for the world economy'. In his view, South Africa's trajectory would 'matter hugely in this story'.

Our country had, rightly or otherwise, become 'an informal spokesman for a continent … a standard bearer for Africa.' And its new president's responsibilities would 'extend beyond the borders of his own country'.

Two years later, in 2020, Ramaphosa held another high office, as chair of the African Union, formalising his spokesmanship for the continent. He did not, however, indicate that he had any intention of moving beyond the familiar terrain of engaging in international posturing based on a pastiche of anti-colonial rhetoric and demands for a seat of influence at the tables of world decision-making. The world, preoccupied with its own concerns, especially the cratered covid-19 economies, took little notice.

In South Africa, though, there were blowbacks from the gesture politics that animated our foreign policy and positioning, illustrating that these weren't cost-free exercises, and that conspicuous acts of national self-harm resulted.

It was perhaps understandable, given the alliances forged in the heat of struggle against apartheid, that there would be a Manichean view of the world by the ANC after it assumed power: 'our allies' (Russia, Cuba, et al) were with us; 'the west' was against us.

Of course, this wasn't strictly true. The armed struggle did far less to topple, or even dent, white-ruled South Africa than the sanctions imposed by the US, the UK and Germany. Moreover, beyond an imagined past, there were the more pressing needs of the much-promised (by every president from Mandela onwards) attraction of foreign investment and interest in the country. And in this scenario, the US and the western world had a big potential role and an influential hand to play, provided South Africa didn't rebuff it.

But there was every indication that is precisely what the play was.

Of all the under-remarked achievements for Africa of the presidency of George W Bush, two are of huge and continuing significance: his multibillion-dollar funding of the President's Emergency Plan For Aids Relief (PEPFAR), which saved millions of lives on the continent; and his championing of the African Growth and Opportunity Act (AGOA), the stated aim of which was to assist the economies of sub-Saharan Africa. Even under protectionist and instinctive Africa-sceptic Donald Trump (he of the 'shithole countries' epithet), the unilateral trade agreement that allowed South Africa and the continent to export, sans restrictions, goods to the US continued.

America is the third-largest export market (after China and Germany) of South African products, but AGOA allows 36 percent of such exports to arrive in the US on preferential terms.[366] Significantly, AGOA is the main reason why this country even has an automotive industry and car manufacturing at all. Principally because of AGOA, South African vehicle exports to the US soared from $298 million in 2001 (the first year of AGOA) to $1.4 billion in 2015, the year AGOA was renewed.[367]

By contrast, while China had become a large export market for South Africa, the terms of trade for this were dire for us: China was actively assisting the de-industrialisation of South Africa, contra to the ANC mantra seeking the opposite, by dumping its state-subsidised ultra-cheap steel exports into the local market, having the decade before helped, in similar fashion, to destroy the local textile industry.

So 2015 might, in the ordinary world, have been when the South African government tipped its hat to such a conspicuous overseas benefactor as the USA. However, in October of that year, when the ANC gathered for its national general council meeting, the section of the reams of documents produced dealing with international relations went beyond the day-before-yesterday ideas in the rest of the policy offers. It was actively hostile to the US, at one point opining that across the world the US was 'toppling progressive democratically elected governments'. Untoppled and undemocratic countries – notably China and Russia (then annexing, illegally and violently, swathes of Ukraine) – received, by contrast, warm approbation as resurging 'two emerging world powers'.

Amid these shrill denunciations, South Africa was hapless about its economic imperatives and interests. At the same ANC policy conflab, party secretary-general Gwede Mantashe denounced an American demand that the government reconsider a bill mandating that 51 percent of local security companies be locally owned (thus forcing foreign owners to sell to ANC-aligned interests likely looking for a fire-sale asset). Actually, the demand was consistent with the AGOA requirement that benefiting countries establish market-based economies 'that protect private property rights'.

Beyond telling the US that South Africa 'would not be taking instructions' from it, Mantashe refused to invite any US or western diplomats to the conference – an unprecedented snub. Since the ban was extended to include representatives from the European Union (EU), which was South Africa's largest trading-bloc partner in the world,[368] it was a hissy fit that wasn't just childish, but damaging – a classic case of cutting off your nose to spite your face.

The best that could be said for the deep vein of anti-American sentiment mined by South Africa was its consistency, from Mandela through to Ramaphosa. And it mattered little to the mandarins in Pretoria whether Barack Obama or Donald Trump was in the White House.

One telling vignette in this regard was buried deep in the pages of Hillary Clinton's otherwise anodyne account of her years as Obama's Secretary of State. She relates in *Hard Choices* a revealing incident that occurred on her last official visit to South Africa in 2012. This was some nine months before the Gupta wedding saga infolded on the apron of the Waterkloof Air Force Base, and the difference between their reception (whisked in and cleared for landing even though it was for a private party) and the treatment meted out to the US's most important official was potent.

Clinton, who was leading a delegation of American business leaders from FedEx, Boeing, General Electric and other major companies from a country which by then was one of South Africa's largest export destination, relates:

[T]he South Africans refused at the last minute ... to allow my diplomatic security team to bring the vehicles and the weapons they needed into the country. My plane sat on the tarmac in Malawi, waiting to hear how the negotiations unfolded. In the end the matter was resolved, and we were finally able to take off.[369]

No doubt the officials in Pretoria delighted in delaying the arrival of a delegation from the world's hyper-power, heedless of the reputational damage this caused. Little wonder Clinton concluded:

In some instances, South Africa could be a frustrating partner ... Thabo Mbeki and Jacob Zuma wanted South Africa to be ... taken seriously on the world stage. That's what we wanted too ... But respect comes from taking responsibility ... Sometimes it was difficult to interpret the reasons behind the government's actions.[370]

By 2019, in the second year of the promise of Ramaphosa's 'investment friendly' administration, the ANC had moved on – it was now also shooting the country in the foot.

CLOWN-CAR DIPLOMACY

In early 2019, an evening with a western diplomat from a leading investor nation in South Africa revealed deep levels of frustration with his host nation. 'Imagine,' he said to me, as we surveyed the sweeping view of Table Mountain from the terrace of a Bishopscourt embassy residence, 'if we'd said during the struggle for democracy here, "It's not our business"? And if we'd added that the future of South Africa couldn't be determined by outsiders, least of all by those from the west? And that there may be terrible violations of human rights in the country, but that was for the government and the people of South Africa to sort out?'

My ambassadorial interlocutor hardly needed to remind me that the ANC in exile had taken a radically different view – it had applied enormous pressure on western governments to put the administrations of PW Botha (with little success) and FW de Klerk (with much better results) under the economic and diplomatic cosh. Now, the ANC in government, in stark contrast to its position in exile, was dusting off the mantra of the NP foreign-affairs playbook: 'no external interference in the internal affairs of other countries'. (Israel was the singular exception to this new-old rule.)

What had really annoyed my otherwise mild-mannered – and now highly frustrated – host that evening was an almost cartoonish and foolish attack by my old department, Dirco, on five western countries, including his. In February 2019 the diplomatic representatives of the US, the UK, Germany, Switzerland and the Netherlands – which between them accounted for 75 percent of all foreign investment in South Africa – were summoned to the Dirco head office in Pretoria, to receive a demarche (a political line of action) registering its displeasure at the conduct of foreign countries.

Some eight months earlier, this ambassadorial quintet had addressed a memorandum in anticipation of an investment summit hosted by Ramaphosa. The ambassadors had met with his 'investment envoys' and at their behest had codified concerns on corruption and other obstacles in the path of foreign investor nations. Notably, the diplomats had flagged concerns at the lack of action on the legal front against state capturers. They had also noted disquiet with government hobbyhorses, from stringent BEE codes to moves to weaken intellectual property rights.

Nothing was heard back until the summons to the Dirco dressing-down.

No doubt the briefly serving foreign minister, Lindiwe Sisulu – who was dropped from this post shortly afterwards – wanted to burnish her anti-western credentials. But my diplomatic friend was both appalled by the clumsy and dilatory action of her department, and nonplussed by the response to a request for suggestions from Ramaphosa's so-called 'listening government'.

But it wasn't so much the diplomatic gaffe by South Africa that stunned even the most sympathetic European envoy stationed here. It was the ruling party, the locus of real power, that gave an unvarnished view of how the government saw things. In one of several bile-filled paragraphs its statement read, in part:

> The ANC has noted with deep concern the interference by the Western imperialist forces like the USA, UK, Germany, Netherlands and Switzerland into the affairs of South Africa … The ANC condemns this dramatic holier-than-thou stance of these former colonisers and we would not like to relate to them on the history of master-slave relations.[371]

A first-year undergraduate probably would have known that, among other things, Switzerland had never colonised anyone, but then again, a first-year student would have been unlikely to pen such a juvenile diatribe.

HOLIER THAN THOU IN THE HOLY LAND

Israel was the one safe space where South African foreign policy felt comfortable to intrude, and suspend the non-interference in domestic politics it offered elsewhere in the world.

In 2014, when Israel invaded Gaza for the second time in five years, the diminutive deputy secretary-general of the ANC, Jessie Duarte, found some outsize language to attack Israel as 'barbaric', suggesting, additionally, that the Israeli occupation of the Palestinian territories was equivalent to the Nazi 'death camps'.[372]

In truth, more than residual anti-Semitism or solidarity with the Palestinians (though both were features of the anti-Israel policy), the enduring reason for the stance of the South African government was a consequence of its anti-western approach. This was given voice in 2015 by Obed Bapela, then head of ANC international relations. He advised a radio station that a proposal to deny South Africans the right to hold dual citizenship with Israel was mooted to prevent local Jews serving in the Israeli Defence Force. Also, he added, it was because 'the ANC is opposed to the imperialist agenda of the US and its allies'.[373]

In that giveaway phrase lay the nub of the issue and the real basis for the anti-Israel prejudice. The Jews are outside 'colonisers' in Araby, and the state of Israel is both a proxy for its US ally and must – as per Ms Duarte – be Nazified to complete the picture. The hypocrisy and historical elisions necessary to arrive at this illogical endpoint are beside the point.

But what was very much in point was, again, the ideological wilfulness on the part of South Africa which, once again, boomeranged against the country's core interests and the most elemental needs of its citizens.

Beginning in 2016, parts of South Africa were gripped by the worst drought in living memory, recording some of the lowest rainfall levels since comprehensive records began in 1904, according to one report.[374] By then, however, chaotic mismanagement and grand theft at the national department of water and sanitation under the baton of Zuma-loving minister Nomvula Mokonyane had raked up billions of rands in unauthorised and wasteful expenditure;

its water boards had been sites of plunder for her hand-picked appointees, and by 2017 her department was bankrupt. Cape Town's 'Day Zero', when the taps would run dry, loomed in 2018.

Just six years earlier, Israel had been in a similarly dire situation; an Israeli hydrologist had spoken of being in 'a situation where we were very, very close to someone opening a tap somewhere in the country and no water would come out'.[375] But Israel had managed to turn the situation completely around. It desalinated its Mediterranean seawater and used its high-tech prowess to recycle wastewater, allowing by 2016 more than half its households, agriculture and industries to receive water that was artificially produced. It became the world leader in innovation for scarce water jurisdictions.

So American-born Arthur Lenk, who had perhaps the most difficult diplomatic task available as the ambassador of Israel in South Africa from 2013 to 2017, decided to highlight the one offer from Israel that surely would resonate in water-scarce South Africa: irrigation and water-saving technologies. At his 'Israeli Water Week' in Cape Town, showcasing innovative successes, however, there was no sign of the ANC, and its provincial secretary, Faeiz Jacobs, claimed that the Western Cape government and other parties in attendance had been captured 'by Israeli lobbyists'. He ladled out righteousness with his scorn adding, 'True to its values, ANC leaders never attended this pro-Israel event.'[376]

Minister Mokonyane did go to the Middle East to check for solutions. But instead of Israel she flew to Iran, and returned with a signed agreement with the Mullahs of Tehran to reduce South Africa's dependence on surface water using Iranian expertise.[377] In fact, Iran had no previous example of exporting its technologies abroad, and its record in its own desert-surrounded country was indifferent. Local water experts there decried the Iranian model for, among other shortcomings, 'water scarcity reappear[ing] just years after each project is finished'.[378]

Nothing more was seen or heard in South Africa of Iranian technologies, but the ANC's ideological purity remained intact. Just like South Africa's water scarcity.

ROGUE DIPLOMATS

Beyond ideological blindness, the cast of characters chosen, with some notable exceptions, to represent the country abroad could have starred in an update of the 1777 comedy of manners, *The School for Scandal.*

The ambassador to Singapore, former SAA cabin staffer Hazel Ngubeni, was recalled after being revealed to be a convicted drug trafficker, for which offence she'd previously served jail time in the US.[379] The high commissioner to Canada was iced out by the Canadians when they discovered that her claimed PhD was false, although the South Africans then piloted Mohau Pheko to Japan, one of our largest trading partners.[380] The high commissioner to Australia, former cabinet minister S'bu Ndebele, was recalled after protests from Canberra that he'd been indicted for fraud and corruption relating to allegations of accepting R10 million in bribes while in office in his former posting as head of the South African national department of transport.[381]

But scandal didn't disqualify a diplomatic posting unless so egregious that the host country recoiled. The enabler of the Gupta wedding party's Waterkloof landing, against all rules and regulations, Bruce Koloane, was given a wrist slap for his misdemeanour but then rewarded with the ambassadorship to The Netherlands (he has since been recalled).[382]

The deputy ambassador to Burundi, Nosithembele Mapisa, who happened to be the sister of the minister of defence, Nosiviwe Mapisa-Nqakula, was 'suspended' after allegedly assisting her sister, the minister, to smuggle a fugitive out of the country using false papers; but she was reinstated and now heads a regional desk at

Dirco, and her sister remains a minister under Ramaphosa.[383]

The defence minister seemingly had a penchant for abusing official airplanes. She hit the headlines again in 2020 for ferrying ANC members on an Air Force jet for a meeting with ZANU-PF leaders. She was reprimanded by Cyril Ramaphosa for an 'error of judgement' and docked three months' salary but retained her ministry.[384]

Even more surreal in the Dirco scandal stakes was the case of the acting ambassador to Sudan regarding the murder of two women in Khartoum in December 2019. The women were reportedly lured into the apartment of the diplomat, Zabantu Ngcobo, and allegedly murdered, according to the killers, 'as a training exercise' to prepare for their real target: the intelligence officer at the embassy who was sending home damaging reports about Ngcobo. Dirco invoked diplomatic immunity against the arrest and prosecution of Ngcobo and her partner, and flew them back to South Africa.[385]

A cynic might conclude that there was something apt in so many of South Africa's excellencies abroad being ensnared in alleged criminal activity, false qualifications and inappropriate behaviour. The face of an ambassador is, after all, the face of their country to the wider world.

CHAPTER 16

Nine signposts: The road ahead

Since its modern inception at Union in 1910, South Africa has lurched through enervating crises: the Spanish flu, far more deadly than the coronavirus; the Great Depression a decade later; its contested entry into World War Two, which split the ruling United Party and presaged its supplanting by the National Party in 1948; the imposition of grand apartheid and the mass African resistance to the system, and the militarisation of the state and emergency rule to interdict change; a siege economy imposed on a recalcitrant government by a world weary of the obduracy of minority rule at the southern foot of Africa, and the violent suppression of dissent by the state equalled in ferocity by the bloody struggles within the Struggle, especially in the killing fields of my home province, KwaZulu-Natal.

On the positive side the entries are shorter but more remarkable for their achievement on the stony soil so inhospitable for so long to a democratic non-racial prospectus taking root: the 'negotiated miracle' of 1994, the beneficent presidency of Nelson Mandela and the inauguration of a modern democratic constitution despite the illiberal canvas on which it was sketched. For a while, a spirit of reconciliation, economic sobriety and political inclusivity held sway at the end of the tumultuous old century, and then continued for a brief moment into the opening years of the new millennium.

But, as this book suggests, the roots planted in 1994 have been energetically ripped out by men and women of zeal, with vigour unmatched by thought of consequence. And toxic weeds have proliferated in the garden planted amid much hope and hype three decades back. Nurturing the soil proved too arduous a task for many entrusted to nourish the fragile plant of democracy. So perhaps that 'golden era' – now much contested, and being rewritten and trampled over – was more a fleeting footnote, or historical interregnum, than a chapter for the ages in our national fable.

It would be an act of intellectual abdication not to suggest where I think we are heading in the future, subject to the caveat that the course of a country doesn't always follow either prediction or existing templates: scenario planners overcome the problem by wisely not offering definitive endgame answers to existential questions but instead positing a range of plausible alternatives.

1. IN A TIME OF PLAGUE

During the time of the enervating coronavirus plague, the whole world was in the same sea although, to borrow a phrase, countries navigated treacherous waters in very different sized and equipped vessels. And about size, it was sobering to be reminded that the entire world was held hostage, or locked down, due to a microscopic parasite 10 000 times smaller than a grain of salt.

Grim precedents from past plagues offer little comfort for the modern world as it confronts the novel virus which at breakneck speed spread across the globe. The Athenian democracy never regained its vigour after its plague in the fifth century BC; the Black Death 1800 years later wiped out nearly half of Europe's population. Although this 21st-century plague isn't nearly as deadly, we can barely fathom when and how it will end – in the words of Canadian academic Wade Davis, 'Pandemics and plagues have a way of shifting the course of history, and not always in a manner immediately evident to the survivors'[386] – but we can estimate that its consequences will be huge.

The most advanced economic powerhouses in the world were revealed, in the main, to be as incompetent and ill-prepared as the most impoverished and backward countries. An equality of misery seemed the default position for most countries, and quite a bit of this had to do with the difficulties in democracies of juggling individual rights with public-health imperatives.

And, of course, there were some impossible choices that even the most gifted and selfless leaders would have been stumped to navigate: It was Wade Davis, again, who expressed it best: 'all the money in the hands of all the nations on Earth will never be enough to offset the losses sustained when an entire world ceases to function, with workers and businesses everywhere facing a choice between economic and biological survival.'[387]

This dire dystopian description – the lived reality of the world circa 2020 – was also a reminder of the feckless and often suboptimal leaders, elected to deal with one imperative, suddenly confronting another, far more intricate and intractable problem, with few precedents or effective tools to interdict an invisible disease.

And like a broken clock that tells the correct time twice a day, Donald Trump in the US was correct on one big thing: China, the largest authoritarian state in the world, had a lot to answer for in the origins and the miscommunication of the spread of coronavirus in Wuhan in December 2019. Its own lockdown and enforcement measures, draconian and effective, were easier to achieve in a country where the ruling party is answerable only to itself and not to the people in whose name it governs.

South Africa was hit by the virus at the precise point at which decades of policy mistakes and inertia, and reckless and (more recently) passive leadership, had rendered its financial immune system and fractured social and political landscapes weak and vulnerable to the new and unprecedented shocks of lockdown economics. The new disease pathogen simply aggravated every political pathology that predated it.

2. FOLLOW THE MONEY

The 'Deep Throat' in the Watergate Scandal that toppled US president Richard Nixon in 1974 advised Bob Woodward and Carl Bernstein of *The Washington Post* to 'follow the money' to finger the culprits. In 2020 a similar back-of-the-envelope calculation reveals the true horror of the South African fiscus and its future trajectory.

In February 2019 the National Treasury recorded that to keep the ship of state afloat, and to pay its army of employees and welfare recipients – two of the biggest-ticket items in the national budget and essential voting pillars for the ANC – the country was obliged to borrow R335.3 billion per year – about R1 billion every day.[388]

By September 2020 we were borrowing R776.9 billion annually[389] – R2 billion a day, more than double in just over a year. And in the zero- or minus-growth environment that characterised highly indebted South Africa, the debt trend line only pointed far and ever farther north. The interest charge on the 2019 debt was an annualised R202.2 billion. A year later it rose to R240 billion, and it looked set to rocket beyond R301 billion in 2021.

Servicing the burgeoning and unchecked public-debt costs and paying the public-sector wage bill cost around 79c of every rand raised by the government through taxation, with hard-pressed and diminished businesses and taxpayers crowded out of economic activity and regeneration. The funding for all this via the annual budget was based increasingly on deficit spending, and here the estimates of National Treasury of a 6.8 percent shortfall between incomings and outgoings for 2020/21 were quickly revised upwards to 15.7 percent, or a monthly gap of around R50 billion.

This, suggested Duncan Artus of Allan Gray, one of South Africa's largest private fund management companies, meant the country was in a 'death spiral' – drowning in debt.[390]

And the numbers went beyond the balance sheet: in the first quarter of 2020, before the coronavirus misery had fully impacted on employment, ten million South Africans were effectively out of a job, while eighteen million were kept going only through social grants, the financing of which tipped the country ever further into insolvency.[391]

3. LAND OF LOUSY OPTIONS

Of all the financial analysts and writers surveying the confidence-shattered and economically devastated covid South African landscape, Claire Bisseker of the *Financial Mail* was in the top tier.

Her appropriately headlined article 'Endgame for South Africa?', published in August 2020, offered little hope and buckets of misery.[392] In the range of choices confronting both the country and its political overlords, no one good path was available; the easy roads had all been missed in the benign years when moderate growth fuelled options. Now, in the cratered landscape of covidonomics, the hard choices ducked earlier stared us full in the face.

All three international credit-rating agencies that had down-graded the sovereign debt to junk status agreed that the country's galloping debt trajectory wouldn't be stabilised, because this outcome depended on sufficient economic growth which, in turn, needed sufficient economic and structural reforms to execute a sharp turnaround. Yet all on offer from the government was a doubling down of the precise failed policies and prescriptions that had landed the country in the economic ditch in the first place.

Addicted to borrowing in lieu of reforming policy and practice, the state funded itself via the bond market; but as yields rose on long-term bonds, the debt trap loomed as the higher interest rate demanded by skittish investors increased the debt obligation: 'As its debt burden keeps increasing, [South Africa] will probably find it harder and harder to find buyers for its bonds. Once it cannot find buyers, the debt trap shuts,' Bisseker warned.

The country was in a classic Catch-22 situation, with escape improbable if not impossible because of the contradictions inherent in the situation. There could be no reform without splitting the ANC, for example, yet a united ANC made reform impossible. And the president of both party and country – of necessity, in that order – announced mid pandemic in August 2020 that he would rather be a weak president than the person who presided over the disunity of his organisation.[393]

And the much-vaunted unity of the ANC – to the extent it actually exists beyond a mutual survival and enrichment pact for its leading lights – was unlikely to survive the likeliest outcome of continuing down the debt death spiral into a fully blown debt crisis: where the country can no longer pay the interest and principal on its enormous debt (the interest costs in 2020 were already gobbling up one fifth of the budget).

This would necessitate going to the IMF, not for the sweetheart low-interest loan it had already received in 2020 which required few concessions from the finance ministry other than lofty promises of reform. No, the next step was a 'structural adjustment' programme, where the dread wizards of Washington (in ANC demonology) would impose the very hard reforms the government had refused to countenance, from stripping the public sector to enforced privatisations.

But back to the Catch-22, since, for the unity of the ANC, conceding on the myth of 'surrendering our sovereignty' would indeed presage the fearful party split. Thus, as Claire Bisseker and others noted, the alternative was a lurch further left into the territory of fantasy economics favoured by many in the party anyway: quixotic policies that run down the domestic savings base (by raiding pension funds for government projects), or adopt coercive levels of taxation, or force the Reserve Bank to print money to bail out the government.

I had watched precisely this economic play at work during my years in Argentina (which held the dubious record for the highest number of sovereign-debt defaults in economic history) and the result was pretty miserable: galloping inflation, a debauched local currency and parallel black-market hunt for restricted US dollars, corroded foreign confidence and a full-blown investment strike, government seizure of private assets and a form of outlaw economics that privileged a few party insiders and left the population at large in conditions of economic hardship.

But Argentina at least produced from its uber-fertile pampas one of the largest crops in the world of soybeans, the staple feed for the planet and its animals. As Bill Clinton noted while on a speaking tour there, 'We don't know the future economics of the world, but we do know that everyone has to eat.'

South Africa's once vaunted unique offer to the world of a minerals treasure chest has become, with every passing year and the birth of new economic life forms and technologies such as electronic cars and big data, less exceptional. Beyond platinum and some other rare earth metal reserves, new offshore oil and gas finds, and our game parks, we're not in the 2020s nearly as unique as we perhaps once thought we were.

Wealthy Argentinians, like rich suburban South Africans, juggled the disadvantages of living in such a perilous economic situation with the lifestyle advantages of Buenos Aires's cosmopolitanism and the rugged joys of polo playing and holidaying in Mendoza's winelands by placing their money offshore or across the River Plate in more stable Uruguay. But many simply decided the best option was to follow their money overseas, and decamp themselves – along with their skills and their tax revenues. South Africa's fragile and shrinking tax and knowledge base seem poised to flow in the same direction.

4. THE CLUNKING HAMMER OF THE STATE

The coronavirus cast the harshest possible light on the paralysis of the state. It couldn't deliver the relief it promised; it couldn't provide basic health care in some places (the Eastern Cape, for example), let alone personal protective equipment for its health personnel or oxygen for its patients.

But the command-and-control model was mightily enjoyed by those exercising power. The ability to ride roughshod over citizens' rights, such as whether you could buy a cigarette (outlawed for five months) or purchase slipslops (disallowed for one month), were utterly laughable. Black markets flourished, as did the appearance of several incompetent ministers offering such absurdities, in faux-camouflage uniforms and berets and sporting mini-Cuban lapel flags.

Taking away basic rights, and allowing the state to intrude ever further into the private sector and private lives of its citizenry, simply fed the appetite of those in charge. Before the onset of the coronavirus, those who'd worshipped at the altar of state control had been somewhat constrained in giving this full expression. The onset of the virus and the imposition of a state of disaster, without much scrutiny or oversight and very little judicial pushback, unleashed the untamed men and women of ideological zeal.

This ceding power to a secretive cabal of ministers in the National Coronavirus Command Council reminded me ominously of the dark 1980s, the time of PW Botha's states of emergency, when a State Security Council, and not Parliament or the courts, determined matters. Helen Suzman described it as 'a creeping coup d'etat by consent'.[394] Billionaire Johann Rupert, whose R1-billion donation at the onset of the plague was initially lauded by Cyril Ramaphosa, was moved, four months later, to describe some of the decisions of the Command Council, operating with the same stealth as the Botha regime, as 'social engineering by decree'.[395]

There was little about the imperatives of public health behind the decision-making, I believe, although this was the ostensible reason offered by Ramaphosa for the off-site process of governing (he didn't address a proper press conference nor make a single parliamentary appearance for five months).

The long lockdown enabled the prohibitionists in government to break cover, although for uncertain health benefits and at a prohibitive economic cost. One alcohol-industry leader, for example, shared with me the results of the cumulative fourteen-week ban on booze imposed in two stages between March and August 2020: R13 billion in deferred or cancelled new investments, around 120 000 job losses and R12 billion forfeited in excise tax.

Small businesses across the beer value chain were decimated: 8 000 taverns and 15 percent of craft breweries were forced to permanently close their doors.

Of course, there was already a plethora of laws on the statute book to curb the nefarious results of excess drinking that had always plagued the country. These, though, required diligent policing and proper enforcement, and neither was evident in the corroded state. Instead, the blunt instrument of a wholesale ban, and the birthing of a thriving illicit market, was the chosen path.

There was another uncomfortable, unconscious mimicking of the discredited past: in 1966 two eminent academics at the University of Natal (as it then was), professors Ronald Albino and Tony Matthews, published an article entitled 'The permanence of the temporary'.[396] It examined the detention laws that allowed the NP regime, 'in the interests of security', to detain citizens without recourse to the courts or other essential liberties. This 'temporary' measure to meet an emergency situation would, the authors prophesied, become a permanent condition. And so it proved as legislated detention, under whose framework shocking abuses and deaths occurred, endured in this country for 25 years after the article was penned.

Likewise, the ANC government, confronting a health and not a security emergency, enjoyed the wide latitude the 2020 state of national disaster conferred on it, and the opportunity to 'reset the economy' on lines congenial to its outdated socialist and statist playbook. Would it, though, cede back the powers it now exercised? This is the most critical question, to which no ready or comfortable answer presents: for how long and at what cost will the economy and citizens be kept under government command and control? Will, indeed, the covid temporary emergency economic regime become the semi-permanent future condition? This seems likely: the state had plucked from its toolbox the hammer of control and would now view every problem as a nail.

5. THE HYENAS FEED

One problem the covid hammer never nailed down was the dark undertow of corruption. South Africa is, of course, hardly alone in the world of politically connected people who use access to state power to enrich themselves unlawfully at the expense of the taxpayer and donor communities, via ripping off government-awarded tenders and contracts.

However, in many other jurisdictions such illicit gains are usually hidden in offshore havens or rendered opaque, and are often rendered untraceable through a network of holding companies and other esoteric financial instruments. Whether it was lack of sophistication or simply the need to show off, many of South Africa's state rip-off skimmers, grifters and rentiers simply parked their proceeds in the garage – literally.

Infamous Zuma-era cabinet minister and current ANC executive member Nomvula Mokonyane received R2.2 million from a 'family friend' as contribution towards her R3-million Aston Martin, who in turn, with the lady's late husband, scored a lucrative deal with the power utility Eskom. Mokonyane declined to disclose this gift in the register of MPs' interests, nor to the taxman, leading the *Financial Mail* to describe her acquisition as 'classic bribery'.[397]

In another case, a former executive of state transport company Transnet, Herbert Msagala, had a fleet of 35 cars seized on various of his properties dotted around the country. He was accused by the Special Investigating Unit (SIU) of profiting from 'corrupt activities' in the form of 'bribes, kickbacks and/or improper benefits' during his tenure as head of the entity's capital projects portfolio. It was further alleged that he had an 'improper and corrupt relationship' with both a company doing business with Transnet and indeed with its former chief executive, Sipho Sithole.[398]

It was the garaging of a Porsche, a Lamborghini, an Audi, Land Rovers and Jaguars that shone the light in October 2019 on Durban mayor Zandile Gumede. The vehicles were found on the properties of her co-accused in a R430-million solid-waste tender scandal for which she was arrested, along with the car owners. Her luxury property in Umhlanga was seized, along with around R50 million of assets found in the accounts and homes of the ten accused of this municipal rip-off which she allegedly had fronted while mayor of eThekweni (greater Durban). Gumede was relieved of her mayoral chain, and released on R50 000 bail pending her court case.

When the ANC national executive, on which no shortage of state profiteers sat and led the ruling party, decreed on 4 August 2020 that 'ethical and moral leadership' was needed in the 'collective fight against corruption',[399] it was responding to public outrage that 60 percent of emergency procurements of the state were revealed to have been spent on businesses that are politically connected or in which 'politically exposed persons' were involved, according to SARS.[400] Ramaphosa described such predators and their predations as 'a pack of hyenas circling a wounded prey.'[401]

At this exact time Madame Gumede re-entered the public frame. On 12 August this 'hyena' was sworn in as an honourable member of the KwaZulu-Natal parliament on behalf of the ANC, her bail conditions allowing her to attend the legislature in addition to sitting in the criminal dock. The ANC, in typical fashion, later squared this awkward circle in an attempt to quiet public outrage by placing her 'on leave', which meant in effect a fully-funded holiday with benefits.

Doubtless Ramaphosa, three days after this spectacle in Pietermaritzburg, was sincere when he wrote to his party members that 'the ANC may not stand alone in the dock, but it does stand as Accused No.1.'[402]

Fine words again, and again he referenced a myriad committees and internal processes, and some state agencies to stop the rot. But the words and the processes had been heard too often by too many victims of state corruption – which included basically the whole country outside the ANC elite, from poor people in ever-increasing need to middle-class taxpayers expected to bail out such profligacies.

The real issue was revealed by the deeply compromised, and by November 2020 criminally accused, Ace Magashule, who controlled the ruling party as secretary-general. He determined who the party disciplined and where its cadres were deployed, and he had a laconic riposte to the demand for a separation of party and state: 'Tell me of one leader of the ANC who has not done business with government.'[403]

This might have been an exaggeration, but it pointed to a broken moral compass. As the *Financial Mail* observed, 'He sounded the death knell for any hope that the party might be able to haul itself out of the grave it has dug … it's effectively dead as an ethical organisation.'[404]

Magashule – with his sinister dark glasses and horrific reputation – might have been the chief gravedigger but the road to perdition had been paved long before, while he sat in provincial obscurity in the Free State. It was embedded in the ANC's policies and practices, and conceived decades back: BEE, state control, cadre deployment, hollowing out independent institutions, and collapsing the wall between party and state. 'Transformation' might have been the cause, but the feeding frenzy of 'the hyenas' was the result.

Is a course correction possible at this late stage? It is, but it's improbable unless Cyril Ramaphosa is willing (or, more aptly, is allowed by his party) to uncouple himself and his government from the cardinal policies that have crashed the ship of state on the rocks of ruin. He can't have it both ways – he can't both purge corruption and continue with the legalised system that enables it.

6. FIGHT OR FLIGHT?

'Living in South Africa now is what it must be like to be married to an addict: there are moments of rare beauty, but mostly all you want for them is to take responsibility and be honest. Unfortunately, it's normally best to leave so that you don't go down with them.'[405]

This was the elegiac conclusion offered in an August 2020 Bisseker article on the parlous economic outlook for the country, an update of the Clash song 'Should I Stay or Should I Go?' that was the background noise and thought that accompanied me during my university years in the 1980s.

By 2020, some forty years later, the volume had been cranked up many decibels. For the middle class, the push factors included some alarming thoughts on the likely path forward – increasing hunger and even food riots, property confiscations and collapsing services, rising taxes, electricity blackouts and growing crime.

Still, there were many in the ranks of the local bourgeoisie who were prepared to tough things out – in conditions of relative comfort, compared to what would likely be reduced lifestyles for the same price elsewhere, provided their financial assets could be warehoused, quite legally, abroad.

(Of course, most South Africans don't have the flight option, being either too poor or too unskilled to consider living abroad, and for the bulk of the country simple survival and getting by is an all-consuming activity.)

Financial analyst Magnus Heystek offered, back in 2014, the last rites on this thought, advising investors that within five years the effects of weakening economic growth and currency decline would see 'jackbooted bankers from the Reserve Bank … overnight, without warning' switch off the offshore-investment tap and impose currency and capital controls on the country. He reminded his reader, 'There are only two types of ex-Rhodesians in the world. Those who took their money out of the country and those who wished that they did.'[406]

A scary prospect indeed – but although the economic skies have darkened considerably in the intervening six years since Heystek's note, the standout fact is that this predicted path hasn't been followed. Prophesy is useful but is never conclusive.

Sandwiched between the emigrants and would-be leavers on the one hand, and the stayers on the other, is a third category. This is the group, mostly younger and idealistic, who have the universal skills set to operate in other, perhaps more congenial, places in the world, but who through conviction and choice envisage a South African future, and determine that by staying they can contribute to country betterment.

I was closely connected to a young woman who passionately belonged to this small tribe, but whose searing experience tipped her into the leavers' camp. She had a doctorate in her academic field and was widely published in peer-reviewed journals. She had a particularly strong track record in community outreach and was keen, in her words, 'to contribute to the transformation agenda in terms of challenging colonial historiography and creating more accurate portrayals of the past'.

In early 2019 three of her professional departmental colleagues at UCT, where she was a post-doctoral fellow, urged her to apply for one of two advertised posts for lectureships in her precise intellectual field of expertise. She knew, in her words, that 'UCT was under pressure to appoint more people of colour', but since this imperative was tied in the advertisement to 'the pursuit of excellence', her head of department encouraged her to apply, and didn't see her whiteness as a total bar to proper consideration.

Having applied, she waited … and waited. Eventually, she was officially told that the application process had been delayed, with no further explanation. A few days later, a senior member of staff called her aside and provided the real reason for the delay: the selection committee had decided to interview only black candidates.

She was later advised by eyewitnesses at the selection committee that the black applicant preferred by the dean didn't have the required PhD in the relevant discipline, so the dean simply 'persuaded the selection committee to hold the position for the applicant until they had graduated with their PhD'.

Her final communication from the UCT human-resources department advised her that her application had 'been carefully considered against the job requirements' but had been unsuccessful. 'What annoyed me most about this email was that it was untrue, as I knew well by this stage that they had never even considered my application,' she told me.

Her hurt was, of course, very personal; but there was also a political aspect. 'The experience forced me to more critically confront some of the narratives I'd held about South Africa, and my place in the society, and ultimately I recognise that some of these ideas no longer make sense to me.'

She dusted off the overseas applications she'd pended months before in the hope of teaching and working at an institution and in a country she loved. She was immediately accepted at a top UK university, where she now works in a thriving atmosphere of intellectual rigour and freedom. She's unlikely to return to live and work in South Africa.

There are many similar tales, and it's easy to dismiss them as some form of 'white privilege nostalgia', grotesquely ill-fitting as it might be of this shunned applicant. But beyond the individual circumstances there is the country condition: ill fares the land that so thoughtlessly dispenses with and exports its knowledge base, especially those deeply committed to its excellence and desirous to contribute to its future.

7. JUDGEMENT DAY

'The liberation dividend' is useful political shorthand for explaining the durability of governing parties whose long years in government are not explicable by achievements in office but due more to voter gratitude for their role in country liberation.

There are many examples, though none has endured forever, as at some point the liberation ticket expires. Usually weary voters, the fed-up citizens enraged by corruption, authoritarian leadership, poor economics or unmet promises, or some combination of these ailments, decide to throw the rascals out.

The longest recorded liberation government in recent history was the Mexican Institutional Revolutionary Party, closely iden-tified with the country's independence. It held power for most of the 20th century – from 1929 to 2000 – using a combination of patronage politics, electoral fraud and ideological flexibility to maintain its grip over seven decades. But deep corruption was its undoing, and although its leader would one more time enter the presidential palace, in 2018 its presidential candidate received only 16.55 percent of the vote, its lowest in history.

Ireland's Fianna Fáil (Soldiers of Destiny), the party founded by Republican hero and president Éamon de Valera, was at the forefront of the barricades for Irish independence. It, too, was long in office as the natural party of government, enjoying some 61 years in power, either alone or in coalition. It, too, presided over epic corruption scandals and managed to lose its monopoly on power in 2011 when it suffered the worst defeat of a sitting government in the history of Ireland.

A downward arc from total power to irrelevant marginalisation was followed by two parties that were correctly credited with the creation of their states in modern form and which dominated government and country for decades. India's National Congress Party – the movement of Gandhi and Nehru – held dominant sway in the world's largest democracy from independence, the achievement of which was its most potent electoral weapon, in 1947 through to 1977, when the authoritarianism of Nehru's daughter, Prime Minister Indira Gandhi, saw it swept from office in a landslide.

It would, under various Gandhi children, return to power again, but in 2017, under yet another Gandhi (grandson Rahul), it obtained a paltry 52 of 542 seats in the Lok Sabha, the lower house of parliament. It's best remembered now for its past achievements, not its future prospects.

Israel's Labour movement, Mapai, and later the Labour Alignment, under its founder and long-serving prime minister, David Ben Gurion, totally dominated modern Israel from its founding in

1948. Opposition leader and later prime minister Ariel Sharon – a famous soldier – ruefully noted that it was impossible to be promoted into the higher ranks of the fabled Israeli Defence Force absent a Labour party membership card. It, too, became complacent in its unchallenged power, corrupt and cavalier in its essential task of safeguarding the country, as the 1973 war proved. It lost power in 1977, and although it would return to office on occasions thereafter, by 2019 it had been reduced to political irrelevance, returning a tiny parliamentary faction of just six seats in the 120-member Knesset. Its return from the political graveyard is improbable, even in the land of biblical miracles and resurrections.

The French Gaullists, France's pre-eminent party of national liberation and post-war government, are today a rump movement. In the 2017 presidential election its candidate, François Fillon, at the centre of a nepotism and corruption scandal, barely scraped twenty percent of the vote in the first round and was eliminated. In the final round voters chose Emmanuel Macron as president. He had started a new party, En Marche, just before the election, indicating French revulsion with 'politics as usual'.

Africa too, in places from Nigeria and Ghana to Senegal and Malawi, has seen the uptick of democracy oust once-dominant parties from power.

This brief electoral laundry list is worth emphasising for two reasons, the obvious one being that there is in the modern democratic world no such thing as an enduring natural majority party of government, absent massive state-aided electoral fraud or some military intervention.

The second reason is allied to the first: each of these longest-serving dominant parties was undone in the end by the very factor that had ensured its longevity: untrammelled power leads to its abuse, and over time, the excesses, and the lack of empathy with ordinary voters bred by arrogant and out-of-touch political potentates, inspires such strong revulsion in voters that, in their numbers, they turn against their political overlords.

Geoffrey Wheatcroft, the British journalist and historian, pinpointed an essential reason why the needs of a liberation struggle are usually unsuited to democratic governance and service delivery: 'All underground movements operate of necessity by basic rules – unconditional loyalty to colleagues, and no questions asked – which become dangerous when carried on into constitutional societies. It is not a coincidence that the parties which began underground, like the French Gaullists and Fianna Fáil in Ireland, have been so prone to corruption.'[407] To which we can now add, of course, South Africa's ANC in 2020.

The further removed a country's citizens are from the clashes and events of liberation and freedom, the more the everyday concerns and fears of voters kick in. By the time the next general election is scheduled in South Africa, in 2024, the ANC will have been in power for an unbroken thirty years, the same time span that saw the removal of the liberation/governing parties of India and Israel for the first time, hastening their future irrelevance.

Voters, either positively by switching sides or passively by abstaining, indicated in 2016 they were happy to eject ANC governments from control of all the major cities in the country bar Durban. They have yet to make the same determination nationally but could so opt in 2024.

This possibility needs to be read with some fat health warnings. The fact that the DA, for example, couldn't maintain its governing grip in the major metros points to the continuation of a problem I identified way back in 2007: nothing divides the South African opposition more than questions of its unity.

Then there's the fact that every significant or small breakaway from the three larger parties (the ANC, the DA and the EFF) has been destroyed by narcissistic ego clashes and policy incoherence, and the latest additions in this column are unlikely to break this mould.

The DA and the EFF are ideologically incompatible and have proven to be unable to cooperate locally, so there are no prospects of closer union there. Unless a crippled 2024 ANC rejoins itself to the EFF to effect a parliamentary majority, a real change in governance awaits a split in the ANC itself – much spoken of but never quite sighted.

Hope lies in the fact that politics is never static, and in the very turbulence of the current economic meltdown and the social misery of so many voters, and the identification of the culprit as the government itself and the ruling panjandrums. Predictions are always perilous, and in a fast-moving and uncertain environment even more so. A popular awakening may then be on the cards, even if its course and destination remain unknowable.

8. WARP SPEED CHANGES EVERYTHING

In 1993 I attended a presentation for MPs on the brave new technological world offered by cellular phones scheduled for arrival in the country the following year. The minister of telecom-munications, Dr Piet Welgemoed, estimated that the likely take-up by consumers of this new device was in the region of 500 000 customers, rising 'in a best-case scenario' to around 900 000.

Today, nearly three decades later, more than 23 million South Africans use or own a smartphone, whose slimline outline contains more computing ability than the entire computer power used to send the first men to the moon in Apollo 11 in 1969; and there are an estimated 103.5 mobile connections in South Africa.[408]

Beyond the inaccuracy of predictions, we're reminded every day, in matters huge or inconsequential, of how fast things are moving.

The internet went public in 1991, and changed our lives. And in the decades since, we've seen the advent of virtual reality, sequencing the human genome and machines that can reason better than people (and replace a lot of their jobs as well).

It wasn't that long ago, in 2004, that Harvard dropout Mark Zuckerberg introduced the world to Facebook. Today it has 2.7 billion active users – but it employs relatively few people. The largest car company, Uber, owns no vehicles, and the biggest accommodation provider, Airbnb, owns no real estate, as *Techcrunch* noted.[409]

But with the world moving at warp speed, the South African government is still in manual mode: the ANC in 2020 still believes in state control and excessive regulatory regimes, while unions have power over unemployed job seekers. The entire paraphernalia of 1950s economics is unsustainable in advancing the broad majority interest in the 2020s.

Either it will have reality forced on it, by leapfrogging technologies and the like, or it will lose control of the very events it seeks to command.

9. 'A THOUSAND POINTS OF LIGHT'

In a now vanished age, back in 1988, George HW Bush made a graceful and powerful speech accepting his party's nomination for the presidency. He identified the binding power of civil society and spoke of the genesis of 'an endless enduring dream' founded in the work of the rich mosaic of community organisations, volunteer associations, philanthropies, social clubs and charities. He described them as 'a brilliant diversity spread like stars, like a thousand points of light in a broad and peaceful sky'.[410]

Decades later, I recalled Bush's majestic words early in the harsh 2020 lockdown in Cape Town, South Africa. Once a week for several months my wife Michal and I would sit at our kitchen table and make peanut-butter sandwiches. The next day we would drop them off at the local Spar supermarket, one of dozens of venues identified by our local community Facebook page as a receiving depot for onward delivery to hungry communities devastated by both the pandemic and the shutdown of the economy.

There was nothing heroic in the individual contributions but there was something extraordinary in the response: every day the trolleys at our dropoff were packed full to overflowing, and as the need expanded, so did the pile of sandwiches.

My stepson Etai once told me that the problem with a lot of my analyses was that I was 'state-centric'. 'If you only look at South Africa through the lens of the government, it's a horror story. But look beyond that into wider society and you'll see a lot of good, sometimes great, things happening,' he advised.

Indeed, South Africa's famously resilient private sector provided some standout examples of world-class managers and innovative product lines, both at home and abroad. For every Steinhoff and Tongaat Hulett accounting scandal,[411] other companies, such as Naspers and Nando's, were shooting out the lights at home and overseas.

And there were hundreds of examples, often of people who had little themselves, of many individual South Africans and a vast array of civil-society groups doing generous things at such a mean time. It was the living embodiment of the national ethos of ubuntu, or common and interactive humanity.

On the edge of the Johannesburg city centre, in Brixton, there was the Brixton Soup Brigade, a battalion of volunteers feeding dozens of at-risk communities. Further up the food chain, as it were, the business-led Solidarity Fund in May 2020 delivered 250 000 food parcels in collaboration with one of the country's finest NGOs, the Muslim-led Gift of the Givers. Likewise, the long-established Jewish organisation Afrika Tikkun used the Judaic concept of 'repair of the world' to do enormous good and practical work to lift young South Africans out of poverty and unemployment.

For every area of state dysfunction there appeared numerous civil-society groups to mind and repair the gap, reaching across race, social stratum and religion. Some rural municipalities, for example, had basic services (provision of water, repair of potholes), long neglected by the local authorities, provided by AfriForum, an Afrikaans-based trade-union-originating organisation. And it was another civic organisation, OUTA, that got rogue former SAA chief Dudu Myeni named as a delinquent director, in the absence of any state prosecution of her.

It's always worth remembering that at moments of deepest peril the country has been rescued often by ordinary individuals prepared to do extraordinary things. Nelson Mandela, who had a genius for acts of reconciliation, recognised the dangers of a potential race war when, on Easter Saturday 1993, ANC and SACP leader Chris Hani was assassinated by two white right-wing killers. He defused this possibility by reminding a national television audience that it was a 'white Afrikaans woman' who'd identified the getaway car and given the information to the police, leading to the capture of the murderers.

That woman, Boksburg housewife Margareta Harmse, today has many successors in all communities: not in averting racial apocalypses, but in everyday acts of kindness and generosity. These bind people and communities ever closer together. Simple gestures of humanity reclaim the famed spirit of resilience which has seen the country survive and prevail in the very worst of times.

One of my democratic heroes, who survived incarceration by the communist regime in Czechoslovakia and emerged afterward as its first democratically elected president, Václav Havel, had the gift of the playwright he once had been to pen a universal formula of hope. His vision of democratic politics underpinned by a strong civil society, and 'rooted in common decency, morality, and respect for the rule of law and human rights', was a transcendent idea because it rose above 'racial, cultural and religious differences'. It was not unrealistic, he reasoned, because in his view it was 'the moral minimum existing at the heart of most faiths and cultures'.[412]

Havel, who died in 2011, lived to see his country split in two because of cultural and ethnic irreconcilabilities. This proves just how hard the signpost he offered is to sight – but it doesn't exempt us from trying, even and especially here on the southern tip of Africa.

This book suggests, based on evidence and personal encounters and impressions, that the odds of achieving the sort of non-racial thriving society, anchored by the rule of law and bolstered by rising levels of prosperity for all its citizens at peace with each other and with the wider world, are long. But that doesn't mean we must surrender the vision of 'a shining city on the hill'. It's an improbable, not an impossible, dream. It requires an optimism of both faith and will, too often in the shortest of supply.

Historian and economist David Landes concluded his magisterial book *The Wealth and Poverty of Nations* with the thought that 'optimism pays' because for both a country – and he deep-dived into many – and its people:

[t]he one lesson that emerges is the need to keep trying. No miracles. No perfection. No millennium. No apocalypse. We must cultivate a sceptical faith, avoid dogma, listen and watch well, try to clarify and define ends, the better to choose means.

'I have set before thee life and death, the blessing and the curse; therefore choose life.' – Deuteronomy 30:19.[413]

Of all our freedoms – personal, psychological and constitutional – exercising that choice is the foundation of all the others. And no government, good, bad or indifferent, can remove it from you.

Abbreviations

AGOA   African Growth and Opportunity Act
ANC   African National Congress
ARV   antiretroviral
BEE   Black Economic Empowerment
BLSA   Business Leadership South Africa
COPE   Congress of the People
Cosatu Congress of South African Trade Unions
DA   Democratic Alliance
Dirco   Department of International Relations and
        Cooperation
EFF   Economic Freedom Fighters
EWC   expropriation without compensation
FNB   First National Bank
GDP   gross domestic product
IMF   International Monetary Fund
IRR   Institute of Race Relations
MEC   member of the executive council
mego   'my eyes glaze over'
MP   member of Parliament
NDP   National Development Plan
NDR   National Democratic Revolution
NEC   national executive committee
NEET   not in employment, education or training
NHI   National Health Insurance
NNP   New National Party
NP   National Party
NPA   National Prosecuting Authority

NUM	National Union of Mineworkers
OUTA	Organisation Undoing Tax Abuse
PAC	Pan Africanist Congress
PFP	Progressive Federal Party
PIC	Public Investment Corporation
RFI	rapid financing instrument
SAA	South African Airways
SACP	South African Communist Party
SADTU	South African Democratic Teachers Union
Santaco	South African National Taxi Council
SAPS	South African Police Service
SARS	South African Revenue Service
SBA	stand-by arrangement
SOE	state-owned enterprise
SRC	Student Representative Council
UCT	University of Cape Town
UIF	Unemployment Insurance Fund
WHO	World Health Organization
Wits	University of the Witwatersrand

Notes

1   Parker, I. 2020. 'Yuval Noah Harari's history of everyone, ever' in *The New Yorker*, 17 &
    24 February. https://www.newyorker.com/magazine/2020/02/17/yuval-noah-harari-
    gives-the-really-big-picture Accessed 1 October 2020.

2   Ganesh, J. 2015. 'Marx was wrong – politics is Darwinian' in *Financial Times*, 17 August.
    https://www.ft.com/content/0884c558-44ca-11e5-b3b2-1672f710807b Accessed
    1 October 2020.

3   Onishi, N and Gebrekidan, S. 2018. 'South Africa vows to end corruption. Are its new
    leaders part of the problem?' in *The New York Times*, 4 August. https://www.nytimes.
    com/2018/08/04/world/africa/south-africa-anc-david-mabuza.html Accessed
    9 December 2020.

4   Johnson, RW. 2020. 'Anatomy of a disappointment' on Politicsweb, 26 August. https://
    www.politicsweb.co.za/opinion/anatomy-of-our-disappointment Accessed
    25 October 2020.

5   Mathe, T. 2018. 'Ramaphosa's campaign team commits to pay back Bosasa donation' on
    Eyewitness News, 18 November. https://ewn.co.za/2018/11/18/ramaphosa-s-
    campaign-team-commits-to-pay-back-bosasa-donation Accessed 7 October 2020.

6   Pilling, D. 2018. 'Cyril Ramaphosa must find a way to make South Africa fairer' in
    Financial Times, 23 May. https://www.ft.com/content/e63103a0-7caa-11e9-81d2-
    f785092ab560 Accessed 7 October 2020.

7   Seccombe, A. 2018. 'SA mines drop off international investment radar' in *Business Day*,
    4 October. https://www.businesslive.co.za/bd/companies/mining/2018-10-04-sa-
    mines-drop-off-international-investment-radar/ Accessed 7 October 2020.

8   SAPA. 2013. 'Malema: Ramaphosa a hypocrite' on IOL, 15 November. https://www.iol.
    co.za/news/malema-ramaphosa-a-hypocrite-1607600 Accessed 7 October 2020.

9   Oriani-Ambrosini, M. 2017. *The Prince and I*. Estate of the late Dr Mario
    GR Oriani-Ambrosini.

10 Smith, C. 2018. 'Ramaphosa: Growing black anger about "lackadaisical" whites with
    power' on Fin24, 13 December. https://www.news24.com/fin24/economy/ramaphosa-
    growing-black-anger-about-lackadaisical-whites-with-power-20181213 Accessed
    7 October 2020.

11 Parkinson, J, Steinhauser, G and Keeler, D. 2018. 'Economic problems exacerbate
    challenges for South Africa's leader' in *The Wall Street Journal*, 26 September. https://
    www.wsj.com/articles/economic-problems-exacerbate-challenges-for-south-africas-
    leader-1537975408 Accessed 7 October 2020.

12   Department of International Relations and Cooperation. 2018. Address by the President of South Africa, Mr Cyril Ramaphosa, to the UN General Assembly, United Nations, New York, USA, 25 September. http://www.dirco.gov.za/docs/speeches/2018/cram0925.htm Accessed 7 October 2020.

13   Merten, M. 2020. 'Social compact for unity and progress – if Ramaphosa has his way and his ministers can deliver' in *Daily Maverick*, 14 February. https://www.dailymaverick.co.za/article/2020-02-14-social-compact-for-unity-and-progress-if-ramaphosa-has-his-way-and-his-ministers-can-deliver/ Accessed 7 October 2020.

14   National Treasury. 2020. Medium Term Budget Policy Statement. 28 October.

15   Democratic Alliance. 2020. State of the Nation Debate / Geordin Hill-Lewis. 18 February. https://www.da.org.za/2020/02/state-of-the-nation-debate-geordin-h-l Accessed 7 October 2020.

16   Worrall, D. 2020. 'Opinion: The ties that bind FW de Klerk, the Democratic Party and the DA' on News24, 6 February. https://www.news24.com/news24/columnists/guestcolumn/opinion-the-ties-that-bind-fw-de-klerk-the-democratic-party-and-the-da-20200206 Accessed 7 October 2020.

17   Naidoo, P. 2020. 'After more than 25 years S. Africa is now junk with Moody's too' on Bloomberg, 27 March. https://www.bloomberg.com/news/articles/2020-03-27/south-africa-gets-full-house-of-junk-ratings-after-moody-s-cut Accessed 7 October 2020.

18   TimesLIVE. 2020. '"If you cannot swallow a rock, stay out of politics," minister Tito Mboweni', 5 May. https://www.timeslive.co.za/politics/2020-05-06-if-you-cannot-swallow-a-rock-stay-out-of-politics-minister-tito-mboweni/ Accessed 7 October 2020.

19   Bateman, C. 2020. 'Business warns of "economic ruin", via Covid-19 lockdown' on BizNews, 14 May. https://www.biznews.com/thought-leaders/2020/05/14/business-government-lockdown Accessed 7 October 2020.

20   Government Communications. 2020. Address by Dr Nkosazana Dlamini Zuma, Minister of Cooperative Governance and Traditional Affairs, at a media briefing on risk-based model to address the spread of the Coronavirus. 25 April. https://www.gcis.gov.za/newsroom/media-releases/address-dr-nkosazana-dlamini-zuma-minister-cooperative-governance-and Accessed 25 October 2020.

21   Saunderson-Meyer, W. 2020. 'Pinning a label to the ANC's failures' on Politicsweb, 3 July. https://www.politicsweb.co.za/comment/pinning-a-label-to-the-ancs-failures Accessed 7 October 2020.

22   *The Economist*. 2019. 'South Africa's president promises big results – eventually'. 13 October. https://www.economist.com/middle-east-and-africa/2019/10/13/south-africas-president-promises-big-results-eventually Accessed 7 October 2020.

23   Erasmus, D. 2020. 'Radical economic transformation best for SA post-Covid-19, says Ramaphosa' in *CityPress*, 6 May. https://www.news24.com/citypress/news/radical-economic-transformation-best-for-sa-post-covid-19-says-ramaphosa-20200506 Accessed 9 December 2020.

24   Masutha, MM. 2020 'Opinion: Why choosing our well-being over tobacco profits and

the tyranny of the markets matter' on News24, 14 May. https://www.news24.com/news24/columnists/guestcolumn/opinion-why-choosing-our-well-being-over-tobacco-profits-and-the-tyranny-of-the-markets-matter-20200514 Accessed 7 October 2020.

25 Serrao, A. 2017. 'Zuma's free education adviser was a spy' on News24, 13 November. https://www.news24.com/news24/southafrica/news/exclusive-zumas-free-education-adviser-was-a-spy-20171113 Accessed 25 October 2020.

26 Johnson, RW. 2020 'The coming showdown (I)' on Politicsweb, 18 May. https://www.politicsweb.co.za/opinion/the-coming-showdown Accessed 22 December 2020.

27 Cele, S and Shoba, S. 2020. 'Covid-19: ANC looks at post-crisis economy' in *Sunday Times*, 31 May. https://www.timeslive.co.za/sunday-times/news/2020-05-31-anc-looks-at-post-covid-19-crisis-economy/ Accessed 7 October 2020.

28 Omarjee, L. 2020. 'Ramaphosa: I see a good future for SAA, Eskom beyond Covid-19' on News24, 31 May. https://www.news24.com/fin24/Economy/ramaphosa-i-see-a-good-future-for-saa-eskom-beyond-covid-19-20200531-2 Accessed 7 October 2020.

29 Johnson, RW. 2020. 'The coming showdown (I)' on Politicsweb, 18 May. https://www.politicsweb.co.za/opinion/the-coming-showdown Accessed 22 December 2020.

30 Godongwana, E. 2020. 'Economic reconstruction'. Presentation, 22 May. https://practicalreasonblog.files.wordpress.com/2020/06/etc-22-may-2020-draft-1.pdf Accessed 23 December 2020.

31 *The Economist*. 2020. 'Covid-19 has throttled South Africa's economy', 18 July. https://www.economist.com/middle-east-and-africa/2020/07/18/covid-19-has-throttled-south-africas-economy Accessed 7 October 2020.

32 Mills, G and Hartley, R. 2020. 'South Africa at a Fork in the Road', 22 July. The Brenthurst Foundation. https://www.thebrenthurstfoundation.org/news/south-africa-at-a-fork-in-the-road/ Accessed 7 October 2020.

33 Russell, J. 2020. 'The light of hope is going out in South Africa' in *The Times*, 16 January. https://www.thetimes.co.uk/article/the-light-of-hope-is-going-out-in-south-africa-zlhr30513 Accessed 23 December 2020.

34 Cillizza, C and Cohen, J. 2012. 'President Obama and the white vote? No problem' in *The Washington Post*, 8 November. https://www.washingtonpost.com/news/the-fix/wp/2012/11/08/president-obama-and-the-white-vote-no-problem/ Accessed 7 October 2020.

35 Van Onselen, G. 2018. 'How the DA learnt to forget and love the ANC' on Politicsweb, 8 July. https://www.politicsweb.co.za/opinion/how-the-da-learnt-to-forget-and-love-the-anc Accessed 7 October 2020.

36 Van Tilburg, L. 2019. 'Is the DA reforming itself into oblivion? – Final report review' on BizNews, 22 October. https://www.biznews.com/leadership/2019/10/22/is-the-da-reforming-itself-into-oblivion-final-report-review Accessed 7 November 2020.

37 Leon, T. 2013. 'This Bill is a pernicious piece of social engineering: Speech in opposition to the Employment Equity Bill, National Assembly, 20 August 1998' on

Politicsweb, 25 October. https://www.politicsweb.co.za/party/this-bill-is-a-pernicious-piece-of-social-engineer Accessed 7 October 2020.

38   Myburgh, J. 2013. 'Has the DA just put a bullet through its brain?' on Politicsweb, 27 October. https://www.politicsweb.co.za/archive/has-the-da-just-put-a-bullet-through-its-brain Accessed 7 October 2020.

39   Zille, H. 2013. 'A plane crash that should have been avoided' on Politicsweb, 7 November. https://www.politicsweb.co.za/party/a-plane-crash-that-should-have-been-avoided--helen Accessed 7 October 2020.

40   Gerber, J. 2018. 'Corruption and confusion: DA stands firm on criminal probe into Patricia de Lille and co' on News24, 25 October. https://www.news24.com/news24/southafrica/news/just-in-de-lille-will-be-subject-of-criminal-investigation-20181025 Accessed 12 December 2020.

41   Smith, A. 2001. 'Marais: I will survive street-name scandal' on IOL, 26 July. https://www.iol.co.za/news/politics/marais-i-will-survive-street-name-scandal-70653 Accessed 25 October 2020.

42   Zille, H. 2016. *Not Without A Fight: The autobiography.* Penguin Random House.

43   Maimane, M. 2015. 'Zuma: A broken man, presiding over a broken society' on Politicsweb, 17 February. https://www.politicsweb.co.za/iservice/zuma-a-broken-man-presiding-over-a-broken-society- Accessed 25 October 2020.

44   Coetzee, R, Leon, T and Le Roux, M. 2019. 'What is wrong with the DA, and how to fix it: A review of the Democratic Alliance – final report' on Politicsweb, 19 October. https://www.politicsweb.co.za/documents/what-is-wrong-with-the-da-and-how-to-fix-it Accessed 27 December 2020.

45   Davis, G. 2016. 'EFF MP ejected from Parly for calling Zuma "corrupt thief"' on EyeWitness News, 24 November. https://ewn.co.za/2016/11/24/eff-mp-labels-president-zuma-a-corrupt-thief Accessed 12 December 2020.

46   Chawane, G. 2018. 'DA promises to double child support – but how?' in *The Citizen,* 5 April. https://citizen.co.za/news/south-africa/1880402/da-promises-to-double-child-support-but-how/ Accessed 7 October 2020.

47   Davis, R. 2017. 'Analysis: Facing factionalism, scandal and a water crisis, is the DA becoming an ANC-lite?' in *Daily Maverick,* 9 October. https://www.dailymaverick.co.za/article/2017-10-09-analysis-facing-factionalism-scandal-and-a-water-crisis-is-the-da-becoming-an-anc-lite/ Accessed 7 October 2020.

48   African News Agency, 2018. 'DA Eastern Cape leader Nqaba Bhanga supports Maimane on "white privilege" comments' on Polity, 7 May. https://www.polity.org.za/article/da-eastern-cape-leader-nqaba-bhanga-supports-maimane-on-white-privilege-comments-2018-05-07 Accessed 7 October 2020.

49   Dreyer, A. 2019. 'From mirror to monster', submission to review panel on May 2019 election results, 1 August.

50   Isaacson, D. 2018. 'Willemse probe: Why Botha and Mallett aren't racist' on TimesLIVE, 20 June. https://www.timeslive.co.za/sport/2018-06-20-willemse-probe-why-botha-and-mallett-arent-racist/ Accessed 7 October 2020.

51 Van Onselen, G. 2019. 'The hollow institution' in *Business Day*, 15 May. https://www.businesslive.co.za/bd/opinion/columnists/2019-05-15-gareth-van-onselen-the-hollow-institution/ Accessed 7 October 2020.

52 Van Onselen, G. 2018. 'The DA's memory hole – Politicsweb' on IRR, 6 April. https://irr.org.za/media/the-das-memory-hole Accessed 7 October 2020.

53 Fisher, A. 2019. 'Photo of "segregated" classroom reopens old wounds in post-apartheid South Africa' on ABC News, 11 January. https://www.abc.net.au/news/2019-01-11/laerskool-schweizer-reneke-race-segretated-photo-sparks-outrage/10708832 Accessed 7 October 2020.

54 Dreyer, A. 2019. 'From mirror to monster', submission to review panel on May 2019 election results. 1 August.

55 Ibid.

56 Ibid.

57 Leon, T. 2019. 'IEC shows mediocrity has become the norm in SA' in *Business Day*, 14 May. https://www.businesslive.co.za/bd/opinion/columnists/2019-05-14-tony-leon-iec-shows-mediocrity-has-become-the-norm-in-sa/ Accessed 8 October 2020.

58 Coetzee, R, Leon, T and Le Roux, M. 2019. 'What is wrong with the DA, and how to fix it: A review of the Democratic Alliance – final report' on Politicsweb, 19 October. https://www.politicsweb.co.za/documents/what-is-wrong-with-the-da-and-how-to-fix-it Accessed 27 December 2020.

59 Ibid.

60 Ibid.

61 Ibid.

62 Ibid.

63 Boonzaaier, D. 2019. 'The curious case of Mmusi Maimane's R4m house' in *City Press*, 16 September. https://www.news24.com/citypress/news/the-curious-case-of-mmusi-maimanes-r4m-house-20190916 Accessed 25 October 2020.

64 *The Citizen*. 2019. 'Maimane's car was a gift from Steinhoff's Markus Jooste, DA confirms', 29 September. https://citizen.co.za/news/south-africa/politics/2184731/maimanes-car-was-a-gift-from-steinhoffs-markus-jooste-da-confirms/ Accessed 8 October 2020.

65 Mokone, T and Deklerk, A. 2019. 'Tony Leon part of delegation sent to ask Mmusi Maimane to quit' in *Sunday Times*, 6 October. https://www.timeslive.co.za/sunday-times/news/2019-10-06-tony-leon-part-of-delegation-sent-to-ask-mmusi-maimane-to-quit/ Accessed 8 October 2020.

66 Cele, S. 2019. 'Herman Mashaba: Tony Leon sought R300m tender from me' on News24, 14 October. https://www.news24.com/citypress/news/herman-mashaba-tony-leon-sought-r300m-tender-from-me-20191014 Accessed 8 October 2020.

67 Makinana, A. 2019. 'Maimane says DA review is "not a referendum" on leadership performance' on TimesLIVE, 7 October. https://www.timeslive.co.za/politics/2019-10-07-maimane-says-da-review-is-not-a-referendum-on-leadership-performance/ Accessed 8 October 2020.

68 Coetzee, R, Leon, T and Le Roux, M. 2019. 'What is wrong with the DA, and how to fix it: A review of the Democratic Alliance – final report' on Politicsweb, 19 October. https://www.politicsweb.co.za/documents/what-is-wrong-with-the-da-and-how-to-fix-it Accessed 27 December 2020.

69 Browder, B. 2015. *Red Notice: A true story of high finance, murder, and one man's fight for justice.* Simon and Schuster.

70 Ibid.

71 February, J. 2016. 'Nkandla judgment: high noon for President Zuma' on ISS Africa, 1 April. https://issafrica.org/iss-today/nkandla-judgment-high-noon-for-president-zuma Accessed 6 October 2020.

72 Wa Afrika, M and Hofstatter, S. 2016. 'Someone is trying to kill me' – Thuli Madonsela in *Sunday Times,* 8 May. https://www.timeslive.co.za/sunday-times/news/2016-05-08-someone-is-trying-to-kill-me-thuli-madonsela/ Accessed 6 October 2020.

73 Van Onselen, G. 2012. 'Seven crooked comrades' on Politicsweb, 27 June. https://www.politicsweb.co.za/documents/seven-crooked-comrades Accessed 27 October 2020.

74 News24. 2014. 'Deputy minister: Madonsela a CIA spy', 8 September. https://www.news24.com/News24/Deputy-minister-Madonsela-a-CIA-spy-20140908 Accessed 6 October 2020.

75 Leon, T. 2016. 'Living in an upside-down world of two sets of laws' in *Business Day,* 26 May.

76 TimesLIVE. 2019. 'Salim Essa: the state-capture mastermind in the shadows', 20 May. https://www.timeslive.co.za/politics/2019-05-20-salim-essa-the-state-capture-mastermind-in-the-shadows/ Accessed 6 October 2020.

77 Goble, P. 2015. '"Good Tsar, Bad Boyars": Popular attitudes and Azerbaijan's future' in *Eurasia Daily Monitor* 12 (30). https://jamestown.org/program/good-tsar-bad-boyars-popular-attitudes-and-azerbaijans-future/ Accessed 6 October 2020.

78 De Klerk, FW. 2020. 'I implore the ANC to turn back from the path it is now on – FW de Klerk'. Politicsweb, 2 February. https://www.politicsweb.co.za/opinion/i-implore-the-anc-to-turn-back--fw-de-klerk Accessed 6 October 2020.

79 *Financial Mail.* 2020. 'Editorial: The end of accountability', 6 August. https://www.businesslive.co.za/fm/opinion/editorial/2020-08-06-editorial-the-end-of-accountability/ Accessed 6 October 2020.

80 Basson, A. 2008. 'ANC rogues' gallery' in *Mail & Guardian,* 18–24 January.

81 *Financial Mail.* 2020. 'Editorial: The end of accountability', 6 August. https://www.businesslive.co.za/fm/opinion/editorial/2020-08-06-editorial-the-end-of-accountability/ Accessed 6 October 2020.

82 Ibid.

83 Bell, T. 2020. 'Echoes of the Hani revolt – and the Broederbond – in the current mess within the ANC' in *Daily Maverick,* 31 August. https://www.dailymaverick.co.za/opinionista/2020-08-31-echoes-of-the-hani-revolt-and-the-broederbond-in-the-current-mess-within-the-anc/ Accessed 6 October 2020.

84 Van Onselen, G. 2008. 'Jacob Zuma, Terror Lekota, and the constitution' on

Politicsweb, 29 October. https://www.politicsweb.co.za/news-and-analysis/jacob-zuma-terror-lekota-and-the-constitution Accessed 27 October 2020.

85 Makunga, M. 2020. 'If incompetence had another name, that would be Gomba' on SowetanLIVE, 30 April. https://www.sowetanlive.co.za/opinion/columnists/2020-04-30-if-incompetence-had-another-name-that-would-be-gomba/ Accessed 6 October 2020.

86 Leon, T. 2016. 'Nkandla excesses expose the glaring gap in founding law' in *Sunday Times,* 24 April. https://www.timeslive.co.za/sunday-times/opinion-and-analysis/2016-04-24-nkandla-excesses-expose-the-glaring-gap-in-founding-law/ Accessed 27 October 2020.

87 Ibid.

88 Keller, B. 2013. 'Could Cyril Ramaphosa be the best leader South Africa has not yet had?' in *The New York Times Magazine,* 27 January. https://www.nytimes.com/2013/01/27/magazine/could-cyril-ramaphosa-be-the-best-leader-south-africa-has-not-yet-had.html Accessed 27 October 2020.

89 Moseneke, DJC. 2014. 'Reflections on South African constitutional democracy – transition and transformation' at the Mistra-Tmali-Unisa conference, 12 November https://constitutionallyspeaking.co.za/dcj-moseneke-reflections-on-south-african-constitutional-democracy-transition-and-transformation/ Accessed 5 November 2020.

90 Taylor, R. 2006. 'Cameron refuses to apologise to Ukip' in *The Guardian,* 4 April. https://www.theguardian.com/politics/2006/apr/04/conservatives.uk Accessed 9 October 2020.

91 BBC News. 2016. 'Clinton: Half of Trump supporters "basket of deplorables"', 10 September. https://www.bbc.com/news/av/election-us-2016-37329812 Accessed 9 October 2020.

92 Associated Press. 2019. '"Trump of the Tropics": Five things you should know about Brazilian leader Jair Bolsonaro's visit with Donald Trump' in *South China Morning Post,* 20 March. https://www.scmp.com/news/world/united-states-canada/article/3002421/trump-tropics-five-things-you-should-know-about Accessed 9 October 2020.

93 Leon, T. 2012. 'No end of lessons for SA from Latin America' in *Business Day,* 20 November. https://www.businesslive.co.za/bd/opinion/columnists/2012-11-20-no-end-of-lessons-for-sa-from-latin-america/ Accessed 9 October 2020.

94 Hoffer, E. 1951. *The True Believer: Thoughts on the nature of mass movements.* Harper & Brothers.

95 Zille, H. 2015. Analysing populism: Keynote address to the 60th Liberal International Congress. https://liberal-international.org/what-we-do/events/congress-meetings/mexico-city-2015/li-deputy-president-helen-zille-analysing-populism-mexico-city-2015/ Accessed 9 October 2020.

96 Smith, D. 2010. 'ANC's Julius Malema lashes out at "misbehaving" BBC journalist' in *The Guardian,* 8 April. https://www.theguardian.com/world/2010/apr/08/anc-julius-malema-bbc-journalist Accessed 26 October 2020.

97 Head, T. 2020. '"This bastard called Cyril…": Malema in explosive rant against
    Ramaphosa' on The South African, 8 June. https://www.thesouthafrican.com/news/
    offbeat/watch-julius-malema-call-ramaphosa-bastard-why-who-are-mennel-family-
    video/ Accessed 9 October 2020.
98 Bendersky, J. 1985. *A Concise History of Nazi Germany.* Rowman & Littlefield.
99 February, J. 2019. 'Reject the EFF's politics that seeks the triumph of violence and an
    unhinged, fascist state' in *Daily Maverick,* 14 July. https://www.dailymaverick.co.za/
    opinionista/2019-07-14-reject-the-effs-politics-that-seeks-the-triumph-of-violence-
    and-an-unhinged-fascist-state/ Accessed 26 October 2020.
100 Leon, T. 2014. 'Seeing different futures in the same old tea leaves' in *Sunday Times,*
    30 November.
101 Steenhuisen, JHS. 2014. *DA Report on Parliament,* August.
102 Steward, D. 2017. 'The origins, meaning and likely consequences of RET' on
    Politicsweb, 27 August. https://www.politicsweb.co.za/opinion/the-origins-meaning-
    and-likely-consequences-of-ret Accessed 31 December 2021.
103 Nicolson, G. 2020. 'Additional arrests expected as VBS Mutual Bank corruption case
    postponed to 2021' in *Daily Maverick,* 8 October. https://www.dailymaverick.co.za/
    article/2020-10-08-additional-arrests-expected-as-vbs-mutual-bank-corruption-case-
    postponed-to-2021/ Accessed 9 October 2020.
104 Mitchley, A. 2018. 'Malema wades further into race debate, calls some black journos
    "house n****rs"' on News24, 25 June. https://www.news24.com/news24/SouthAfrica/
    News/malema-wades-further-into-race-debate-calls-some-black-journos-house-
    nrs-20180625 Accessed 9 October 2020.
105 Van Onselen, G. 2017. 'Malema's Indian bigotry' in *Business Day,* 31 July. https://www.
    businesslive.co.za/bd/opinion/columnists/2017-07-31-gareth-van-onselen-malemas-
    indian-bigotry/ Accessed 9 October 2020.
106 Zille, H. 2015. Analysing populism: Keynote address to the 60th Liberal International
    Congress. https://liberal-international.org/what-we-do/events/congress-meetings/
    mexico-city-2015/li-deputy-president-helen-zille-analysing-populism-mexico-
    city-2015/# Accessed 9 October 2020.
107 Malema, M. 2020. 'Legacy of white arrogance continues to haunt us' on Politicsweb,
    26 July. https://www.politicsweb.co.za/documents/legacy-of-white-arrogance-
    continues-to-haunt-us--j Accessed 9 October 2020.
108 Feketha, S. 2020. 'Malema on 7 years of EFF: We've represented those who have lost
    hope' on IOL, 26 July. https://www.iol.co.za/news/politics/malema-on-7-years-of-eff-
    weve-represented-those-who-have-lost-hope-a63c104a-c9cf-4a3a-92e9-f6722f790671
    Accessed 9 October 2020.
109 Uys, S. 1959. 'Dr Hendrik Frensch Verwoerd, Prime Minister Of South Africa' in *Africa
    South* Vol 3 No 2 Jan-Mar.
110 Verwoerd, H. 2008. 'The Jewish Question in South Africa – Hendrik Verwoerd' on
    Politicsweb, 3 April. https://www.politicsweb.co.za/documents/the-jewish-question-
    in-south-africa--hendrik-verwo Accessed 9 October 2020.

111 Ibid.

112 Packer, G. 2019. *Our Man: Richard Holbrooke and the End of the American Century.* Alfred A Knopf.

113 Van Onselen, G. 2013. 'FW de Klerk: the ultimate "joiner"' on Inside Politics, 7 March. https://inside-politics.org/2013/03/08/fw-de-klerk-the-ultimate-joiner/ Accessed 25 October 2020.

114 Byman, D and Pollack, KM. 2019. 'Beyond Great Forces: How individuals still shape history' in *Foreign Affairs,* November/December.

115 Madisa, K. 2020. 'It was not De Klerk's kindness that Mandela was released from prison – Ramaphosa' on SowetanLIVE, 11 February. https://www.sowetanlive.co.za/news/south-africa/2020-02-11-it-was-not-fw-de-klerks-kindness-that-mandela-was-released-from-prison-ramaphosa/ Accessed 8 October 2020.

116 SAPA. 2006. 'PW and Tambo were partners for new SA – Mbeki' on IOL, 3 November. https://www.iol.co.za/news/politics/pw-and-tambo-were-partners-for-new-sa-mbeki-301587 Accessed 26 October 2020.

117 BBC News. 2020. 'FW de Klerk and the South African row over apartheid and crimes against humanity', 18 February. https://www.bbc.com/news/world-africa-51532829 Accessed 8 October 2020.

118 Buso, O. 2018. 'Investigation proves EFF and Malema benefitted from VBS heist – analyst' on 702, 21 November. http://www.702.co.za/articles/328019/investigation-proves-eff-and-malema-benefitted-from-vbs-heist-analyst Accessed 8 October 2020.

119 Al Jazeera. 2020. '"Murderer in house": South African president's address disrupted', 13 February. https://www.aljazeera.com/news/2020/2/13/murderer-in-house-south-african-presidents-address-disrupted Accessed 8 October 2020.

120 Gerber, J. 2020. 'Notion that apartheid is a crime against humanity is Soviet propaganda meant to agitate – FW de Klerk Foundation' on News24, 14 February. https://www.news24.com/news24/southafrica/news/notion-that-apartheid-is-a-crime-against-humanity-is-soviet-propaganda-meant-to-agitate-fw-de-klerk-foundation-20200214 Accessed 8 October 2020.

121 BBC News. 2020. 'FW de Klerk and the South African row over apartheid and crimes against humanity', 18 February. https://www.bbc.com/news/world-africa-51532829 Accessed 8 October 2020.

122 Rich, N. 2019. 'Swiveling man' in *The New York Review of Books*, 21 March. https://www.nybooks.com/articles/2019/03/21/saul-bellow-swiveling-man/ Accessed 8 January 2021.

123 Mbeki, T. 2000. State of the Nation Address, 4 February. South African History Online. https://www.sahistory.org.za/archive/2000-president-mbeki-state-nation-address-4-february-2000 Accessed 26 October 2020.

124 Myburgh, J. 2016. 'A descent into racial madness' on Politicsweb, 14 January. https://www.politicsweb.co.za/documents/a-descent-into-racial-madness Accessed 23 November 2020.

125 Nicolson, G. 2018. 'Velaphi Khumalo's posts on whites declared hate speech' on *Daily Maverick*, 5 October. https://www.dailymaverick.co.za/article/2018-10-05-velaphi-

khumalos-posts-on-whites-declared-hate-speech/ Accessed 8 October 2020.

126 Dexter, P. 2016. 'Only whites can be racist' on Politicsweb, 19 January. https://www.
     politicsweb.co.za/opinion/only-whites-can-be-racist Accessed 8 October 2020.

127 Hart, C. 2016. Twitter. 3 January. https://twitter.com/chrishartZA/
     status/683658092467339264 Accessed 1 January 2021.

128 Hogg, A. 2016. 'Chris Hart quits Standard Bank following suspension over "racist"
     tweet' on BizNews, 15 March. https://www.biznews.com/undictated/2016/03/15/
     chris-hart-quits-standard-bank Accessed 8 October 2020.

129 Kalenga, A. 2016. 'Gareth Cliff removed from *SA Idols* judging panel' on Eyewitness
     News, 9 January. https://ewn.co.za/2016/01/09/Gareth-Cliff-removed-from-SA-
     Idols-judging-panel Accessed 8 October 2020.

130 Morrow, L. 2020. 'An honest conversation about race?' in *Wall Street Journal,* 2 July.
     https://www.wsj.com/articles/an-honest-conversation-about-race-11593728522
     Accessed 8 October 2020.

131 IRR. 2018. *Race Relations in South Africa: Reasons for Hope 2018 – Holding the Line.* South
     African Institute of Race Relations.

132 Ibid.

133 Brett, S. 2017. 'America's best university president' on University of Chicago,
     20 October. https://www.uchicago.hk/news/americas-best-university-president/
     Accessed 8 October 2020.

134 Jansen, J. 2016. Talk at Franschhoek Literary Festival, May.

135 Baran, PA. 1961. 'The commitment of the intellectual' in *Monthly Review,* 1 May.
     https://monthlyreview.org/1961/05/01/the-commitment-of-the-intellectual/
     Accessed 8 October 2020.

136 Artworks Task Team (UCT). 2017. *Art Under Threat at the University of Cape Town.*
     February. https://arttimes.co.za/wp-content/uploads/2017/07/Art-Under-Threat-at-
     University-of-Cape-Town-Dossier.pdf Accessed 8 October 2020.

137 Powell, I. 2017. 'The art of UCT's Max Price: Siding with ignorance and
     misperception' in *Maverick Life,* 4 August. https://www.dailymaverick.co.za/
     article/2017-08-04-the-art-of-ucts-max-price-siding-with-ignorance-and-
     misperception/ Accessed 26 October 2020.

138 Wood, G. 2017. 'Is UCT justified in taking down artworks that could cause offence?' in
     Financial Mail, 17 August. https://www.businesslive.co.za/fm/life/art/2017-08-17-is-
     uct-justified-in-taking-down-artworks-on-its-campus-that-could-cause-offence/
     Accessed 8 October 2020.

139 Bobin, F. 2015. 'Disputes damage hopes of rebuilding Afghanistan's Bamiyan Buddhas'
     in *The Guardian,* 10 January. https://www.theguardian.com/world/2015/jan/10/
     rebuild-bamiyan-buddhas-taliban-afghanistan Accessed 8 October 2020.

140 Schama, S. 2015. 'Artefacts under attack' in *Financial Times,* 13 March. https://www.
     ft.com/content/5f5e1bec-c80e-11e4-8fe2-00144feab7de Accessed 8 October 2020.

141 Thatcher, G. 1985. 'Why Soviets restore Czarist splendor to Leningrad' in *The Christian
     Science Monitor,* 4 September. https://www.csmonitor.com/1985/0904/oczar.html
     Accessed 8 October 2020.

142 Morton, S. 2016. 'It's a pity UCT cancelled Flemming Rose lecture' in *Cape Argus*, 28 July. https://www.iol.co.za/capeargus/its-a-pity-uct-cancelled-flemming-rose-lecture-2050702 Accessed 8 October 2020.

143 Manjra, S. 2016. 'Students and youth are reasserting their new identities' on News24, 11 October. https://www.news24.com/news24/SouthAfrica/News/students-and-youth-are-reasserting-their-new-identities-20161011 Accessed 8 October 2020.

144 Galgut, E. 2017. 'When a university loses its mind' on Politicsweb, 23 November. https://www.politicsweb.co.za/opinion/when-a-university-loses-its-mind Accessed 8 October 2020.

145 Cherry, M. 2020. 'All we get from her UCT colleagues is a deafening silence' in *Business Day*, 8 July. https://www.businesslive.co.za/bd/opinion/2020-07-08-all-we-get-from-her-uct-colleagues-is-a-deafening-silence/ Accessed 8 October 2020.

146 Ibid.

147 Ibid.

148 Nattrass, N. 2020. 'Power at UCT: When the "Executive" follows the BAC's lead, individuals are trampled' in *Daily Maverick*, 22 June. https://www.dailymaverick.co.za/article/2020-06-22-power-at-uct-when-the-executive-follows-the-bacs-lead-individuals-are-trampled/ Accessed 8 October 2020.

149 Cherry, M. 2020. 'All we get from her UCT colleagues is a deafening silence' in Business Day, 8 July. https://www.businesslive.co.za/bd/opinion/2020-07-08-all-we-get-from-her-uct-colleagues-is-a-deafening-silence/ Accessed 8 October 2020.

150 James. C. 2007. *Cultural Amnesia: Notes in the margin of my time.* Norton.

151 Smith, C. 2016. 'Super rich ditching SA – report' on Fin24, 29 February. https://www.news24.com/fin24/economy/super-rich-ditching-sa-report-20160229 Accessed 2 October 2020.

152 BusinessTech. 2020. 'This is how many millionaires live in South Africa right now'. 5 April. https://businesstech.co.za/news/wealth/235761/this-is-how-many-millionaires-live-in-south-africa-right-now/ Accessed 2 October 2020.

153 Whitfield, B. 2020. 'Why SA needs its rich' in *Financial Mail*, 27 February. https://www.businesslive.co.za/fm/special-reports/2020-02-27-bruce-whitfield-why-sa-needs-its-rich/ Accessed 2 October 2020.

154 Cameron, J. 2019. 'Adrian Gore: SA is larger, more relevant than we think' on *BizNews*, 2 September. https://www.biznews.com/wef/wef-africa/2019/09/02/adrian-gore-sa-larger-relevant Accessed 2 October 2020.

155 *Financial Mail.* 2019. 'Rupert: SA at point of no return'. 25 July.

156 Ibid.

157 Olifant, N and Pillay, T. 2016. 'Edward Zuma opens charge of corruption against Johann Rupert' on TimesLIVE, 26 March. https://www.timeslive.co.za/politics/2016-03-26-edward-zuma-opens-charge-of-corruption-against-johann-rupert/ Accessed 2 October 2020.

158 Business Insider SA. 2020. 'Here's how much Rupert, Oppenheimer will be worth after donating R1 billion each'. 24 March. https://www.businessinsider.co.za/johann-rupert-

and-nicky-oppenheimer-donate-r1-billion-to-small-businesses-to-help-with-coronavirus-heres-their-net-worth-2020-3 Accessed 2 October 2020.

159 Sharma, R. 2013. 'South Africa should forget the Brics era' in *Financial Times,* 27 March. https://www.ft.com/content/b529da46-96d5-11e2-a77c-00144feabdc0 Accessed 2 October 2020.

160 Sharma, R. 2018. 'The millionaires are fleeing. Maybe you should, too' in *The New York Times,* 2 June. https://www.nytimes.com/2018/06/02/opinion/sunday/millionaires-fleeing-migration.html Accessed 2 October 2020.

161 Speckman, A. 2020. 'Going another round with Moody's' in *Sunday Times,* 9 February. https://www.timeslive.co.za/sunday-times/business/2020-02-09-going-another-round-with-moodys/ Accessed 2 October 2020.

162 Smith, C. 2016. 'Super rich ditching SA – report' on Fin24, 29 February. https://www.news24.com/fin24/economy/super-rich-ditching-sa-report-20160229 Accessed 26 October 2020.

163 Wilson, N. 2020. 'Luxury homes flood the market' in *Sunday Times,* 8 March. https://www.timeslive.co.za/sunday-times/news/2020-03-08-luxury-homes-flood-the-market/ Accessed 4 October 2020.

164 World Bank Group. 2016. Doing Business Economy Profile 2017: South Africa. World Bank, Washington, DC. © World Bank. https://openknowledge.worldbank.org/handle/10986/25626 License: CC BY 3.0 IGO Accessed 26 October 2020.

165 Malope, L. 2018. 'Banking Association shoots down Investec's "SA high risk" comments' on Fin24, 3 June. https://www.news24.com/fin24/companies/financial-services/banking-association-shoots-down-investecs-sa-high-risk-comments-20180601 Accessed 5 November 2020.

166 ANC – FNB. 2013. 'FNB apologises to ANC for posting research clippings online' on PoliticsWeb, 25 January. https://www.politicsweb.co.za/party/fnb-apologises-to-anc-for-posting-research-clippin Accessed 2 January 2021.

167 Jeffery, A. 2014. 'The ANC govt's war on economic rationality' on Politicsweb, 27 March. https://www.politicsweb.co.za/news-and-analysis/the-anc-govts-war-on-economic-rationality Accessed 4 October 2020.

168 *The Economist.* 2014. 'Bashing business for votes', 27 March. https://www.economist.com/baobab/2014/03/27/bashing-business-for-votes Accessed 4 October 2020.

169 Business Leadership South Africa. 2019. 'Business welcomes the ANC Manifesto', 15 January. https://blsa.org.za/business-welcomes-the-anc-manifesto/ Accessed 4 October 2020.

170 Industrial Development Corporation (IDC). 2013. *South African Economy: An overview of key trends since 1994.* December.

171 Myburgh, J. 2019. 'The extraordinary race-blindedness of the transformationists' on Politicsweb, 22 November. https://www.politicsweb.co.za/opinion/the-extraordinary-raceblindedness-of-the-transform Accessed 4 October 2020.

172 Johnson, RW. 2015. *How Long Will South Africa Survive? The looming crisis.* Jonathan Ball.

173 Johnson, RW. 2019. 'The ANC's last chance' on Politicsweb, 10 June. https://www.

politicsweb.co.za/opinion/the-ancs-last-chance Accessed 4 October 2020.

174 Reuters. 2020. 'Explainer: Why South Africa's public wage bill is a problem', 27 February. https://www.reuters.com/article/safrica-economy-wages-idUSL5N2AR33A. Accessed 26 October 2020.

175 Bloomberg. 2019. 'South Africa's R172 billion free education plan unlikely to deliver skills: World Bank' on BusinessTech, 22 January. https://businesstech.co.za/news/government/294756/south-africas-r172-billion-free-education-plan-unlikely-to-deliver-skills-world-bank/ Accessed 3 January 2021

176 Mboweni, T. 2020. Twitter, 10 January. https://twitter.com/tito_mboweni/status/1215441642892746752 Accessed 3 January 2021

177 Cotterill, J. 2020. 'South Africa's central bank slashes rates to post-apartheid low' in *Financial Times*, 14 April. https://www.ft.com/content/ef404f4f-bb45-4e8d-a15a-5fde900a8d9c Accessed 3 January 2021

178 Mills, G and Hartley, R. 2020. 'Brink of a breakdown: South Africa has reached a critical fork in the road (Part 2) in *Daily Maverick*, 28 July. https://www.dailymaverick.co.za/article/2020-07-28-brink-of-a-breakdown-south-africa-has-reached-a-critical-fork-in-the-road-part-2/ Accessed 4 October 2020.

179 Maltz, J. 2019. 'Jews are leaving South Africa once again – but don't blame BDS' in *Haaretz*, 16 June. https://www.haaretz.com/world-news/asia-and-australia/.premium-jews-are-leaving-south-africa-once-again-but-don-t-blame-bds-1.7366376 Accessed 4 October 2020.

180 SA Monitor. 2015. 'Populist fury against whites resembles past anti-Semitism – BDlive – 24 November 2015', 24 November. https://sa-monitor.com/populist-fury-whites-resembles-past-anti-semitism-bdlive-24-november-2015/ Accessed 26 October 2020.

181 Stephens, B. 2019. 'The secrets of Jewish genius' in *The New York Times*, 27 December. https://www.nytimes.com/2019/12/27/opinion/jewish-culture-genius-iq.html Accessed 4 October 2020.

182 Stone, S. 2017. 'ANC's dirty war' in *City Press*, 15 January. https://www.news24.com/news24/SouthAfrica/News/ancs-dirty-war-20170115-3 Accessed 4 October 2020.

183 Elon, A. 2002. *The Pity of it All: A history of the Jews in Germany, 1743–1933*. Metropolitan Books.

184 Ibid.

185 Cameron, E. 2013. 'Constitution holding steady in the storm' in *Sunday Times*, 30 June. https://www.pressreader.com/south-africa/sunday-times-1107/20130630/281925950594851 Accessed 4 October 2020.

186 Goldman Sachs. 2013. *Two Decades of Freedom: What South Africa is doing with it, and what now needs to be done*, 4 November https://www.goldmansachs.com/insights/archive/colin-coleman-south-africa/20-yrs-of-freedom.pdf Accessed 4 October 2020.

187 Leon, T. 2013. 'The many faces of "Government Sachs" reports' in *Business Day*, 12 November; Hartley, R. 2013. 'Is the glass half full or half empty?' in *Sunday Times*, 10 November.

188 Cameron, E. 2013. 'Constitution holding steady in the storm' in *Sunday Times*, 30 June.

189 Keller, B. 2013. 'The Heretic' in *New York Review of Books*, 26 March.

190 Malan, R. 1990. *My Traitor's Heart*. The Bodley Head.

191 Ibid.

192 Malan, R. 2004. 'South Africa: The cape of new hope' in *The Telegraph*, 24 January. https://www.telegraph.co.uk/travel/destinations/africaandindianocean/southafrica/729534/South-Africa-The-Cape-of-new-hope.html Accessed 2 October 2020.

193 Mbeki, T. 2004. 'State of the Nation Address', 6 February. South African History Online. https://www.sahistory.org.za/archive/2004-president-mbeki-state-nation-address-6-february-2004-national-elections Accessed 2 October 2020.

194 In November 1991 Nelson Mandela announced that the first constitutional talks would take place at the World Trade Centre in Kempton Park, Johannesburg, where the Convention for a Democratic South Africa (CODESA I) ultimately signed a Declaration of Intent. By 1993 the multiparty Negotiating Forum had reached agreement on many issues and the Interim Constitution for South Africa was drafted. It came into effect on 27 April 1994 to govern South Africa's first one-person-one-vote election.

195 Harvard School of Public Health News, 2009. 'The cost of South Africa's misguided AIDS policies'. https://www.hsph.harvard.edu/news/magazine/spr09aids/ Accessed 2 October 2020.

196 Hartley. R. 2014. *Ragged Glory*. Jonathan Ball.

197 Rosling, H. 2018. *Factfulness: Tens reasons we're wrong about the world - and why things are better than you think*. Sceptre.

198 Ng, C. 2007. 'The "Developmental State" and Economic Development'. Paper written for Master's at Oxford University.

199 Department of Research and Information. 2013. *South African Economy: An overview of key trends since 1994*. December. Industrial Development Corporation. https://www.idc.co.za/wp-content/uploads/2018/11/IDC-RI-publication-Overview-of-key-trends-in-SA-economy-since-1994.pdf Accessed 2 October 2020.

200 Ibid.

201 Giliomee, H. 2017. 'South Africa's exceptional history' on Politicsweb, 4 April. https://www.politicsweb.co.za/opinion/south-africas-exceptional-history Accessed 2 October 2020.

202 BusinessTech. 2018. 'Here's how South Africa's crime rate compares to actual war zones.' 18 September. https://businesstech.co.za/news/lifestyle/271997/heres-how-south-africas-crime-rate-compares-to-actual-warzones/ Accessed 2 October 2020.

203 Dawood, Z. 2019. 'Hillcrest businessman bludgeoned to death' in *Daily News*, 6 June. https://www.iol.co.za/dailynews/news/kwazulu-natal/hillcrest-businessman-bludgeoned-to-death-25292041 Accessed 2 October 2020.

204 Makgoale, O. 2018. 'Life Esidimeni: Horror story under the ANC's watch' in *Daily Maverick*, 29 January. https://www.dailymaverick.co.za/opinionista/2018-01-29-life-esidimeni-horror-story-under-the-ancs-watch/ Accessed 2 October 2020.

205 Jika, T. 2019. 'Hawks probe R111m hospital fraud' in *Mail & Guardian,* 18 April.

206 Harding, A. 2020. 'Coronavirus in South Africa: Inside Port Elizabeth's "hospitals of horrors"' on BBC News, 14 July. https://www.bbc.com/news/world-africa-53396057 Accessed 2 October 2020.

207 *Mail & Guardian.* 2012. 'Education system worse than under apartheid: Ramphele', 23 March. https://mg.co.za/article/2012-03-23-education-system-worse-than-under-apartheid-ramphele/ Accessed 2 October 2020.

208 Masuabi, Q. 2017. 'Study shows SA kids "can't read for meaning"' on HuffPost News, 5 December. https://www.huffingtonpost.co.uk/2017/12/05/south-african-learners-worst-at-reading-in-world-shows-international-study_a_23297219/ Accessed 3 January 2021.

209 Kirchner, C. 2012. Address at UN General Assembly, 25 September. https://www.cfkargentina.com/address-by-cristina-kirchner-at-un-general-assembly-2012/ Accessed 4 October 2020.

210 *The Economist* .2015. 'The hollow state', 16 December. https://www.economist.com/middle-east-and-africa/2015/12/16/the-hollow-state Accessed 4 October 2020.

211 Hartley. R. 2014. *Ragged Glory.* Jonathan Ball.

212 Diagnostic Overview: National Planning Commission. The Presidency of the Republic of South Africa. https://nationalplanningcommission.files.wordpress.com/2015/02/diagnostic-overview.pdf Accessed 4 October 2020.

213 Russell, A. 2013. 'Zuma warns west's 'colonial' corporates in *Financial Times,* 3 March. https://www.ft.com/content/7824cc28-83ed-11e2-b700-00144feabdc0 Accessed 4 October 2020.

214 Manuel, T. 2013. Speech on implications of the National Development Plan for the public service. Conference of the Senior Management Service. https://www.gov.za/speech-trevor-manuel-minister-presidency-national-planning-commission-implications-national-0 Accessed 4 October 2020.

215 McMahon, F. 2000. *Road to Growth: How lagging economies become prosperous.* Atlantic Institute for Market Studies, Halifax, NJ.

216 Ibid.

217 Manuel, T. 2013. Speech on implications of the National Development Plan for the public service. Conference of the Senior Management Service. https://www.gov.za/speech-trevor-manuel-minister-presidency-national-planning-commission-implications-national-0 Accessed 4 October 2020.

218 *The Economist.* 2018. 'After Zuma, the hangover: South Africa's new president will have to dish out bitter medicine'. 22 February.

219 Joffe, H. 2019. 'Without growth, fiscal disaster looms' in *Sunday Times,* 27 October. https://www.timeslive.co.za/sunday-times/business/2019-10-27-hilary-joffe-without-growth-fiscal-disaster-looms/ Accessed 4 October 2020.

220 Donnelly, L. 2020. 'SA's catastrophic shortfall in tax revenue could pave road to IMF' in *Business Day,* 5 May. https://www.businesslive.co.za/bd/economy/2020-05-05-sas-catastrophic-shortfall-in-tax-revenue-could-pave-road-to-imf/ Accessed 4 October 2020.

221 Mokone, T. 2020. 'Ramaphosa unveils R100bn fund to create 800,000 public sector jobs' on TimesLIVE, 15 October. https://www.timeslive.co.za/politics/2020-10-15-ramaphosa-unveils-r100bn-fund-to-create-800000-public-sector-jobs/ Accessed 27 October 2020.

222 *Financial Mail.* 2019. 'Editorial: A tragedy of fiscal failure foretold', 28 November. https://www.businesslive.co.za/fm/opinion/editorial/2019-11-28-editorial-a-tragedy-of-fiscal-failure-foretold/ Accessed 4 October 2020.

223 Hogg, A. 2019. 'MTPBS in a nutshell' on BizNews, 30 October. https://www.biznews.com/budget/2019/10/30/mtpbs-nutshell Accessed 4 October 2020.

224 Van Onselen, G. 2017. *Political Musical Chairs: Turnover in the national executive and administration since 2009.* South African Institute of Race Relations, August.

225 Ibid.

226 Kane-Berman, J. 2020. 'The worst of the ANC's great and many failures' on Politicsweb, 17 March. https://www.politicsweb.co.za/opinion/water-the-worst-of-the-ancs-great-and-many-failure Accessed 4 October 2020.

227 Skiti, S. 2019. 'Consultants a fruitless waste' in *Mail & Guardian*, 28 June. https://mg.co.za/article/2019-06-28-00-consultants-a-fruitless-waste/ Accessed 4 January 2021

228 Manuel, T. 2013. Speech on implications of the National Development Plan for the public service. Conference of the Senior Management Service. https://www.gov.za/speech-trevor-manuel-minister-presidency-national-planning-commission-implications-national-0 Accessed 27 October 2020.

229 Myburgh, J. 2019. 'Transformation is killing South Africa' on Politicsweb, 26 September. https://www.politicsweb.co.za/opinion/transformation-is-killing-south-africa Accessed 4 October 2020.

230 Johnson, RW. 2019. *Fighting for the Dream.* Jonathan Ball Publishers.

231 *Olmstead v United States* 22 US 438. 1928. Justia: US Supreme Court. https://supreme.justia.com/cases/federal/us/277/438/ Accessed 5 October 2020.

232 Umraw, A. 2019 'Brian Molefe, Siyabonga Gama and Anoj Singh "architects of state capture" at Transnet' on TimesLIVE, 7 May. https://www.timeslive.co.za/politics/2019-05-07-brian-molefe-siyabonga-gama-and-anoj-singh-architects-of-state-capture-at-transnet/ Accessed 5 October 2020.

233 Khumalo, K. 2020. 'ANC top 6 leaders ignored Prasa corruption – Popo Molefe' in *Sunday World*, 29 June. https://sundayworld.co.za/politics/anc-top-6-leaders-ignored-prasa-corruption-popo-molefe/ Accessed 5 October 2020.

234 Pauw, J. 2017. *The President's Keepers: Those keeping Zuma in power and out of prison.* Tafelberg.

235 The Money Show. 2020. Bruce Whitfield interviews CNN's Richard Quest at the 2020 World Economic Forum in Davos, on Radio 702, 26 January. https://www.youtube.com/watch?v=xQnNn9svVX4 Accessed 5 October 2020.

236 Maughan, K. 2020. 'House of cards: Is Hermione Cronje hiding an ace?' in *Financial Mail,* 15 October. https://www.businesslive.co.za/fm/features/cover-story/2020-10-15-house-of-cards-is-hermione-cronje-hiding-an-ace/ Accessed 27 October 2020.

237 Leon, T. 2015. 'Deconstructing the ANC's agenda', speech delivered on 10 June 2004 at Johannesburg Press Club, on Politicsweb, 20 April. https://www.politicsweb.co.za/documents/deconstructing-the-ancs-agenda--tony-leon Accessed 5 October 2020.

238 African National Congress. 1998. 'The state, property relations and social transformation' in *Umrabulo,* No 5, Third Quarter.

239 African National Congress. 1996. 'The National Democratic Revolution: Is it still on track?' in *Umrabulo*, Fourth Quarter.

240 African National Congress. 1997. 'Nation-formation and nation building: The national question in South Africa.' in *Umrabulo*, No 3, July.

241 African National Congress. 1999. 'Accelerating the pace of change: Assessing the balance of forces in 1999' in *Umrabulo,* No 7, Third Quarter.

242 Ibid.

243 Leon, T. 2013. 'This Bill is a pernicious piece of social engineering: Speech in opposition to the Employment Equity Bill, National Assembly, 20 August 1998' on Politicsweb, 25 October. https://www.politicsweb.co.za/party/this-bill-is-a-pernicious-piece-of-social-engineer Accessed 5 October 2020.

244 Ibid.

245 Myburgh, J. 2019. 'Transformation is killing South Africa' on Politicsweb, 26 September. https://www.politicsweb.co.za/opinion/transformation-is-killing-south-africa Accessed 4 October 2020.

246 Ibid.

247 MiningMx. 2013 'BEE deal not forced on Gold Fields'. 23 September. https://www.miningmx.com/off-the-wires/17633-bee-deal-not-forced-on-gold-fields/ Accessed 5 October 2020.

248 Southern African Legal Information Institute. 2013. *Naidoo v Minister of Safety and Security and Another* (JS 566/2011) [2013] ZALCJHB 19; [2013] 5 BLLR 490 (LC); 2013 (3) SA 486 (LC); (2013) 34 ILJ 2279 (LC) (15 February 2013) http://www.saflii.org/za/cases/ZALCJHB/2013/19.html Accessed 5 October 2020.

249 Phakathi, B. 2020. 'Support for ailing tourism sector will be guided by BEE, says minister' in *Business Day,* 7 April. https://www.businesslive.co.za/bd/national/2020-04-07-support-for-ailing-tourism-sector-will-be-guided-by-bee-says-minister/ Accessed 7 November 2020.

250 Tau, P, Yende, SS and Stone, S. 2020. 'Councillors accused of looting food parcels meant for the poor' in *City Press,* 19 April. https://www.news24.com/citypress/News/councillors-accused-of-looting-food-parcels-meant-for-the-poor-20200419 Accessed 5 October 2020.

251 BusinessTech. 2020. '"Thieves were waiting at the door" as soon as South Africa announced coronavirus budgets, says Mboweni'. 5 August. https://businesstech.co.za/news/government/423250/thieves-were-waiting-at-the-door-as-soon-as-south-africa-announced-coronavirus-budgets-says-mboweni/ Accessed 5 October 2020.

252 Broughton, T. 2020. 'Court finds government failed to feed children' on TimesLIVE, 17 July. https://www.timeslive.co.za/news/south-africa/2020-07-17-court-finds-government-failed-to-feed-children/ Accessed 27 October 2020.

253 Seeletsa, M. 2020. 'Zwane was "unaware" of requirements of his job as MEC, Zondo commission hears' in *The Citizen*, 25 September. https://citizen.co.za/news/south-africa/state-capture/2362778/zwane-was-unaware-of-requirements-of-his-job-as-mec-zondo-commission-hears/ Accessed 27 October 2020.

254 Niselow, T. 2017. 'It's the economy, stupid: 7 times business, politicians shocked us in 2017' on Fin24, 28 December. https://www.news24.com/fin24/economy/its-the-economy-stupid-7-times-business-politicians-shocked-us-in-2017-20171228 Accessed 27 October 2020.

255 Hausmann, R. 2017. 'Is South Africa about to make an historic mistake?' CDE Insight, 9 June. https://www.cde.org.za/wp-content/uploads/2018/06/CDE-Insight-Professor-Ricardo-Hausmann-Is-South-Africa-about-to-make-a-historic-mistake.pdf Accessed 5 October 2020.

256 Leon, T. 2019. 'Do Cyril and Tito dare break the racial quota taboo at Eskom?' in *Sunday Times*, 20 February. https://select.timeslive.co.za/ideas/2019-02-20-do-cyril-and-tito-dare-break-the-racial-quota-taboo-at-eskom/ Accessed 12 December 2020.

257 Van Damme, P. 2019. Twitter, 13 February. https://twitter.com/zilevandamme/status/1095655116919750656 Accessed 4 January 2021

258 Cape Business News, 2019. 'Eskom's millionaire managers demand more money, crying "it's unfair"', 7 August. https://www.cbn.co.za/featured/eskoms-millionaire-managers-demand-more-money-crying-its-unfair/ Accessed 9 December 2020.

259 Thompson, W. 2019. 'Time for government to act, says Capitec CEO' in *Business Day*, 27 September.

260 Leon, T. 2012. *On the Contrary: Leading the opposition in a democratic South Africa*. Jonathan Ball.

261 *The Economist*. 2020. 'Bernie Sanders, nominee', 27 February. https://www.economist.com/leaders/2020/02/27/bernie-sanders-nominee Accessed 5 October 2020.

262 Judt, T and Snyder, T. 2012. *Thinking the 20th Century*. Penguin.

263 *BusinessTech*. 2019. 'Government's plan to "nationalise" all sports, clubs and gyms in South Africa'. 22 December. https://businesstech.co.za/news/government/363014/government-wants-to-nationalise-all-sports-clubs-and-gyms/ Accessed 5 October 2020.

264 African National Congress. 2020. 'Reconstruction, growth and transformation: Building a new, inclusive economy' on Politicsweb, 10 July. https://www.polity.org.za/article/reconstruction-growth-and-transformation-building-a-new-inclusive-economy-2020-07-10 Accessed 4 January 2021

265 Donnelly, L. 2017. 'SAA flies rings round weary fiscus', in *Mail & Guardian*, 27 July.

266 FlightGlobal. 2001. 'Ex-SAA chief in £29m pay-and-misrule claim'. 19 June. https://www.flightglobal.com/ex-saa-chief-in-29m-pay-and-misrule-claim-/38056.article Accessed 27 October 2020.

267 Vermeulen, A and Williams, B. 2001. 'SAA "ran at a loss under Coleman Andrews"' on IOL, 10 June. https://www.iol.co.za/news/south-africa/saa-ran-at-a-loss-under-coleman-andrews-67904 Accessed 27 October 2020.

268 Skiti, S. 2020. 'Without a clear plan, SAA stood no chance' in *Mail & Guardian*,

16 April. https://mg.co.za/article/2020-04-16-without-a-clear-plan-saa-stood-no-chance/ Accessed 27 October 2020.

269 Korhonen, M. 2017. 'Analysis: For all the billions, SA Airways bailout money not enough to buy Emirates' on Africa Check, 30 October. https://africacheck.org/2017/10/30/analysis-billions-sa-airways-bailout-money-not-enough-buy-emirates/ Accessed 4 January 2021

270 De Villiers, J. 2018. '5 things SAA can learn from Ethiopian Airlines – now Africa's most profitable airline' on Business Insider, 9 June. https://www.businessinsider.co.za/5-things-saa-can-learn-from-ethiopian-airlines-now-africas-most-profitable-airline-2018-6 Accessed 5 October 2020.

271 Nortier, C. 2020. 'SAA racks up new losses during lockdown, KwaZulu-Natal the new one to watch and no word on schools reclosing' in *Daily Maverick*, 20 July. https://www.dailymaverick.co.za/article/2020-07-20-saa-racks-up-new-losses-during-lockdown-kwazulu-natal-the-new-one-to-watch-and-no-word-on-schools-reclosing/ Accessed 6 October 2020.

272 Paton, C. 2020. 'Police and education the biggest losers to fund SAA' in *Business Day*, 28 October. https://www.businesslive.co.za/bd/national/2020-10-28-police-and-education-the-biggest-losers-to-fund-saa/ Accessed 6 November 2020.

273 Bruce, P. 2020. 'That screeching was Tito Mboweni hitting the brakes on promises to cut spending' in *Business Day*, 28 October. https://www.businesslive.co.za/bd/opinion/columnists/2020-10-28-peter-bruce-that-screeching-was-tito-mboweni-hitting-the-brakes-on-promises-to-cut-spending/ Accessed 6 November 2020.

274 Maughan, K. 2020. 'Dudi Myeni's move' in *Financial Mail*, 27 February. https://www.businesslive.co.za/fm/features/2020-02-27-dudu-myenis-move/ Accessed 11 December 2020.

275 *Organisation Undoing Tax Abuse and South African Airways Pilots Association v Duduzile Cynthia Myeni and Others*. Case 15966, July 2020. https://outa.co.za/web/content/113110 Accessed 11 December 2020.

276 Business Insider SA. 2019. '21 CEOs in 10 years: A guide to all the executive drama at SAA and Eskom', 3 June. https://www.businessinsider.co.za/all-the-ceos-at-eskom-and-saa-2019-6 Accessed 11 December 2020.

277 *Organisation Undoing Tax Abuse and South African Airways Pilots Association v Duduzile Cynthia Myeni and Others*. Case 15966, July 2020. https://outa.co.za/web/content/113110 Accessed 11 December 2020.

278 Maughan, K. 2020. 'Dudi Myeni's move' in *Financial Mail*, 27 February. https://www.businesslive.co.za/fm/features/2020-02-27-dudu-myenis-move/ Accessed 11 December 2020.

279 Ibid.

280 Maughan, K. 2020. 'Murky details behind Dudu Myeni's silence at Zondo inquiry' in *Business Day*, 9 November. https://www.businesslive.co.za/bd/national/2020-11-09-news-analysis-murky-details-behind-dudu-myenis-silence-at-zondo-inquiry/ Accessed 11 December 2020.

281 Business Insider SA. 2020. 'Seven things you need to know about Dudu Myeni – including how silence could land her in jail', 5 November. https://www. businessinsider.co.za/dudu-myeni-what-you-need-to-know-2020-11 Accessed 11 December 2020.

282 African News Agency. 2020. 'Zondo to lay criminal charges against Myeni' on Polity, 27 November. https://www.polity.org.za/article/zondo-to-lay-criminal-charges-against-myeni-2020-11-27 Accessed 11 December 2020.

283 News24. 2020. 'Whistleblower hits back at Dudu Myeni'. *The Witness*, 6 November. https://www.news24.com/witness/news/kzn/whistleblower-hits-back-at-dudu-myeni-20201106 Accessed 11 December 2020.

284 Maughan, K. 2020. 'Dudi Myeni's move' in *Financial Mail*, 27 February. https://www. businesslive.co.za/fm/features/2020-02-27-dudu-myenis-move/ Accessed 11 December 2020.

285 Ensor L. 2017. 'Zola Tsotsi links Zuma to Eskom capture' in *Business Day*, 22 November. https://www.businesslive.co.za/bd/national/2017-11-22-tony-gupta-threatened-to-fire-me-says-zola-tsotsi/ Accessed 11 December 2020.

286 Ibid.

287 *Organisation Undoing Tax Abuse and South African Airways Pilots Association v Duduzile Cynthia Myeni and Others*. Case 15966, July 2020. https://outa.co.za/web/content/113110 Accessed 11 December 2020.

288 Ibid.

289 Ibid.

290 Ibid.

291 Ibid.

292 Ibid.

293 Haffajee, F. 2018. 'Nene's testimony thrusts light on Zuma, the classic kleptocrat' in *Daily Maverick*, 4 October. https://www.dailymaverick.co.za/article/2018-10-04-nenes-testimonythrusts-light-on-zuma-the-classic-kleptocrat/ Accessed 11 December 2020.

294 *Organisation Undoing Tax Abuse and South African Airways Pilots Association v Duduzile Cynthia Myeni and Others*. Case 15966, July 2020. https://outa.co.za/web/content/113110 Accessed 11 December 2020.

295 Ibid.

296 Ibid.

297 Ibid.

298 Pilling, D and Cotterill, J. 2017. 'Jacob Zuma, the Guptas and the selling of South Africa' in *Financial Times*, 30 November. https://www.ft.com/content/707c5560-d49a-11e7-8c9a-d9c0a5c8d5c9 Accessed 5 October 2020.

299 Coen, C. 2020. 'Mkhwebane loses ConCourt bid to appeal Vrede dairy farm judgment' in *The Citizen*, 28 August. https://citizen.co.za/news/south-africa/courts/2351053/mkhwebane-loses-concourt-bid-to-appeal-vrede-dairy-farm-judgment/ Accessed 5 October 2020.

300 SABC News. 2019. 'Corruption has cost SA close to R1 trillion: Ramaphosa',

15 October. https://www.sabcnews.com/sabcnews/corruption-has-cost-sa-close-to-r1-trillion-ramaphosa/ Accessed 5 October 2020.

301 *Cape Messenger,* 6 March 2018.

302 Ibid.

303 Cairns, P. 2017.' Jonas: All institutions in SA are under threat' on Moneyweb. 12 October. https://www.moneyweb.co.za/news/south-africa/jonas-all-institutions-in-sa-are-under-threat/ Accessed 5 October 2020.

304 *Mail & Guardian.* 2016. 'Key comments from the Concourt's Nkandla ruling', 31 March. https://mg.co.za/article/2016-03-31-key-comments-from-the-concourt-in-nkandla-ruling/ Accessed 6 November 2020.

305 Pilling, D and Cotterill, J. 2017. 'Jacob Zuma, the Guptas and the selling of South Africa' in *Financial Times,* 30 November. https://www.ft.com/content/707c5560-d49a-11e7-8c9a-d9c0a5c8d5c9 Accessed 5 October 2020.

306 Ibid.

307 Harford, T. 2016. The hazards of a world where mediocrity rules, 14 September. https://timharford.com/2016/09/the-hazards-of-a-world-where-mediocrity-rules/ Accessed 5 October 2020.

308 Delaney, S. 2016. 'How Lynton Crosby (and a dead cat) won the election' in *The Guardian,* 20 January. https://www.theguardian.com/politics/2016/jan/20/lynton-crosby-and-dead-cat-won-election-conservatives-labour-intellectually-lazy Accessed 19 December 2020.

309 Hogg, A. 2015. 'Counting cost of ANC Cadre Deployment Policy – SOEs losing tens of billions' on BizNews, 15 August. https://www.biznews.com/leadership/2015/08/14/counting-cost-of-anc-cadre-deployment-policy-soes-losing-tens-of-billions Accessed 6 October 2020.

310 Ibid.

311 *Mail & Guardian.* 2005. 'The ANC's oilgate'.

312 SAPA. 2009. 'Oilgate: Judge criticises public protector' on IOL, 1 August. https://www.iol.co.za/news/politics/oilgate-judge-criticises-public-protector-453558

313 News24. 2016 'Hlaudi gets another massive pay increase', 30 September. https://www.news24.com/channel/TV/News/hlaudi-gets-a-million-rand-pay-increase-and-jets-off-to-mauritius-20160930 Accessed 27 October 2020.

314 BusinessTech. 2020. 'Government has spent R187.4 billion bailing out state companies over the last 20 years: Mboweni', 26 August. https://businesstech.co.za/news/government/428898/government-has-spent-r187-4-billion-bailing-out-state-companies-over-the-last-20-years-mboweni/ Accessed 27 October 2020.

315 Gernetzky, K. 2020. 'Land Bank confirms default on R50bn of debt' in *Business Day,* 24 April. https://www.businesslive.co.za/bd/companies/financial-services/2020-04-24-land-bank-confirms-default-on-r50bn-of-debt/ Accessed 6 October 2020.

316 Maughan, K. 2020. 'State finally has a solid case against alleged Transnet looters' in *Business Day,* 28 April. Accessed 6 October 2020.

317 Mantu. R. 2020. 'Phoenix to arise from old SAA – DPE' on Politicsweb, 3 May.

https://www.politicsweb.co.za/politics/saa-leadership-compact-a-ground-breaking-initiativ Accessed 6 October 2020.

318 Bisseker, C. 2020. 'Our economy has run out of road, yet we are still hobbling down SAA's runway' in *Business Day*, 4 May. https://www.businesslive.co.za/bd/opinion/columnists/2020-05-04-claire-bisseker-our-economy-has-run-out-of-road-yet-we-are-still-hobbling-down-saas-runway/ Accessed 6 October 2020.

319 Quintal, G. 2020. 'Ramaphosa appoints presidential council to reform state-owned enterprises' in B*usiness Day*, 11 June. https://www.businesslive.co.za/bd/national/2020-06-11-ramaphosa-appoints-presidential-council-to-reform-state-owned-enterprises/ Accessed 6 October 2020.

320 Prince, C and Wa Afrika, M. 2018. 'Brian Molefe's R19bn Transnet "lie"' in *Sunday Times*, 17 June. https://www.timeslive.co.za/sunday-times/news/2018-06-16-brian-molefes-r19bn-transnet-lie/ Accessed 1 October 2020.

321 Myburgh, P. 2017. *The Republic of Gupta: A story of State Capture.* Penguin Random House.

322 Prince, C and Wa Afrika, M. 2018. 'Brian Molefe's R19bn Transnet "lie"' in *Sunday Times*, 17 June. https://www.timeslive.co.za/sunday-times/news/2018-06-16-brian-molefes-r19bn-transnet-lie/ Accessed 1 October 2020.

323 Ramaphosa, C. 2019. 'Blood River: Dingane's Zulu warriors were freedom fighters' on Politicsweb, 16 December. https://www.politicsweb.co.za/documents/blood-river-dinganes-zulu-warriors-were-freedom-fi Accessed 26 October 2020.

324 Ramaphosa, C. 2019. 'Address by President Cyril Ramaphosa on the occasion of the National Day of Reconciliation, Bergville Community Sports Complex, Okhahlamba Local Municipality'. South African Government. https://www.gov.za/speeches/president-cyril-ramaphosa-national-day-reconciliation-16-dec-2019-0000 Accessed 1 October 2020.

325 Schoeman, J. 2019. 'Afrikaners are not "invaders" – Afrikanerbond' on Politicsweb, 19 December. https://www.politicsweb.co.za/politics/afrikaners-are-not-invaders--afrikanerbond Accessed 1 October 2020.

326 Judt, T and Snyder, T. 2012. *Thinking the 20th Century.* Penguin.

327 Nkanjeni, U. 2019. 'Cyril Ramaphosa admits to visiting Medupi only once, and Mzansi has questions' on SowetanLIVE, 10 December. https://www.sowetanlive.co.za/news/south-africa/2019-12-10-cyril-ramaphosa-admits-to-visiting-medupi-only-once-and-mzansi-has-questions/ Accessed 26 October 2020.

328 Fallon, I. 2019. 'Power cuts halt Ramaphosa campaign to resurrect South Africa' in *The Times,* London, 22 December. https://www.thetimes.co.uk/article/power-cuts-halt-ramaphosa-campaign-to-resurrect-south-africa-jtb5qf9jp Accessed 1 October 2020.

329 Stephens, B. 2016. 'Who did this to us?' in *Wall Street Journal*, 29 August. https://www.wsj.com/articles/who-did-this-to-us-1472513066 Accessed 6 October 2020.

330 Le Roux, K. 2020. 'Between 1923 and 2008 Eskom received no fiscal support – not a cent', 5 March. http://www.capetalk.co.za/articles/376882/between-1923-and-2008-85-years-eskom-received-no-financial-support-not-a-cent-from-taxpayers Accessed 6 October 2020.

331 Manuel, T. 2020. 'Our problem: spending more on the past than the future' in *Business Day*, 12 March. https://www.businesslive.co.za/bd/opinion/2020-03-12-trevor-manuel-our-problem-spending-more-on-the-past-than-the-future/ Accessed 6 October 2020.

332 Burke, E. 1790. *Reflections on the Revolution in France.* James Dodsley.

333 Janse van Rensburg, A. 2018. 'ANC using land as camouflage to attack white people – Moeletsi Mbeki' on News24, 15 May. https://www.news24.com/news24/southafrica/news/anc-using-land-as-camouflage-to-attack-white-people-moeletsi-mbeki-20180515 Accessed 6 October 2020.

334 Institute of Race Relations. 2018. *Empowering the State, Impoverishing the People.*

335 Mbeki, M. 2009. 'Why BEE should be abolished' on IOL, 29 November. https://www.iol.co.za/news/politics/why-bee-should-be-abolished-466121 Accessed 27 October 2020.

336 Mbeki, M. 2011. 'Only a matter of time before the bomb explodes' on Leader, 12 February. http://www.leader.co.za/article.aspx?s=23&f=1&a=2571 Accessed 27 October 2020.

337 Ibid.

338 Ibid.

339 Mahlakoana, T. 2018. 'Cyril Ramaphosa says NHI is on its way – whether you like it or not' in *Business Day*, 22 June. https://www.businesslive.co.za/bd/national/health/2018-06-22-cyril-ramaphosa-says-nhi-is-on-its-way--whether-you-like-it-or-not/ Accessed 6 October 2020.

340 South African Government. 2020. Twitter, 2 March. https://twitter.com/GovernmentZA/status/12344.

341 Van den Heever, A. 2019. 'Only a failing government could have come up with the NHI' in *The Citizen*, 24 August. https://citizen.co.za/news/south-africa/health/2170905/only-a-failing-government-could-have-come-up-with-the-nhi/ Accessed 6 October 2020.

342 Steward, D. 2014. 'The "Second Phase" vs the NDP' on Politicsweb, 27 May. https://www.politicsweb.co.za/news-and-analysis/the-second-phase-vs-the-ndp Accessed 6 October 2020.

343 Institute of Race Relations. 2018. *With a Little Help from our Friends: 89th Annual Report.* IRR.

344 Ibid.

345 Ibid.

346 Africa News. 2018. 'Let's work in unity of purpose in ANC – Magashule's closing address at Gauteng conference', 23 July. https://www.africanews24-7.co.za/index.php/voices/political-input-delivered-anc-sg-ace-magashule/ Accessed 6 October 2020.

347 FW de Klerk Foundation. 2020. 'Speech: 30 Years After 2 February 1990', 31 January. https://www.fwdeklerk.org/index.php/en/latest/news/976-speech-30-years-after-2-february-1990 Accessed 6 October 2020.

348 Magubane, K. 2019. 'Magashule speech takes aim at Reserve Bank, again' on Fin24,

18 July. https://www.news24.com/fin24/Economy/magashule-speech-takes-aim-at-reserve-bank-again-20190718 Accessed 6 October 2020. Importantly, according to the report of this speech, the secretary-general's written text on the SA Reserve Bank was elided from the speech when delivered.

349 Arendt, H. 1951. *The Origins of Totalitarianism.* Schocken Books.

350 Pauw, J. 2017. *The President's Keepers: Those keeping Zuma in power and out of prison.* Tafelberg.

351 Montalto, PA. 2019. 'Election preview: What comes after is key' on Intellidex, 3 May. https://www.intellidex.co.za/our-services/capital-markets-research/capital-markets-research-notes/ Accessed 6 November 2020.

352 Maughan, K. 2019. 'Edwin Cameron blasts land officials in his last judgment' in *Business Day,* 23 August. https://www.businesslive.co.za/bd/national/2019-08-23-news-analysis-edwin-cameron-blasts-land-officials-in-his-last-judgment/ Accessed 6 November 2020.

353 Ibid.

354 Constitution of the Republic of South Africa Bill (Second Reading Debate): Proceedings of the Constitutional Assembly. 1996. 6 May. https://static.pmg.org.za/docs/2005/9605const.htm Accessed 6 October 2020.

355 Ibid.

356 Syrian Observatory for Human Rights. 2020. 'Nearly 585,000 people have been killed since the beginning of the Syrian Revolution'. 4 January. https://www.syriahr.com/en/152189/ Accessed 9 October 2020.

357 Statement by Amb. Xolisa Mabhongo. United Nations Security Council. 29 April 2020.

358 Mandela, N. 1993. 'South Africa's future foreign policy' in *Foreign Affairs* (72)5, November/December.

359 Kurmanaev, A. 2019. 'Venezuela's collapse is the worst outside of war in decades, economists say' in *The New York Times,* 17 May. https://www.nytimes.com/2019/05/17/world/americas/venezuela-economy.html Accessed 27 October 2020.

360 Fabricius, P. 2018. 'Washington sleeps easy: SA envoy to Venezuela calls off "plans" for military action against US' in *Daily Maverick,* 17 August. https://www.dailymaverick.co.za/article/2018-08-17-washington-can-sleep-easy-again-sa-envoy-calls-off-plans-for-military-action-against-us/ Accessed 9 October 2020.

361 Grattan, S, Polanco, A and Armas, M. 2019. 'Two killed as Maduro sends troops to block Venezuela aid convoys' in *The Mercury News,* 23 February. https://www.mercurynews.com/2019/02/23/two-killed-as-maduro-sends-troops-to-block-venezuela-aid-convoys/ Accessed 6 November 2020.

362 *Business Day.* 2019. 'SA diplomats fluff it again in Venezuelan crisis', 15 February 2020. https://www.businesslive.co.za/bd/opinion/editorials/2019-02-15-editorial-sa-diplomats-fluff-it-again-in-venezuelan-crisis/ Accessed 9 October 2020.

363 Ramaphosa, C. 2020. Twitter, 28 April. https://twitter.com/CyrilRamaphosa/status/1255088582957637635 Accessed 6 January 2021.

364 *The Economist*. 2019. 'Security questions for Jeremy Corbyn', 9 November. https://www.economist.com/britain/2019/11/09/security-questions-for-jeremy-corbyn Accessed 9 October 2020.

365 Rachman, G. 2018. 'Why South Africa matters to the world' in *Financial Times*, 12 February.

366 Theobald, S. 2018. 'Expropriation without compensation puts preferential access to US markets at risk' in *Business Day*, 13 August. https://www.businesslive.co.za/bd/opinion/columnists/2018-08-13-stuart-theobald-expropriation-without-compensation-puts-preferential-access-to-us-markets-at-risk/ Accessed 9 October 2020.

367 Lamprecht, N and Tolmay, AS. 2017. 'Performance of South African automotive exports under the African Growth and Opportunity Act from 2001 to 2015' in *International Business & Economics Research Journal*. March. 16(2):131.

368 ka'Nkosi, S. 2015. 'Mantashe: We won't be dictated to by US' on IOL, 9 October. https://www.iol.co.za/business-report/economy/mantashe-we-wont-be-dictated-to-by-us-1927254 Accessed 9 October 2020.

369 Clinton, H. 2014. *Hard Choices*. Simon & Shuster.

370 Ibid.

371 Umraw, A. 20109. 'ANC slams "interference by imperialist forces" over corruption warning' on TimesLIVE, 4 February. https://www.timeslive.co.za/politics/2019-02-04-anc-slams-interference-by-imperialist-forces-over-corruption-warning/ Accessed 9 October 2020.

372 Polity. 2014. ANC: Statement by Jessie Duarte, ANC Deputy Secretary General, on the situation in the Gaza Strip (10/07/2014). https://www.polity.org.za/article/anc-statement-by-jessie-duarte-anc-deputy-secretary-general-on-the-situation-in-the-gaza-strip-10072014-2014-07-10 Accessed 9 October 2020.

373 Modise, T. 2015. 'Obed Bapela on dual citizenship, "imperialism" & why the ANC's not naïve' on News24, 11 September. https://www.news24.com/fin24/biznews/obed-bapela-on-dual-citizenship-imperialism-why-the-ancs-not-naive-20150911 Accessed 9 October 2020.

374 Joubert, J. 2016. 'SA drought not broken after driest year in history' on TimesLIVE, 8 September. https://www.timeslive.co.za/news/south-africa/2016-09-08-sa-drought-not-broken-after-driest-year-in-history/ Accessed 28 October 2020.

375 Kershner, I. 2015. 'Aided by the sea, Israel overcomes an old foe: drought' in *The New York Times*, 29 May. https://www.nytimes.com/2015/05/30/world/middleeast/water-revolution-in-israel-overcomes-any-threat-of-drought.html Accessed 9 October 2020.

376 Leon, T. 2016. 'There is water aplenty – if only the ANC knew where to find it' on TimesLIVE, 22 June. https://www.timeslive.co.za/news/south-africa/2016-06-22-the-big-read-there-is-water-aplenty-if-only-the-anc-knew-where-to-find-it/ Accessed 9 December 2020.

377 *WaterWorld*. 2016. 'Drought-quenching desalination plants to be built by South Africa/Iran partnership', 11 May. https://www.waterworld.com/international/desalination/article/16202878/droughtquenching-desalination-plants-to-be-built-by-south-africairan-partnership Accessed 10 October 2020.

378 Mirchi, A and Madani, K. 2016. 'A grand but faulty vision for Iran's water problems', in *The Guardian*, 9 May. https://www.theguardian.com/world/2016/may/09/iran-desalination-water Accessed 10 October 2020.

379 Wa Africa, M. 2016. 'SA high commissioner's past as drug smuggler exposed' on TimesLIVE, 2 October. https://www.timeslive.co.za/sunday-times/news/2016-10-02-sa-high-commissioners-past-as-drug-smuggler-exposed/ Accessed 10 October 2020.

380 SAPA. 2015. 'Mohau Pheko regrets faking doctorate' on SowetanLIVE, 27 February. https://www.sowetanlive.co.za/news/2015-02-27-mohau-pheko-regrets-faking-doctorate/ Accessed 10 October 2020.

381 TMG Digital. 2017. 'Corruption case against S'bu Ndebele likely to be dropped – report' on SowetanLIVE, 26 March. https://www.sowetanlive.co.za/news/2017-03-26-corruption-case-against-sbu-ndebele-likely-to-be-dropped-report/ Accessed 6 January 2021.

382 Van Diemen, E. 2019. 'Bruce Koloane resigns as ambassador after state capture testimony on Guptas' Waterkloof landing' on News24, 4 September. https://www.news24.com/news24/SouthAfrica/News/just-in-bruce-koloane-resigns-as-ambassador-after-state-capture-testimony-on-guptas-waterkloof-landing-20190904 Accessed 28 October 2020.

383 *The Citizen*. 2017. 'Axed SA embassy official "scapegoated" to protect Mapisa-Nqakula and sister'. 16 January. https://citizen.co.za/news/south-africa/1397411/axed-sa-embassy-official-made-scapegoat-protect-mapisa-nqakula-sister/ Accessed 10 October 2020.

384 Mokhoali, V. 2020. ANC expected to pay back R105,000 for trip to Zimbabwe on Air Force jet' on EyeWitness News, 30 September. https://ewn.co.za/2020/09/30/anc-expected-to-pay-back-r105-000-for-trip-to-zimbabwe-on-air-force-jet Accessed 28 October 2020.

385 Fabricius, P. 2020. 'South Africa's acting ambassador to Sudan accused in assassination and murder plot' in *Daily Maverick*, 13 October. https://www.dailymaverick.co.za/article/2020-10-13-south-africas-acting-ambassador-to-sudan-accused-in-assassination-and-murder-plot/ Accessed 27 November 2020.

386 Davis. W. 2020. 'The unraveling of America' in *Rolling Stone*, 6 August. https://www.rollingstone.com/politics/political-commentary/covid-19-end-of-american-era-wade-davis-1038206/ Accessed 10 October 2020.

387 Ibid.

388 National Treasury. 2019. Budget Review. February. Republic of South Africa. http://www.treasury.gov.za/documents/national%20budget/2019/review/FullBR.pdf Accessed 10 October 2020.

389 National Treasury. 2020. Supplementary Budget Review. http://www.treasury.gov.za/documents/national%20budget/2020S/review/FullSBR.pdf Accessed 28 October 2020.

390 Baron, C. 2020. 'SA edging up to "death spiral", says Allan Gray's Duncan Artus' in *Sunday Times*, 23 August. https://www.timeslive.co.za/sunday-times/business/2020-08-23-sa-edging-up-to-death-spiral-says-allan-grays-duncan-artus/ Accessed 10 October 2020.

391 Bisseker, C. 2020. 'Endgame for South Africa?' in *Financial Mail*, 6-12 August.

392 Ibid.

393 Gibson, D. 2020. 'Opinion: Ramaphosa is a decent man but a weak president' in *The Star*, 18 August. https://www.iol.co.za/the-star/opinion-analysis/opinion-ramaphosa-is-a-decent-man-but-a-weak-president--307141d5-ce6d-4d3f-87fd-9b73f49350d1 Accessed 10 October 2020.

394 Wren, C. 1989. 'Pretoria decentralizes security system' in *The New York Times*, 29 November. https://www.nytimes.com/1989/11/29/world/pretoria-decentralizes-security-system.html Accessed 10 October 2020.

395 Rose, R. 2020. 'Schools and taxis — the emperor is naked' in *Financial Mail*, 27 July. https://www.businesslive.co.za/fm/opinion/2020-07-27-rob-rose-schools-and-taxis-the-emperor-is-naked/ Accessed 10 October 2020.

396 Matthews, AS and Albino, RC. 1966. 'The permanence of the temporary: An examination of the 90- and 180-day detention laws' in *South African Law Journal* (83).

397 Marrian, N. 2020. 'Mama Aston's bribery blind spot' in *Financial Mail, 10 September*. https://www.businesslive.co.za/fm/opinion/state-of-play/2020-09-10-natasha-marrian-mama-astons-bribery-blind-spot/ Accessed 10 October 2020.

398 Mashego, A. 2020. 'SIU seizes Transnet exec's houses, a farm and 35 cars' in *City Press*, 16 August. https://www.news24.com/citypress/news/siu-seizes-transnet-execs-houses-a-farm-and-35-cars-20200815 Accessed 6 January 2021.

399 BizNews. 2020. 'ANC: "We are embarrassed by corruption"', 5 August. https://www.biznews.com/sa-investing/2020/08/05/anc-corruption Accessed 28 October 2020.

400 Wicks, B. 2020. 'Sars finds 17 PPE tenders of R1.2bn involving "politically exposed persons"' in *The Citizen, 21 August*. https://citizen.co.za/news/south-africa/parliament/2346540/sars-finds-17-ppe-tenders-of-r1-2bn-involving-politically-exposed-persons/ Accessed 28 October 2020.

401 Chutel, L. 2020. 'South Africa's big coronavirus effort tainted by corruption' in *The New York Times*, 24 August 2020. https://www.nytimes.com/2020/08/19/world/africa/coronavirus-south-africa-aid-corruption.html Accessed 10 October 2020.

402 Feketha, S. 2020. 'The ANC may not stand alone in the dock, but it does stand as Accused No.1 – Ramaphosa' on IOL, 23 August. https://www.iol.co.za/news/politics/the-anc-may-not-stand-alone-in-the-dock-but-it-does-stand-as-accused-no1-ramaphosa--055183b7-61d2-4fb6-b968-80d8a860a967 Accessed 10 October 2020.

403 Madia, T. 2020. 'Show me one leader of the ANC who hasn't done business with the state - Ace Magashule' on News24, 7 August. https://www.news24.com/news24/southafrica/news/watch-show-me-one-leader-of-the-anc-who-hasnt-done-business-with-the-state-ace-magashule-20200807 Accessed 10 October 2020.

404 *Financial Mail*. 2020. 'Editorial: Ace's ANC eulogy'. 13 August. https://www.businesslive.co.za/fm/opinion/editorial/2020-08-13-editorial-aces-anc-eulogy/ Accessed 10 October 2020.

405 Bisseker, C. 2020. 'Endgame for South Africa?' in *Financial Mail*, 6-12 August.

406 Heystek, M. 2014. 'South Africa: The death of the rainbow nation …' on SAPeople,

19 November. https://www.sapeople.com/2014/11/19/death-rainbow-nation-south-africa/ Accessed 7 January 2021.

407 Wheatcroft, G. 1996. *The Controversy of Zion: Jewish nationalism, the Jewish state, and the unresolved Jewish dilemma.* Addison Wesley Publishing.

408 Kemp, S. 2020. *Digital 2020: South Africa.* https://datareportal.com/reports/digital-2020-south-africa Accessed 10 October 2020.

409 Goodwin, T. 2015. 'The battle is for the customer interface' on TechCrunch, 4 March. https://techcrunch.com/2015/03/03/in-the-age-of-disintermediation-the-battle-is-all-for-the-customer-interface/ Accessed 10 October 2020.

410 Bush, GHW. 1988. RNC Acceptance Speech, 18 August.

411 Cameron, J. 2019. 'Another Steinhoff! Tongaat Hulett, Deloitte trickery blows up in fresh corporate scandal' on BizNews, 4 June. https://www.biznews.com/sa-investing/2019/06/04/steinhoff-tongaat-hulett-deloitte Accessed 7 November 2020.

412 Paul Wilson, his translator, provided this precis of Václav Havel in the *New York Review of Books,* 9 February 2012. https://www.nybooks.com/articles/2012/02/09/vaclav-havel-1936-2011/ Accessed 7 January 2021.

413 Landes, D. 1999. *The Wealth and Poverty of Nations: Why some are so rich and some so poor.* WW Norton & Co.

Index